D1176216

A HISTORY OF VICARAGES IN THE MIDDLE AGES

A HISTORY OF VICARAGES IN THE MIDDLE AGES

BY

R. A. R. HARTRIDGE

M.A., CAMB., PH.D., LOND.

SOMETIME SCHOLAR OF EMMANUEL COLLEGE, CAMBRIDGE
AND SIR WILLIAM MEYER STUDENT, UNIVERSITY COLLEGE,
LONDON

Thesis approved for
the Degree of Doctor of Philosophy
in the University of London

BARNES & NOBLE, Inc.
NEW YORK
PUBLISHERS & BOOKSELLERS SINCE 1873

First published, 1930
Reprinted, 1968
by permission of the Cambridge University Press

L. C. Catalog Card Number: 68-23763

Printed in the United States of America

254
H334h
176305

GENERAL PREFACE

THERE is only too much truth in the frequent complaint that history, as compared with the physical sciences, is neglected by the modern public. But historians have the remedy in their own hands; choosing problems of equal importance to those of the scientist, and treating them with equal accuracy, they will command equal attention. Those who insist that the proportion of accurately ascertainable facts is smaller in history, and therefore the room for speculation wider, do not thereby establish any essential distinction between truth-seeking in history and truth-seeking in chemistry. The historian, whatever be his subject, is as definitely bound as the chemist "to proclaim certainties as certain, falsehoods as false, and uncertainties as dubious." Those are the words, not of a modern scientist, but of the seventeenth-century monk, Jean Mabillon; they sum up his literary profession of faith. Men will follow us in history as implicitly as they follow the chemist, if only we will form the chemist's habit of marking clearly where our facts end and our inferences begin. Then the public, so far from discouraging our speculations, will most heartily encourage them; for the most positive man of science is always grateful to anyone who, by putting forward a working theory, stimulates further discussion.

The present series, therefore, appeals directly to that craving for clearer facts which has been bred in these times of storm and stress. No care can save us altogether from error; but, for our own sake and the public's, we have elected to adopt a safeguard dictated by ordinary business commonsense. Whatever errors of fact are pointed out by reviewers or correspondents shall be publicly corrected with the least possible delay. After a year of publication, all copies shall be provided with such an erratum-slip without waiting for the chance of a second edition; and each fresh volume in this series shall contain a full list of the errata noted in its immediate predecessor. After the lapse of a year from the first publication of any volume, and at any

Mills College Library
Withdrawn
MILLS COLLEGE
LIBRARY

time during the ensuing twelve months, any possessor of that volume who will send a stamped and addressed envelope to the Cambridge University Press, Fetter Lane, Fleet Street, London, E.C. 4, shall receive, in due course, a free copy of the *errata* in that volume. Thus, with the help of our critics, we may reasonably hope to put forward these monographs as roughly representing the most accurate information obtainable under present conditions. Our facts being thus secured, the reader will judge our inferences on their own merits; and something will have been done to dissipate that cloud of suspicion which hangs over too many important chapters in the social and religious history of the Middle Ages.

G. G. C.

July 1930

AUTHOR'S PREFACE

A PORTION of the present work was awarded a Sudbury-Hardyman Research Prize of Emmanuel College, Cambridge, in 1927. In the following year a revised and enlarged version was awarded the Prince Consort Prize of Cambridge University. For the help and encouragement that I received from these awards, I must express my deepest gratitude.

The book is not a complete history of vicarages in all countries in the obedience of the Popes in the Middle Ages, but rather a study centred intensively on our own country and spreading over the neighbouring lands with diminishing intensity. The reader will find that the Swiss and German examples are taken from one or two documents that offer corroborative testimony of great value, but that the descriptions of French conditions are founded on a considerable mass of documents. Italian conditions, which, as I understand, have peculiar characteristics, have not, as yet, found any place at all in my studies. Nevertheless, it may be hoped that my work is the more valuable for having overstepped our insular boundaries.

The minor subject of choral vicars in cathedrals and collegiate churches has been left untouched, as lying, in spite of its similarities, outside the scope of parochial institutions. It is to be hoped, however, that some student of those corporations will soon give us an adequate account of non-parochial vicars.

My supervisor in research in the University of London was the Rev. Professor Claude Jenkins, whose gentle and patient guidance has been one of the most charming influences in my education. The authorities of University College, whose award of the Sir William Meyer Studentship made this work possible, have shown the greatest kindness throughout, and forbearance when unavoidable circumstances interrupted my studies. The Master and Fellows of Emmanuel College, Cambridge, by means of a research grant and by their hospitality, gave me invaluable assistance. To all these kindest of friends I offer my heartiest thanks.

My debt to the editor of this series, Dr G. G. Coulton, must be most apparent. He has devoted many hours of his time to discussion of my difficulties, corresponded with me constantly, and always treated me with such friendliness that never at any time have I felt myself, by weight of his authority, forced towards any conclusion at which I could not honestly arrive. To Mrs Coulton I am indebted for useful advice concerning the Index.

To the Syndics of the Press I offer sincere thanks for their generous kindness in publishing this volume.

R. A. R. H.

EMMANUEL COLLEGE
CAMBRIDGE
July 1930

CONTENTS

CHAPTER I

ORIGINS

It would be pleasant and easy for the present author to leap straight from a touch-line marked "General Lateran Council 1215". A brief survey must, however, first be made of the early medieval tithe system. There is already an extensive and growing literature on the subject, which is one on the details of which learned authorities will probably for ever disagree. Imbart de la Tour, Dr Ulrich Stutz and other writers[1] trace the general medieval tithe system as far back as the fifth century A.D. It was based on the Jewish system of tithes instituted by the Mosaic law, as interpreted by early writers such as St Ambrose, who declared that the Christian bishops, priests and deacons, respectively represented the high priest, priest and levite of the older Dispensation. At first by free will and then under the solemn laws of the Church, the Christian converts paid tithes like the Jews of old to their spiritual advisers and fathers. Gradually the system of parishes within well-defined dioceses came into existence, and still more gradually the parish tithes came to be considered part of the normal endowments of the parish church. The actual process by which this came to pass gives occasion for the display of great erudition on the part of our authorities, but does not matter here.

Of more importance for the purpose of this study is the famous letter of Pope Gelasius[2] in 494, which determined that the revenues of the churches in Lucania, Bruttium and Sicily should be divided into four equal parts, one for the bishop, one for the ministering clergy, one for alms to the poor and one for the Church fabric. Authorities are agreed in regarding this decision as of the greatest importance, not only because canonists chose to make it a Decretal Letter, but from the more immediate point of view of historical development. Gregory I recom-

[1] I am here trying to find some highest common factor of these authorities, not to describe their quarrels even on details of importance.

[2] Binius, *Concilia Generalia*, Cologne, 1606, II, p. 246 *a*.

mended it to our St Augustine of Canterbury[1]. It appears that the rule came to be regarded as general and as applying not only to episcopal churches but also to all parochial churches. Such a development takes time, but no authority seems to doubt that it was a perfectly natural and real development, not one brought about at a later time by the fictions of lawyers. The bishop seems to have dropped out of the sharing, and there was left a threefold division, subject to certain regular episcopal dues. Certainly the number three does seem to recur in a most significant way in later divisions of the proceeds of Church revenues, as will appear in the documents quoted in this book.

The ecclesiastical development was complicated by the attitude of lay lords, who, we are told, claimed a *dominium* over the parish priests, which the ecclesiastical authorities strove to whittle down as small as possible. Monsieur P. Thomas[2] represents the parochial system as starting with a fairly complete *dominium* of the lay lords. Hence ensued a long struggle for mastery between Pope and bishops on the one hand, and lay potentates and lords on the other, ending in a settlement which left the right of patronage to laymen as a piece of real property, but, in theory at least, denied them other rights over churches, although abuses (*i.e.* survivals) of lay control lasted until the end of the Middle Ages.

Our authorities declare that the parish was normally part of the lord's domain, but not necessarily so, it being sometimes created entirely regardless of domains. Often it corresponded with the old *villa* of late Roman times, but neither was this necessary, for it might be a group of *villae* or only a portion of a *villa*. It came to replace the *villa* as a unit, and to prepare for, even create, the village. It was not simply another name for any lay unit, but it was close enough in appearance to be locally often confused with lay units of land.

The influence of the lay lords in the establishment of the Christian organisation must not be under-estimated. Stutz maintains that parish churches were mainly set up by local lords in place of the old heathen temples, and these lords held the

[1] Stutz, *Kirchl. Benef.* p. 29, n. 19.

[2] *Le Droit de Propriété des Laïques*, dealing with the problem on similar lines to those of Imbart de la Tour and Stutz but more definitely as a struggle between lay and ecclesiastical potentates.

same powers over them as they had over the temples; the glebe was a legacy from heathen days, and to it was added the Jewish-Christian custom of tithes. The parish priest was nearly always in practice, and sometimes in the troublous times of the Dark Ages even legally, the lord's "man". A lord in a tenth-century charter declared: "I give thee this church for life; but I will resume it if you commit any injustice towards me". Another declared: "I give thee this church...saving my service", thereby denoting expressly the feudal relation between the lord and his priest "man"[1].

It is agreed that the authority of the local lay lords over the parish churches was almost universal before A.D. 1000, but the extent to which they took tithes for their own use is a much more obscure question. Phillimore[2], in his *Ecclesiastical Law* (2nd ed. pp. 217 *seq.*), says that it was from confusion of parochial boundaries that there arose the first alienation of tithes and oblations from the immediate uses of bishops and clergy. Except when deliberately founded by outside powers, such as that of the bishop, the parish usually had no limits other than the possessions of its founders. When new fiefs were created out of parts of these possessions, to whom should the tithe then be paid? In practice the new lords bequeathed their tithes where they thought fit. Such a practice was very attractive, as it gained a cheap reputation for piety for the lords and gave them a powerful influence over ecclesiastical foundations. Yet it is probable that Phillimore has mistaken the sequence. Imbart de la Tour and Stutz adopt the view that the right of conferring tithes at will on anyone in orders or to any religious corporation preceded the more rigid rule that tithes should be paid to the local parish priest. Be this as it may, the practice of conferring tithes at will, just as if they were properly belonging absolutely to the lay lord, was quite general. In such a way did Baldwin de Lille, Count of Flanders, in 1067 give all the tithes of the villages of Ghyvelde and Quaedypre to the abbey of St Winoc at Bergues. Where in later days we find that a "pension" in a church was due to a monastic foundation, we can often trace this to such a transference of part of the tithes.

[1] Imbart de la Tour, *Les Paroisses Rurales*, p. 306.
[2] Phillimore, 1st ed. p. 265.

There was, however, a tendency to go even further, and deprive the tithes of all spiritual significance. For example, Ulric de Bagé, in 994, settled on his wife, Ermengarde, the mediety of a church dedicated to St Martin. Between 943 and 964 one Hildegard possessed the mediety of a church of St Christophe and the fourth part of a church of St Pierre and she gave them to the abbey of Cluny[1]. The church of Aluze was possessed *jure hereditario* by Bernard and Hugh, brothers, and by Walter and Robert, their cousins[2]. In 1034 a lay lord[3] granted two churches to a monastery, declaring that he himself had held even the "altar" under the name of vicar. One supposes that the services of these churches were performed by the lord's chaplain or some other stipendiary, or else not at all. This, indeed, was a most exceptional case.

There is sometimes, however, reasonable room for doubt whether a lay lord, who in his documents declared that he is "giving" tithes to a monastery, was actually giving away something that he had himself enjoyed. In 1094 Hugh de Berzé granted to Cluny the parish church of Berzé-le-Châtel, "with sepulture and cemetery, with the oblations also of the living and the defunct, and also a half of the tithes of bread and wine of the whole parish". This donation was made with the assent of the priest Bernard, who served the parish and who now abandoned his rights. The church was said to belong to Hugh de Berzé *jure hereditario*[4]. It seems as if Hugh was granting away the income of the priest, and not anything that he had himself ever enjoyed. The hereditary right was probably a vague one, amounting to something like the powers the lord might have over the miller and his mill, although the mill would not have normal periods of vacancy as did the church.

So it is probable that many of the so-called "gifts" of tithes from laymen to monasteries were very cheap gifts: that, in fact,

[1] L. Baecker, *Les Flamands, etc.* pp. 256, 264.

[2] Charmasse, *Les Origines des paroisses rurales, etc.* p. 44.

[3] Quoted in D'Arbois de Jubainville, *Histoires des comtes de Champagne*, I, p. 471: *ego, Gilduinus videlicet miles,... Ecclesias igitur, quas apud Pontemleviatum, unam virgini dicatam Mariae, matri Domini, alteram vero beato Petro, apostolorum principi, tenebam, cujus etiam altare sub vicarii nomine possidebam, qui ibi Deo assidue serviant, monachis perpetualiter concedo, ita libere et absolute, ut illas tenere dignoscor.*

[4] Charmasse, *Les Origines des paroisses rurales, etc.* p. 53.

the laymen were giving away what was not theirs to give. What could be more natural an abuse than that the lord, having a completely feudal idea of himself as the lord of the parish priests on his lands, should consider that he had the right to grant away the priests' fees, when they fell vacant?

The local lord and his feudal dependents would generally be the chief, and sometimes the only, contributors towards the income of the parish church, whether in tithes or in other payments. Consequently, the ancient idea of a discretionary payment of tithes to any church might be combined with the idea of feudal relationship, when the lord "gave" away the income of the parish church or part of it.

It is impossible to say whether or not the bishop's consent was often procured to lay donations of tithes in times previous to A.D. 1100. It is true that few episcopal confirmations exist or are mentioned, but this must not be taken as conclusive evidence that the bishops did not consent generally to such donations. After about A.D. 1100, probably under the stricter canonical regulation[1], such episcopal confirmations became frequent, but this may only mean that they were more zealously preserved through a greater fear of the episcopal authority. So when Fulk de Lailly and Mary his wife in 1129 wished to transfer to the monks of Vauluisant, diocese of Sens, all the tithes which those monks paid to them from lands in the parish of Lailly, these tithes were resigned "into the hands of" the archbishop of Sens[2]. The archbishop apparently completed the good work by inducing the parish priest of Lailly to surrender his part of similar tithes in return for a yearly pension in perpetuity of wheat and manure from the monks. During the twelfth century monasteries were striving hard to secure episcopal and Papal confirmations[3] of their property, the legality of which was now liable to be questioned. There was usually no ultimate difficulty made about granting these confirmations provided all the necessary expenses were paid. By the end of the twelfth century most of the gifts of churches of old standing had been ratified by Papal confirmations, and the new laws left no room for doubt that all

[1] For a discussion of the subject see Van Espen, *Jus Eccl. Univ.* Venice, 1781, III, pp. 178 *seq.*

[2] Paris, MS. lat. 9901, fol. 42.

[3] See pp. 28, 29.

fresh alienations must be approved by special acts of the bishops, and even of their deans and chapters.

In the religious revivals of the eleventh and twelfth centuries many laymen who had uneasy consciences about their ownership or who wished to found monasteries, or to give alms so that they might have the prayers of the religious after their death, conferred tithes and churches (*altaria*[1] as the continental documents usually call them) on the religious. Their descendants often perhaps challenging the right of their fathers to alienate their inheritance, or forgetful of the documents that their fathers had sealed, or maliciously determined to blackmail the monasteries, engaged in lawsuits that usually ended in the same way. The monks nearly always kept the churches, the laymen nearly always acquired a good sum of ready money. It is the normal story of early charters. Whether the grantors were kings, ecclesiastics, nobles or knights, there were always some of them who tried this kind of blackmail. The remedy was a rigid formalism of documents and ceremonies, and a deep reverence for the written and sealed document. The story of these legal squabbles may be told a hundred times with different actors.

The example of the church of Naveil[2] is very interesting. Fulbert, bishop of Chartres, between 1007–29 authorised the monks of Marmoutier to make the acquisition of the church of Naveil from the knight Hilgod, who held it from him. They did so and also bought back the rights which the vassal, Robert, held in it. After that they were to have free and tranquil possession of the whole church. Yet a little later, Hilgod appears to have taken it away violently from the monks and he compelled them to buy it back from him for 40*s*. At the same time he engaged to defend them from all ulterior claims. The children of Robert also claimed back some of the church property. Arnulfe, son of Robert, was induced to renounce his claim before the bishop and in the presence of his mother and sister. In 1075 the abbey was forced to make payments to various lay claimants. Even before this the abbey had been forced to pay 41*s*. indemnity to Archdeacon Hugh, who had, at one time, possessed one quarter

[1] I do not think *altaria* here means altarages (see p. 36) in the complete thirteenth-century sense. The word seems to include all the duties and income of the parish priest.

[2] M. de Tremault, *Chart. de Marmoutier*, pp. 1–12.

of the church. The story is very complicated, and the number of claimants indicate that the parish was very fat. Similarly (1104–24) the abbey was forced to give a palfrey and 40*s*. to the knight Robert Montlandai, a claimant, and also one-quarter of the tithes of Lancé.

The Church in the twelfth century rigidly set its face against lay tithe-owning, and with very great success. Pope Alexander III wrote to Henry II, bishop of Bayeux (*c*. 1165–81)[1]:

> Know you that it has come to our hearing that certain laymen, wishing to vindicate for themselves the right of patronage in certain churches of your diocese, keep for themselves two garbs of the tithes which lawfully belong to the churches, allowing the third only to go to the churches[2]. Since therefore you should provide lest from their insolence such an evil example should issue forth to others, we order your Fraternity to warn those laymen more diligently and induce them to allow the aforesaid two garbs, as also the third, to go to the churches and not to require any similar thing in churches of their patronage.

If this would not suffice the bishop was to smite them with excommunication. In 1230 Gregory IX addressed a letter to the archbishop of Auch complaining of the same thing[3]. In 1198 Innocent III allowed the chapter of Bayeux to buy back tithes from the hands of laymen, an indulgence that proves that no spiritual thunders had sufficed to make all of them part with these ill-gotten gains[4]. This permission became a frequent last resource in the war against lay tithe-holders, from whom nothing but a good cash payment could free the tithes. In 1249, it was granted to the abbey of St Nicholas-des-Prés[5], in the diocese of Tournai, by Pope Innocent IV, and (1295–1305) to the chapter of Thérouanne by Boniface VIII even in parishes outside their own diocese. The frequency with which such indulgences recur only adds to the evidence that it was not until the end of the thirteenth century in France that tithes in lay

1 *Antiq. Cart. Ecclesiae Baiocensis* (*Liber Niger*), Rouen and Paris, 1902, I, p. 206.

2 An eminent authority has, however, urged upon me that this withholding of two garbs was a formal act of protest by the laymen, and the document does not prove any real lay ownership of them. My reading is based on the assumption that 'two garbs,' like the common medieval *duae partes*, implies two thirds, and the mention of the third garb seems to clinch the argument.

3 *Cart. de Ste Marie d'Auch*, pp. 143–4.

4 *Antiq. Cart. Eccl. Baioc.* II, p. 50.

5 *Tournai Soc. Hist. et Lit. Mémoires*, XII, p. 269.

hands were very abnormal. Whereas this abuse had quite early died out in England it still flourished in France, possibly because government and authority were so much weaker.

Ivo of Chartres says that he will not spare abbots and heads of monasteries if they accept from laymen the tithes and oblations that cannot belong to laymen. Neither ought they to accept gifts that encroach on the anciently instituted stipends of the parish priests. The False Capitularies had already insisted that it was the layman's duty to surrender his tithes back to the Church. The three great Lateran Councils of the twelfth century (1st: canon 5—1123; 2nd: canon 10—1139; 3rd: canon 14—1179) all declared it illegal for one layman to transfer tithes to another. "If the receiver give them not up to the bishop, let him be denied Christian burial." The Council of 1179 forbade the religious to receive tithes from the laity without consent of the bishop, and empowered the bishop to make proper provision for the spiritual work of appropriated parishes. As Dr Coulton points out, these decrees went no further than to discourage or forbid lay ownership of tithes. They did not command the layman to give his tithes to a monastery. In Germany, indeed, tithe-owning by the lay lords continued right up to the time of the Reformation. The 1496 Visitation records for the diocese of Worms[1] show this quite clearly. In this diocese by that time most of the churches were appropriated to religious corporations, and it seems that in a very large number pensions from the tithes were held by laymen. In a few cases this is definitely stated, in many others merely suggested. The Elector Palatine held one-third of the great tithe of Wiesloch[2], and the whole of the great tithe of Friesenheim[3], and since he bore important church burdens at Labacher Hof[4] it is reasonable to suppose that he held important tithes in that church. Nor are these the only examples. The Count of Nassau was under obligation to keep up the nave and ornaments of Kirchenarnbach[5], and possibly held proportionate tithes there. At Wachenheim an der Pfrimm[6] it was "truly necessary to enquire into the matter of the fabric, because laymen receive for themselves" the appro-

[1] *Zeitschrift...Oberrheins*, XXVII.
[2] *Ibid.* p. 443. [3] *Ibid.* p. 233. [4] *Ibid.* p. 320.
[5] *Ibid.* p. 321. [6] *Ibid.* pp. 271–2.

priate dues. The *glebe*[1] of Alsheim[2] was perpetually alienated to a certain layman who burdened the vicar with an annual pension for the use of it. The glebe of Leiselheim[3] was also alienated. Such are the most obvious cases of lay claims on the tithes and lands of the parish churches revealed in this visitation at the very end of the Middle Ages.

Yet widespread as was the custom of lay tithe-owning on the Continent previous to A.D. 1200 one hesitates to adopt the view that has been suggested that the subsequent monastic rights in tithes were, in the main, merely the lay alienations re-assumed by the Church. "Appropriation" of churches by monasteries, and other corporations, was the formal acquisition by them of the income of the churches. The parish priest who received the full income of the church was called the Rector. The appropriating monastery acquired for itself the rectory and was itself the Rector Appropriate, or Impropriate[4] to use the phraseology of seventeenth-century lawyers. We shall see how the bishops insisted on the appointment of parish priests by the Appropriators, and the assignment to them of suitable endowments. Such a parish priest was called a Vicar, that is to say, one who performed the parochial duties *vice* the rector. The first necessity for the complete system was a formal appropriation deed, sealed or signed by the bishop who granted the rectory to the corporation to their own uses (*in proprios usus*). Then the bishop instituted the appropriator in the same way as he would have instituted a rector sole, but without demanding personal residence[5]. Finally he "ordained" the vicarage by a formal document in which he set aside the suitable portion (*congrua portio*) of the vicar. The vicarage was then a complete and "perpetual", that is, life-long, benefice by itself. This, however, was a development of the twelfth century, as will be seen.

The Council of Mainz in the year 847 made the following regulation:

Let none of the monks...presume to accept parishes of churches without the consent of the bishop: but for those titles in which they

[1] *dos*—foundation endowment of a church as apart from dues; hence principally the glebe.

[2] *Zeitschrift...Oberrheins*, XXVII, p. 244.

[3] *Ibid.* p. 250.

[4] The usual modern custom is to talk of ecclesiastical appropriators and lay impropriators.

[5] For an account of an appropriation ceremony, see *Vic. County Hist.* (*London*), I, p. 205.

shall have been appointed let them make reasonable return to the bishop or his vicar, and when convoked, let them come to the synod.

From this it is clear that monks, either singularly or corporately, had already been accepting parish churches, although their religious profession bound them to retire from the world to the cloister. It cannot be denied that the rule of a parish was incompatible with the utmost severity of St Benedict's Rule. Whether the Rule ought to have been relaxed is entirely another question: it is quite indubitable that the monk was meant to live away from the world and to leave the souls of laymen to the immediate care of secular priests. The monk existed to pray for men's souls, not to minister to their daily needs.

At another Council of Mainz[1] in 852 it was decreed:

We determine that throughout the churches of monks or laymen and the demesne or beneficed chapels where tithes are given, the bishops be received with worthy honour that they may be able to fulfil their ecclesiastical office.

At a Council of Coblenz in 922, it was decreed:

This also is determined, that the churches of any monks whatever, situate in the respective dioceses of the bishops, be submitted as it behoves to the rule of divine service, and that due ceremony be observed in exercising matters relating to the ecclesiastical cure. These monks should without any doubt obey their bishops in everything.

These decrees leave no doubt of the antiquity of monastic church-owning in the sense that the monks received the proceeds of the rectories, and show that it was very early necessary to insist that such churches should continue to be part of the ordinary organisation of the diocese under its secular authorities.

Frequently in these early times, Phillimore[2] says, churches were given to sole corporations spiritual, such as abbots and priors, with the idea that they themselves could perform the parochial duties. It was a very common practice to found a new abbey or priory in a parish church, the revenues of which were annexed to the abbacy. Imbart de la Tour[3] gives the example of the abbey of St Sernin of Toulouse, in about 990, and in the

[1] Stutz, *Kirchl. Benef.* p. 169, n. 73.

[2] Phillimore, 2nd ed. p. 219.

[3] Imbart de la Tour, *Les Paroisses Rurales*, pp. 247–8; also Charmasse, *Les Origines des paroisses rurales, etc.* p. 48.

eleventh century the abbeys of St Jean of Angély, St Cyprien and Bèze. It also appears to him, however, that the parochial duties were quite early performed in these churches, not by the abbot, but by clerks appointed by him to hold from the convent, yet before about A.D. 900 there seems no idea of a vicar with security of tenure. The practice by which a rector hired a priest to perform his parochial duties for him had already appeared. Hincmar at the end of the ninth century refers to one Seminatus, who held a church and who hired one Grimo, a priest, to sing in that church in his stead (*ad illius vicem*) until he should come to ordination in the space of a year and a half. Imbart de la Tour has found his first reference to a *vicarius sacerdos* in a text of 926, where we read that a clerk received in usufruct the church of Villa Tervicus, *i.e.* Trivy[1]. He delegated the spiritual rule of it to a *vicarius sacerdos* charged with the service of the parish. The church belonged to a man named Gaison, *ex suo proprio*. He declared that the carelessness of its priests had led to an almost complete destruction of the building (*quae incuria sacerdotum adnulla erat graviter et pene destructa*). On October 9th, 926, at a synod at a place called *Exigium* (unidentified) the tithes were, by Gaison's request, given to the nephew of the archdeacon. The bishop consented to it. The nephew was to become a priest and enjoy the church for his lifetime, on condition of restoring the building. A *vicarius sacerdos* was to be appointed, after being approved by the archpriest and satisfying all canonical requirements. In the chartulary of the abbey of Montiérender, there is a deed of Manasses[2], bishop of Troyes, dated April 9th, 991. The deed appears to be authentic, although it reveals an advanced stage of development for so early a date. It recounts how the Abbot Adso begged that the bishop should concede to the abbey three "altars" of places now known as Lassericourt, St Christophe, and St Leger-sous-Brienne. "To whose petition willingly acceding, we have granted to that place these three altars so that it may have and possess them on this condition, however, that it should thereupon present to us vicars, who should faithfully take charge of souls. And if those vicars shall have departed this life, others again shall be pre-

[1] Migne, *P.L.* t. 126, col. 539.
[2] Lalore, *Cartulaires du diocèse de Troyes*, IV, p. 143, n. 18.

sented, saving, however, the episcopal ordering." There is nothing said here about the payment of the vicars, and it is fairly safe to assume that they were stipendiaries, and not the holders of separately ordained benefices.

The use of the word "altar" in this document indicated "a parish church with its spiritual duties". It is a common use, although, since there is a more technical use of the word, very confusing. In the eleventh century, St Abbo, abbot of Fleury, wrote a letter to the kings, Hugh and Robert of France, in which he said: "There is another very grave error by which the Altar is said to belong to the Bishop, and the Church (*Ecclesia*) to a certain other lord: since from the consecrated house and the altar is made a certain thing that is called a church, as a man consists of body and of soul. See, most just Princes, whither avarice leads us, while charity grows cold"[1]. The church referred to here is a bishop's church but the argument is the same for parish churches. By "altar" is here meant the duties of the church, which may not be sold, and the dues attached to them; by "ecclesia", the building and its dependent property. This distinction would naturally be a cause of the abuse by which laymen or monasteries gained the revenues of churches without episcopal grant. They could plead that they had only been granted the ecclesia, which had no spiritual significance, and were not usurping the altar. When the altar was granted to a monastery, a custom of feudal analogy grew up, that the bishop exacted a payment called the *Redemptio altarium*. This was a feudal relief, and, as part of the tendency to feudalise the church, was justly condemned by the highest authorities. Pope Urban II's Council of Clermont[2] of 1095 declared that an altar granted to a monastery, if there were no written privilege or confirmation, should revert to the bishop after the death of the beneficiary; but Gratian and the Codex Cencii add a clause which declares simoniacal the old French custom of *Redemptio altarium*, and determine that every monastery that had held for thirty years an altar, or a tithe, obtained by a *redemptio* should keep it for ever, saving, however, to the bishops the annual dues which they were wont to have from those altars. In the twelfth century the

[1] P. Thomas, *Le Droit de Propriété, etc.* p. 77.
[2] Hefelé, *Conciles*, v, p. 401; Migne, *P.L.* t. 187, col. 547.

Abbot Godefroid de Vendôme[1] wrote to the Papal legate complaining that the bishop of Angers tried to make these decrees of no effect, by demanding an annual payment from their simplicity. Because the monks had refused to pay, he had placed them under an interdict. It does not appear whether this annual payment was really an excessive payment, or only the dues allowed to the bishop by the qualifying clause of the decree.

Even bishops joined in the general movement. In 1069 Bishop Drogo of Thérouanne[2], conferred on his cathedral chapter two whole altars, two parts of ten others, and one-third of two others. He added besides the church of Pernes with five day-works of land. This wholesale donation or confirmation reveals how far matters had already moved. The same Drogo gave also (1073–8) to the collegiate priory of Licques[3] the parochial altar there, doubtless expecting the prior or one of his canons to serve the altar. In 1074 the bishop of Troyes conceded the altar of the church of Margérie-Hancourt to the abbey of Montiérender at the request of the abbot. He expressly allowed the church to be served by a canon vicar. The yearly payment allowed to the bishop as a compensation for the loss of episcopal rights in appropriated churches appears in several documents of the eleventh century. In 1035 the bishop of Troyes[4] confirmed the altar of Ste Marguerite at Rosnay l'Hôpital to the abbey of Montiérender, while the canons agreed to pay the bishop 3*s*. a year. Earl Manasses at the same time renounced all his rights in the Church and made them over to the abbey. In 1071 the bishop of Laon[5] granted to the abbey of St Hubert-en-Ardenne the church of Evergnicourt: and was promised a yearly pension of 2*s*. In 1084 Bishop Gérard[6] of Thérouanne notified and confirmed the gift of the altar of Framecourt, made by the knight Acard to the abbey of Ham. He declared this altar free from all exaction on condition that the said religious should pay each year to the cathedral church the sum of 12*d*. At the same time he similarly freed from episcopal dues the church of Hautecloque. When we reach this stage, it becomes

[1] Migne, *P.L.* t. 157, col. 68.
[2] *Cart. de Thérouanne*, I, p. 79. [3] *Ibid.* p. 82.
[4] Lalore, *Cartulaires du diocèse de Troyes*, IV, p. 177.
[5] *Cart. de St Hubert*, p. 36.
[6] *Regestes de Thérouanne*, I, p. 89.

apparent that the procedure had established itself as an ordinary and regular piece of business approved of by the ecclesiastical authorities.

Bishop White Kennett says:

> Another fair Pretext of the Religious to gain Appropriations, was to desire no more than two parts of the Tyth and Profits to be so appropriated to them; leaving a *Third* to the free and quiet enjoyment of the Parish Priest, whom at the same time they eased from the Burthen of Repairing the Church and Relieving the Poor, and took that charge upon themselves. This again was a Colour that lookt well; for it was but a Returning to the Old Institution of dividing the Profits of a Parish into three Parts, one to the Priest, one to the Church, and a third to the poor[1].

For example, *two parts* of the tithe of Loo were transferred from the abbey of Corbie[2] to that of St Pierre-de-Loo in 1164. In 1121, or earlier, it was arranged that the proceeds of the parish of Neuville-sous-Brienne[3] should be divided into three parts, one of which went to the abbey, one to the incumbent and a third to a certain clerk named Guido. On the death of Guido his part was to go to the abbey, which so gained *two parts* of the church. We shall see how frequent it was for the incumbent to receive a third of the church revenues, the monastery retaining the other two-thirds. Moreover, the monks were regarded as poor men, and alms to them as the charity that clothes the naked and feeds the destitute. Ivo of Chartres[4], about 1150, stated that the tithes and oblations of the faithful could be shared not only by monasteries, but even by *xenodochia*, the sick, and pilgrims. He said that:

> though tithes and oblations are owed in the first place to those who do the clerical work—*clericali militiae*—yet the church may hold what it possesses in common with all the poor: how much more, then, with those poor who have left their own possessions, and, bearing Christ's Cross not by compulsion, are following the poor Christ.

The practice by which laymen conferred tithes on monasteries was by 1150 ancient, and was generally approved by men who did not adopt the rigid uncompromising attitude of Ivo.

[1] Kennett, *Impropriations*, p. 27.
[2] *Thérouanne Reg.* I, p. 149.
[3] Lalore, *Cartulaires du diocèse de Troyes*, IV, p. 194.
[4] Migne, *P.L.* t. 162, col. 200.

This negative counsel[1] might easily be interpreted as a positive precept in favour of the monasteries. This transpires from a late eleventh-century Breton charter which is all the more significant because its appeal to canon law seems to owe a great deal to the drafter's imagination. It runs[2]:

"Be it known unto all men, both present and future, that I, Barbota, possessed patrimonially the church of St. Brévin, so that I was wont, without contradiction from any man, to place in that church whatsoever chaplain I would, by the year or by the month. But, having learned from Benedict bishop of Nantes, and from many others that the Court of Rome had, in several councils, commanded the bishops to smite with the sword of excommunication, until they should make proper satisfaction, all patrimonial patrons of churches who should neglect to grant such churches to monks or canons or other servants of God, therefore since I would rather save my soul than commit it to the everlasting torments of hell, by the counsel of my lord Benedict, bishop of Nantes, and of my friends I have granted the aforesaid church in perpetuity to the monks of St. Aubin on condition that they make monks of my two sons, Evan and Daniel, and that they provide for me until my death. The monks, therefore, by the counsel of their abbot Gérard, and their whole chapter, and with the assent of Benedict bishop of Nantes, have appointed a chaplain to that church, to whom they have granted the third part of the whole revenues thereof, reserving two parts for themselves. Afterwards I and my friends humbly besought the monks and they granted a third portion of their own two parts to my daughter, Domeline, for the term of her natural life: and if this my daughter aforesaid bear to her husband a male child, who attains to the office of priesthood, the monks have agreed to grant him for life that third part together with the chaplaincy of the church; after his death the monks are to have his third part also."

The bishop was to receive a gold piece yearly from the church in recognition of his assent to the transaction[3].

Yet the twelfth century produced dissentient voices even among the monks themselves. The monks, as professional poor, had a right to the alms of the faithful, but there were some monks who discerned a tendency for them to become professional alms-takers. An early account of the origin of the Cistercian order under the sub-heading *Instituta monachorum*

[1] Coulton, in *Hist. Teach. Misc.* III, p. 179, Dec. 1925.

[2] A. de la Borderie, *Recueil d'actes inédits, etc.* Rennes, 1888, p. 65.

[3] Or more likely as a payment for the loss of episcopal dues and sequestrations (*pro sequestris*). This payment is quite normal in later centuries.

Cisterciensium de Molismo venientium[1] mentions that the monk has no part in the old fourfold division of the tithes, and that if he claims such a right he is taking away unjustly from the rights of others. Abélard[2], as a monk, went no further than his orthodox antagonist, St Bernard, when he said that "we usurp those things that belong to the [parochial] clergy, and by diverse means acquire the revenues of parishes in tithes and in oblations". The early Cistercians considered it contrary to their profession to take the revenues of the parishes, and attacked the Cluniacs and Benedictines for so doing. In a deed of 1158, Henry II, bishop of Liège, declared that he had remitted, with the consent of his cathedral church and under certain conditions, to Bernard, abbot of Clairvaux, the church of Alne[3], with its dependencies, that he might establish there an abbey of his order. The abbey was founded in 1147 by Francon de Morvaux, who was sent with monks from Clairvaux. "But since that same church possessed certain altars, tithes, serfs and handmaids, which men of that Order cannot regularly hold, the aforesaid abbot returned all of them into my hand, that I and all my successors should possess them perpetually." It was thus that St Bernard put his ideals into practice, but in later years his Order quite ceased to think as he did on this matter. In his great apology for the Cluniac Order to St Bernard, Peter the Venerable[4] of Cluny replies to St Bernard who has posed the question: "What reason or authority has conferred on you the possessions of parish churches, of first fruits and of tithes, since these do not belong to monks, but to clerks by canonical sanction?" Peter appeals to the Catholic Church for his authority, and declares that the monks who wait on the divine service day and night have every right to share in the inheritance of the tribe of Levi. "For who receive the offerings of the faithful more justly, the monks who assiduously pray for the sins of those who offer, or the clerks who now, as we see, seeking temporal things with the utmost diligence, rate altogether lower spiritual things and those that pertain to the salvation of souls?" Although the monks do not administer the sacraments, they

[1] Dugdale, *Monasticon*, 1682 ed. I. p. 699; Caley ed. V, p. 224.
[2] Migne, *P.L.* t. 178, col. 588. Sermon on St John the Baptist.
[3] Devillers, *Descr. Anal. des Cart.* I, p. 247.
[4] Migne, *P.L.* t. 189, col. 141, lib. I, epist. 28. Contrast also with St Bernard's Epistle 397, to the monks of Marmoutier.

watch over the safety of the greatest part of the faithful. If the clerks may live of the church revenues in return for their ministration of baptism, of penance, of preaching and of the other sacraments, why should not monks share in them in return for prayers, for Psalms, for tears, for alms, and for manifold good things offered for the salvation of the people to God. Peter quotes the canon[1] by which a bishop is allowed to set up a monastery in a parish church, and another that allows the bishop to give away his share of the proceeds of a parish church. Hence he claims that the Cluniacs possess their churches and tithes, "freely, justly, and canonically".

Yet, though he refused "altars" for monasteries of his own Order, St Bernard apparently did not altogether condemn the practice of appropriation. In 1143 Bishop Haton of Troyes[2] begins a grant to the Augustinian house of St Loup in these words:

> I Haton, by the grace of God bishop of Troyes, will that it be known to all, as well present as future, that dom[3] Bernard, of good memory, Abbot of Clairvaux, sought from us that we should concede the church of Lusigny to the canons of the Blessed Loup of Troyes: and since we hold this abbot on account of his sanctity in such veneration, that we wish to withhold nothing at all from him that he justly seeks of us, we conceded in perpetuity the aforesaid church to the above mentioned canons, that is to say, to dom[4] Everard the abbot, and the rest of the brothers serving (*famulantibus*) God under his rulership and to their successors, saving our episcopal right.

The brothers were allowed to present either a regular or a secular to the cure. It seems that St Bernard had no objection to the appropriation of a church when it was to be served by a regular canon. The importance of this cannot be over-emphasised. Did not Bernard say that parish churches do not belong to monks, but rather to clerks by canonical sanction? Then it appears that he must have regarded the canon as resembling in some particulars rather a clerk than a monk. I cannot believe that St Bernard made a complete *volte-face* on this matter, and came to sanction appropriations to monks as well, and in view

[1] Canon XII, q. 2, Si episcopus.
[2] Lalore, *Cartulaires du diocèse de Troyes*, I, p. 25.
[3] (*donnus*.) [4] (*donno*.)

of the frequent dispensations to Austin canons to serve churches the above explanation seems certainly the true one.

The correct procedure by which the bishop received the churches or tithes from the laymen and then in his own right conferred them on the monastery is shown in a document of 1122. In this, Geoffrey, bishop of Chartres[1], gave his consent to the gift of the churches of Crucherai and Nourrai to the abbey of Marmoutier, by one Barthélemy, who held them from his predecessors. As the bishop could not attend in person he sent the archpriest of the Vendômois to receive the churches from Barthélemy, and transfer them to the monks. This was the procedure which Peter the Venerable regarded as canonical, although he deduced it from the meaning of the canons, rather than found it expressly enjoined there. He admitted that the canon only said the "bishop's own part" but pointed out that it did not forbid the gift of the whole church by the bishop. While refusing to follow Peter's interpretation of the canon, it is only fair to add that this procedure soon became recognised as the only regular one and that it became a strong safeguard against many abuses. The power so given to the bishop was very large, but time was to prove that many bishops could use it well and wisely.

In France in the twelfth century the canon allowing the foundation of monasteries in parish churches had given rise to numbers of priories with cure (*Prioratus Curatus*). These tended to be little more than two or three monks living under the rule in the rectory house attached to the church. The serving of cures by monks and canons demands closer attention and must be deferred to a later chapter.

The monastic privileges at times covered other rights than that of serving cures by their own monks. Jean I, bishop of Thérouanne[2], in confirming (1111–13) the donation made to the abbey of La Capelle by Count Eustace III of the altars of March, Oye, Offekerque, and Nouvelle-Eglise, freed them all from all sinodical rights and all other diocesan charges. Innocent II in 1138, while confirming the nunnery of Bourbourg[3] in possession of the altar of Coutiches, exempted it from all

[1] M. de Tremault, *Chart. de Marmoutier*, p. 382.
[2] *Thérouanne Reg.* I, p. 108. [3] *Bourbourg Cart.* p. 37.

exaction on the part of the diocesan bishop. Whether this included the ordinary dues is not quite clear. Some time before 1175, the church of St Mary at Whitby was exempted from the payment of sinodals[1], when it was confirmed *in proprios usus* to Whitby Abbey. About 1160 the abbot of Darley in the diocese of Coventry and Lichfield was recognised as dean over all the churches of the abbey in Derbyshire, and was empowered to hold a decanal council of their own secular clergy to prevent anyone demanding more than the accustomed dues[2]. Yet in 1122 the Lateran Council had forbidden the office of parish priests to monks, who should have their churches served by vicars. The 1179 Council of Lateran[3] ordered the monks to present priests to the bishop who should make these priests responsible for the cure of souls. A council held at Avranches[4], under Alexander III in 1172, not only forbade laymen to receive any part of the oblations of a church (canon 3), but expressly forbade several other practices arising from the appropriation of parochial revenues. Churches should not be committed to annual vicars, who were appointed for one year only, nor should churches be given to an annual farm, that is, the rectory be leased for the space of one year (canons 4, 7). Nothing should be taken away from that third part that belonged of right to the parish priest (canon 8).

The Council of Westminster 1102 had enacted[5]:

> That monks do not accept churches without the bishop's consent, nor so rob the revenues of those which are given them that the priests who serve them lack that which they need for themselves and their churches.

Alexander III, in 1179, forbade the archbishop and chapter of York to detract from the due incomes of the clergy serving their churches, and commanded all monks of the diocese of Canterbury to present fit priests to their churches. He also wrote to the bishop of Norwich that a vicar who had obtained another benefice should be deprived of his vicarage, and again to the

[1] *Whitby Cart.* (Surtees Soc. no. 69), p. 57.

[2] Mus. Britt. MS. Cott. Titus, CIX, p. 132 or fol. 154: *ut predictus abbas et quisque successorum eius sit decanus de omnibus ecclesiis que dicte sunt ecclesie sue in Derbisira....*

[3] Thomassin, *Anc. et nouv. disc.* I, col. 1493.

[4] Mansi, *Concilia*, t. 22, col. 139.

[5] Wilkins, *Concilia*, I, p. 383, col. 22.

same effect to the bishop of Ely. He wrote to the bishop of Norwich that no vicar could appoint a substitute to perform the duties of his benefice. Honorius III declared that vicars should be compelled to reside in their benefices, and become priests, under penalty of the loss of the fruits of the benefices[1].

John of Salisbury[2] in the twelfth century already complained of the evil of absentee rectors who only served the churches by others. He said:

> Those who live—not to say luxuriate, as the people reckon—of the altar, do not wish to be burdened with the priesthood, or to serve the altar, but have introduced certain parsonages, of which by law the burdens belong to one and the emoluments to another. And although the Apostle says "He who works not neither shall he eat" (II. Thess. 2.) yet he who deserves less receives more, and enters upon burdensome and outside labours.

So it was not only the monasteries that were absentee rectors, but also secular clerks for one reason or another. Regulations about vicarages were quite as necessary where the rector was a non-resident secular as where the position was occupied by a religious corporation.

Pope Innocent III was responsible for the great work of systematising these parochial relations. In 1199, in a decretal letter to the archbishop of Canterbury[3], he protested against a habit that had arisen by which the laity conferred two parts or the whole of their tithes not on their own parish church but on other institutions. It is unreasonable that they who perform the spiritual duties should not receive the temporal offerings. In this he was only repeating the bull of Pope Celestine III[4] in 1195 to Archbishop Hubert, against the free disposal of tithes according to the will of the parishioners. Innocent also, in 1199, required the archbishop to annul all new pensions that had recently been imposed on parish churches in his province, contrary to the canons. At the great Lateran Council (IV) of 1215, canon 32 was enacted as follows:

> A vicious custom that must be extirpated has grown up in certain parts, where patrons of parish churches, and certain other persons

[1] *Decret. Greg.* IX, lib. I, tit. XXVIII, cc. i–iv.
[2] Migne, *P.L.* t. 199, col. 678.
[3] *Ibid.* t. 214, col. 672.
[4] Kennett, *Impropriations*, p. 13.

claiming the profits for themselves leave to the priests deputed to the service of them, such a scanty portion that from it they cannot be suitably (*congrue*) sustained. For as we have learned for certain, there are some regions where the parish priests have for their sustentation only the fourth of a fourth, to wit, the sixteenth part of the tithes; whence it cometh that in those regions scarce any parish priest can be found who is even moderately well-educated[1]. Since therefore it is not lawful to muzzle the ox that treads the corn, but he who serves the altar should live of the altar: we have ordained that by a certain custom of the bishop or patron, not withstanding any other, a sufficient portion be assigned for the priest.

Where possible, the rector was to reside and officiate but elsewhere

he should take care to have a *perpetual* vicar canonically instituted, who (as is aforesaid) should have a fit portion of the profits of the church.

Further, the assignment of a pension away from the revenues of a parish church was totally forbidden.

This canon may be termed the Magna Carta of the parish priest. Often ignored, often overridden, often misinterpreted, it stood firm throughout the Middle Ages, as the bedrock of the vicarage system. The *perpetual* vicar, to whom it refers, that is, the vicar who was instituted by the bishop and who could not be removed save by force of judicial procedure, and who had a separate endowment of his own, is the typical vicar of that system. A *perpetual* holder of any benefice could only be removed by the proper authorities for crimes and misuse of his office, and could not even resign his benefice without special permit. He was wedded to it for life. Perpetual vicars had been mentioned before: we find the phrase in an English provincial enactment of about 1173 at Westminster, but never before had their office been so authoritatively defined as this. This canon[2] runs: "Perpetual vicars who are bound by a faithful oath to their parsons, shall not raise themselves up against their parsons". Probably this enactment was made because some vicars, after lengthy residence in their churches, had seen fit to claim the entire proceeds of the church and attempt to persuade the

[1] *Unde fit ut in his regionibus pene nullus inveniatur sacerdos parochialis qui vel modicam habeat peritiam litterarum.*

[2] Wilkins, *Concilia*, I, p. 475, cap. 27.

authorities to recognise them as the true parsons. It is quite probable that the perpetual vicar of 1173 had had a separate endowment in tithes. From 1215 onwards a perpetual vicar could claim such an endowment as his by express canonical right. One must, however, be cautious against exaggeration. The 1215 canon certainly did not create the vicarage endowment, as Lalore's collection of chartularies for the diocese of Troyes proves over and over again. It did recognise that endowment was essential to the office of a perpetual vicar, and gave a powerful weapon to well-disposed bishops for the defence of the parish church against all intruders.

CHAPTER II

ENGLISH VICARAGES "BEFORE THE COUNCIL"

ENGLISH appropriations before the Norman Conquest, if they occurred at all, must have been rare. One need not go so far as Bishop Kennett in denying all probability of them, and an attempt has already been made in the previous chapter to show that lay lords did confer on religious corporations more rights in churches than they had actually enjoyed themselves, yet Kennett's opinion is worth quoting here. He quotes Selden[1] as saying:

That in Saxon times many Appropriated churches are found.... He refers to the Recitals of the Charters of King Bertulph, King Beored, and King Edred made to the Abby of Croyland and inserted in Ingulphus.

But these are spurious. Even if they are not,

they do no more than convey the Churches with their Tythes (*i.e.* so endow'd) to those Religious Corporations who had thereby no other Right conveyed to them, than what the Lay Lords before had; which was a right of Protection and Commendation to the Church, not a Right of converting the Profits to their own strict Property and use. I confess, the consequence was much to the same purpose.

King Edgar's grant of the churches and churchyards on the manor of Lewisham, which included Greenwich, Woolwich, Mottingham and Coombe, to the abbey of St Peter's, Ghent[2], in 964, if genuine, probably was no more than a grant of advowson. Saxon deeds, usually forged ones, were a favourite hobby of the monastic historian, whose aim frequently was to prove the age and antiquity of his monasteries and its possessions. The arguments in the register of Bishop de Pontissara[3] as to whether the king or the bishop was the founder of St Swithin's Priory at Winchester, bear eloquent testimony to this. It will be wise for

[1] Kennett, *Impropriations*, pp. 22–3. Also Selden, *Hist. of Tithes* (1618), p. 370.

[2] *Reg. Hethe*, p. 32.

[3] *Reg. Pontissara*, p. 609.

us to resist the temptation to fight over again all these old unprofitable battles of historians. Pegge[1] says:

For some time after the Norman Conquest (for I think there were not many appropriations before that aera) patrons who were chiefly lords of manors and erectors of the parish churches, gave the respective rectories at their own will and pleasure, and without consulting with any body, to whatever religious foundation they pleased. Churches, therefore, at this time were all donatives, and the monks in this case collated themselves to the cures. And afterwards, to avoid a multiplicity of institutions and inductions, they obtained license from the King and the ordinary, and sometimes from the Pope himself to be perpetual incumbents of their appropriated churches without those forms.

Authorities agree that the lords certainly conferred the rectories "at their own will and pleasure", but whether without express or implied consent on the part of the diocesan bishops is a matter for doubt. The scarcity of documents giving such consent may only be due to a general failure to recognise the importance of this documentary evidence. The true solution of the problem is probably that sometimes the lords gave without any such consent, and sometimes there was an episcopal document which was afterwards lost and not recorded: that there was, in fact, a total lack of system and no recognised correct method of procedure. The lawyer's passion for system and uniformity is usually most misleading in the morning twilights of history. The twelfth-century Lateran Councils in effect selected what seemed the best and most consistent of the multitudinous local customs, created from them a system and then assumed that that system had existed throughout the early centuries of the Church.

Pegge says that the monks collated themselves to the cures. This same opinion is found, only with a greater assumption of legality, in a document concerning assart tithes in the chartulary of St Evroul's Abbey[2], which will be quoted later. The appropriated churches of these early times do seem occasionally to have been served by monks, but it is doubtful whether this was the general intention. The abuse most frequently dealt with by

[1] *Life of Grosseteste,* App. VII, p. 322. This quotation, I find later, is taken almost verbally from Sir Henry Spelman's *Larger Worke of Tithes* (1647), p. 152.

[2] See pp. 70 *seq.*

the twelfth-century councils is not the service of churches by monks, but the inadequate service of them by the underpaid clerks hired by the monks. In England it is especially doubtful whether monks often served the churches themselves. The opinion of the present writer, which the sources are inadequate to prove, is that in the appropriated churches of eleventh- and twelfth-century England, the "mercenary" priest, removable at pleasure and without a settled benefice in endowments, was the rule and the monk incumbent the rare exception. While examples can be found of such mercenaries, examples of monk incumbents by no means leap to the eye.

There are an immense number of twelfth-century deeds of gift of parish churches and their appurtenances in England. Dugdale's *Monasticon Anglicanum* contains some such deeds for most of the monasteries that were already existing by this time. Of these early deeds it is difficult to decide which only conferred the advowson on the monks, and which gave to them the tithes of the rectory. In 1119 Burel, we learn, gave the church of Holywell[1] and the tithe of his mill and of all his belongings to Chester Abbey. This seems to indicate that he conferred the advowson of the church and his own tithes only, not the whole proceeds of the rectory. Bishop Richard of Coventry and Lichfield (1161–82) confirmed the grant to Chester Abbey by Ralph de Mold, steward of the Earl of Chester, of the church of Neston. He had gained the consent of his mother, of whose dowry it was part, for this gift, and the late rector, William de Mold, his brother, had resigned the church that it might be converted to the uses of the monks. It is quite clear that this was an appropriation made by consent of the bishop[2]. A simple gift of advowson did not require the consent of the bishop, although such consent might prove a safeguard to the receiver. In 1160 one Aelgar, a priest, entered the monastery of Christchurch, Canterbury, and gave as his dowry to the monastery the church which he had hitherto held. Obviously there was something unusual, even possibly irregular, about this procedure, and one may surmise that Aelgar had been both patron and incumbent of the church. It was stipulated that the next of kin to Aelgar should always hold the vicarage, or, if the next of kin were not

[1] *Chester Chart.* (Chetham Soc.), I, p. 41. [2] *Ibid.* I, p. 119.

in holy orders, some other person was to be presented whose appointment should be profitable to the monastery[1]. The name of the church is not stated, a fact which makes it more likely that the story was true, and not invented for ulterior motives. There is another document[2], however, of about 1150 by which the church of St Mary's, Bothaw, was given to the monastery by the priest who was its absolute proprietor. This priest continued to act as vicar, paying 5*s*. pension to the monastery. It looks as if these two documents refer to the same transaction.

A more wholesale grant was that of Robert de Crèvecœur[3] made between 1125 and 1136 for the good of his own soul and that of his uncle, Hamo, the steward to the canons of Leeds Priory in Kent, of all the churches on his lands. These were Leeds with the chapel of Bromfield, Chatham, Rainham, Goudhurst, Lamberhurst, Farleigh and Teston. The same Priory also received the church of Wateringbury (1174–6) from Hamo, son of Richard of Wateringbury. Letters of Bishop Walter of Rochester notified the formal institution of the priory to the church at the presentation of the lord of the manor, and on the resignation of the last parson[4]. Tonbridge parish church[5] was appropriated to the Knights of the Hospital of St John of Jerusalem by Walter, bishop of Rochester, after its advowson had been granted to them for that purpose by Roger de Clare, Earl of Hereford (between 1152 and 1172). Another grant to the Hospitallers was that of the rectories of Halse and Heathfield[6], made by Robert de Arundell and confirmed by Reginald, bishop of Bath, some time between 1174 and 1192. Often the grants were made for specific purposes as a number of documents relating to the diocese of Winchester reveal. In 1172[7] the chapels of Chilcomb, Morestead, Whitchurch, Compton and Wyke were confirmed to St Swithin's priory for the anniversaries of founders and benefactors. The condition that prayers should be made for the benefactor is quite general, and this is a more definite form of it that often occurs. In 1162 the church of All Saints[8] with the chapel of St Mary, Ellingham, were granted by William de Solariis to the abbey of St Saviour's,

[1] *Litt. Cant.* (R.S.), III, p. 356.
[2] *Ibid.* III, p. 357.
[3] *Reg. Hethe*, p. 12.
[4] *Ibid.* pp. 12–13.
[5] *Ibid.* pp. 15–16.
[6] *Buckland Cart.* p. 172, no. 317.
[7] *Reg. Pontissara*, p. 624.
[8] *Ibid.* p. 411.

Coutances, for the upkeep of monastic buildings in perpetual alms. This was part of the endowment of the daughter priory of Ellingham. Part of the church of Elendon was possessed in 1172 by St Swithin's Priory for writing books and for repairing organs. Whitchurch[1] was assigned to the same priory for the sacristy. Littleton[2] was appropriated in 1171 to the office of guestmaster of the priory.

There were also in this century many grants of tithes that did not amount to the whole proceeds of a church, but were confirmed by the bishops to the monasteries as annual pensions. St Hugh, bishop of Lincoln[3], in a general confirmation of churches in Oxfordshire to Eynsham Abbey, 1197–8, mentioned pensions of 1 mark in the church of Stainton, 2 marks in Souldern, half a mark in Barton, 5 marks in Charlbury, 4*s.* in Norton churches and others elsewhere. From another church the abbey received a pound of wax yearly, and from yet another one pound of pepper. Probably these were commutations of tithe dues. Chester Abbey (1174–80) was granted a pension of 2*s.* yearly in the church of Handley by Hente de Boydell[4]. When Strood Hospital in the diocese of Rochester[5] was founded in 1193, Bishop Gilbert de Glanville appropriated to it the chapel of St Margaret, but reserved a pension of half a mark of the oblations of St Margaret's day to the monks of his cathedral chapter. This was a compensation for the loss of dues on the church being received into mortmain. It was confirmed[6] to Rochester Priory by the same bishop, who also confirmed 40*s.* from its mother altar of St Nicholas of Strood, 2 marks from Aylesford Church (both pensions being reservations from grants to the new Hospital at Strood), 10 marks from Dartford, and 7*s.* from Woolwich. He also granted 2*s.* yearly from Barming[7] Church to Leeds Priory.

The church of Higham, in the diocese of Rochester, affords an example of the quarrels that arose at this time concerning churches and tithes. About 1148 St John's Abbey[8], Colchester, surrendered the church to Mary, daughter of King Stephen,

[1] *Reg. Pontissara*, p. 625.
[2] Rev. J. C. Cox, LL.D., F.S.A., *Vic. County Hist.* (*Hants.*), II, p. 111 *b*.
[3] *Eynsham Chart.* I, pp. 44–5.
[4] *Chester Chart.* I, p. 92.
[5] *Reg. Hethe*, p. 1.
[6] *Ibid.* p. 42.
[7] *Ibid.* p. 13.
[8] *Ibid.* p. 27.

for her foundation of nuns there. This act was duly notified and confirmed by Bishop Walter. Yet later (1166–79) Gilbert Foliot, bishop of London and Simon, abbot of St Albans, as Papal legates, had to decide the ownership of the church, for Colchester Abbey claimed it back again. They decided that the nuns were to have the church in return for a piece of land, worth 30*s*. yearly, which land was to be restored if the nuns could procure for the abbey the land called Blunt's Hall in exchange. Whether the original price had never been paid by the royal foundress to the abbey, or whether this payment was but legalised blackmail, does not appear. It appears also that there was a risk for monasteries of losing much of the profits of their churches by prolonged vacancies during which bishops drew the revenues. The monks of Eynsham[1] carefully transcribed into their chartulary a bull of Pope Innocent II or III to the archbishop of Canterbury and his suffragans, that had been granted in reply to questions of the monks of R. (*sic*). This bull stated that the churches belonging to monastic houses were never vacant, and that until parsons or vicars are instituted the monks should receive all the fruits. This expressly prohibited the bishop from drawing the profits of vacant vicarages. It was also, unhappily, a temptation to the monks to leave their benefices vacant for an undue length of time.

Churches were granted to cathedral chapters and in cases of non-monastic chapters came to be used as prebends for canons of the cathedral. For instance, in 1192, King John granted to Lichfield Cathedral the church of Bakewell[2] in the same diocese. The conditions made were that reasonable sustenance was to be found for the three prebendaries who served the church, and that a daily mass was to be said for John both before and after his death. This grant was originally to the bishop himself, but Bishop William de Cornhill (1215–23) made over two-thirds of the church to the use of the chapter.

Papal confirmation was the surest safeguard of the monasteries and was, sooner or later, sought by every monastery for all its more important possessions, among which churches ranked very high. The chartulary of practically every monastery

[1] *Eynsham Chart.* I, p. 18.
[2] Cox, *Notes on the Churches of Derbyshire*, II, p. 5.

of this period contains such a confirmation, and probably bitter experience taught that a little money spent in procuring legal assistance at Rome was a good and necessary investment. Pope Eugenius III, in 1146, confirmed seven churches to the Benedictine abbey of Abingdon[1] in Berkshire, although it is impossible to discover exactly what rights the abbey possessed in these churches. Probably it was only the advowson that was meant, but possibly tithe rights also. In 1173 Pope Alexander III confirmed all the possessions of the Benedictine abbey of Sherborne[2] in Dorsetshire including the parish church of Sherborne, which the abbot held *in prebendam* from the church of Salisbury, with its chapels, lands, tithes and adjacent belongings. A number of other churches were also confirmed to the abbey, some such as Littleham, and St Ishmael of Pennalt expressly with their lands, tithes and appurtenances. In 1191 Pope Celestine III[3] confirmed the church of Buckland, in the diocese of Bath and Wells, and thirteen other churches to Gloucester Abbey *in proprios usus* and in 1192 Yalding[4] with Brenchley chapel, Mereworth, and Stradishall and its chapel to Tonbridge Priory. Such are a few examples of confirmations by twelfth-century popes of English churches to English monasteries. By 1200 the practice of appropriation had become very frequent, and for the rest of the Middle Ages Papal confirmations flowed out from the Curia with unceasing regularity. It was indeed time for an Innocent III to appear who should insist on the rights of the parish clergy as strongly as he approved of the just privileges of the monks.

In twelfth-century England the churches were served, so far as one may gather, by vicars under terms made locally without any reference to a general system. The earliest mention of an English parochial vicar, so called, that I have come across, is at Pershore in 1147. Simon, bishop of Worcester, signified that at the instance of Athelard, the parson, and Edwin, the priest ruling the vicarage by the presentation of the prior and monks of Malvern, he had dedicated the church and granted an Indulgence to votaries resorting thither.

[1] Dugdale-Caley, *Monasticon*, I, p. 522 *b*. [2] *Ibid.* I, p. 339 *a*, *b*.
[3] *Hist. and Cart. Gloucs.* III, p. 11. Notwithstanding the opposition of the diocesan bishop or the prohibitions of the Lateran Council. See p. 32.
[4] *Reg. Hethe*, p. 18.

In an Inquisition[1] into the manors belonging to the Dean and Chapter of St Paul's in 1181, there is also an account of churches on these manors. The introduction to this is of very great interest, setting forth as it does the necessity for a distinction of persons between the "farmer" of the manor and its church and the incumbent of the church:

lest by promiscuity in acts the spheres of office of the things be disordered[2], let there be always in the same village a distinction of persons; let there be one who has charge of temporal matters, and another who ministers to spiritual needs: let there be one who pays tithes, and another who receives them. Let there, moreover, be ordained a vicar in the churches according to the disposition of the chapter, who if the means (*facultates*) of the church allow, while he serves the altar may be content with the altar: if they do not allow, let provisions be supplied to the chaplain from the tithes, to such an extent that he may always be self-respecting. The rest of the fruits, however, which they shall have cultivated in the church at their own expense, and also the greater tithes, shall be reserved to the canons, and shall either be handed over to the chaplains for a yearly payment or to other clerks at farm. As a regular proceeding it shall be done as we have stated above, unless urgent necessity for a while compel some other course of action for some temporary reason or great usefulness to the chapter. Let there, however, be ordained in the churches a vicar according to the disposition both of the Dean and Chapter.

I have been able to discover few indubitably twelfth-century vicarages in England, and so am led to consider the vicarage system in England as a growth of the early thirteenth, with its roots, indeed, in the past, but scarcely shooting above ground until those early years of the thirteenth century when it grew with such amazing rapidity. The miscellaneous character of the twelfth-century vicarages recorded in Appendix A is quite obvious and they can in no wise be held to constitute a system. They were but sporadic attempts to provide for the proper payment of ministers who should perform the regular service of the churches. They make it clear, however, that the work of Popes and bishops in fostering the system was, after all, but the adoption into universal practice of what the best conscience of the appropriating monks had already, in scattered places, produced spontaneously.

[1] *Domesday of St Paul's* (Camden Soc.), 1858, pp. 146 *seq.*
[2] *Ne promiscuis actibus rerum turbentur officia.*

In 1204, the bishop of Ely[1] sent to Innocent III a long letter of queries about difficulties of canon law, which was answered patiently with a mild protest that the Pope had many and other things to occupy his time. The answer is of great importance as a declaration of law on many difficult points, and the question of appropriations, and of vicarages, looms large. It is clear evidence of the importance that bishops assigned to these matters.

"You have asked", said Innocent[2], "whether it is lawful for religious men, who have been granted permission from the Apostolic See to convert their churches to their own uses, to enter them, on the death of the parsons, on their own authority or whether they ought rather to be inducted by the diocesan. To which we reply that unless by chance it is contained in the indulgence of the Pope expressly 'without the consent of their bishop' it is not lawful for them to enter in possession of them because we do not believe an indulgence of this kind to be derogatory to episcopal rights."

This decision gave the bishop chance to protest against any appropriation by Papal authority that he knew to be unjust though he might often in fact protest vainly. Moreover, it is clear that monasteries, being rectors, should be inducted in the person of their representatives into their benefices as rectors with all the usual ceremony. On the other hand, the express permission to appropriate on voidance without consent of the bishop or archdeacon was not rarely given. Silkstone Rectory[3], in County York, by a bull of 1255 was to be so appropriated to Pontefract Priory, but in 1284 Archbishop Wickwane saw fit to perform the appropriation himself in order to save his face, acknowledging the *fait accompli* of 1281, when on the promotion of the rector to the bishopric of Bath and Wells the monks of Pontefract "intruded" into the church. The archbishop had even called in the power of the king to expel the monks, but as soon as this was removed for some cause not stated, the monks had entered again. Another case of this express permission to enter "without consent of the Bishop or Archdeacon" is that given to Roche Abbey[4], diocese of York, in 1256 to apply to its

[1] Eustace—also vice-chancellor and keeper of the Royal Seal, and ultimately chancellor. "In all the tangled events and in the various councils of this stirring period Eustace took a leading part" (*D.N.B.* VI, p. 915 *a*).

[2] Migne, *P.L.* t. 215, cols. 481–2.

[3] *Reg. Wickwane*, pp. 273–4, 292–4.

[4] *Cal. Pap. Let.* I, p. 331.

own uses any church whose patronage should canonically be made over to them.

Similarly, when Archbishop Odo Rigaldi of Rouen summoned the monks of the abbey of Eu to answer why they had appropriated certain of their churches without consent of the diocesan bishop, they claimed letters and privileges allowing them to do so. A year later the archbishop woefully wrote in his Register, "For the churches appropriated by their own authority they have not hitherto paid us well", referring of course to the usual dues[1].

It was a bad policy, striking a terrible blow at local church discipline, and encouraging the monks in their frequent insubordination to the bishops.

The bishop of Ely also asked Pope Innocent whether it was lawful for the bishop to perform appropriations "without the consent of the Pope or the consent of his own chapter, and in spite of the Statute of the 3rd Lateran Council that had forbidden the increase of old pensions in churches or the assignment of new ones to monasteries". The Pope replied that the bishop could not do these things without the consent of the Pope, except by the will of his chapter. As a consequence of this rule, there is frequently inserted in the episcopal registers the document giving the consent of the chapter, as well as that of the bishop that enjoined the appropriation.

A third question relating to these matters was: If the bishop, having received the permission of the patron, simply says to a monastery, "we concede to you that church", should that be taken as conferring the appropriation or only the patronage of the rectory? The Pope ruled that the bishop thus by these words conferred all the temporal rights he himself possessed in the church, save the sinodal dues. Even if the bishop himself possessed no such rights these words were to be taken as conferring all the proceeds of the church, but if the donation was to be legal, the consent of the chapter was required[2]. It might be suggested that Innocent was historically wrong, because many early grants of churches may only have been grants of

[1] *Reg. Rigaldi*, pp. 269, 300.

[2] It seems to be assumed that the capitular body was always an interested party when there was question of a complete appropriation of a church. Hence its permission was normally to be regarded as essential for legality.

advowson, but at any rate, the legal issue that had so long been dubious, was settled, and the mere fact of definition was a gain to the canon law.

These decisions are typical of this great period of definition of church law, and show how the legal mind was becoming the ruler of the Church. Innocent III was a magnificent lawgiver, because he was not afraid to make original decisions of a clear-cut nature. The bishop of Ely is in this instance acting in a fashion typical of an age when English bishops were keen administrators of law, keener indeed on destroying anomalies than on sweeping away abuses, it is true, but above all anxious for definitions[1]. It was a necessary work, and was on the whole well carried out, although rather spoilt by the irresponsibility of the Papal Curia. The medieval Pope was so far above law that the exceptions he was able to make tended to ruin the neatness, precision, and efficacy of the law he created. As yet, however, these things did not come to pass and the work of definition proceeded most effectively. The whole work of thirteenth-century vicarage founding is the product of an age of lawyers, with the inspiration of a few who were not only administrators but also moralists, like Grosseteste.

The early years of the century, even before the Lateran Council of 1215, show the work of vicarage foundation being carried on. The vicarage that existed at Walkern[2] in Hertfordshire, even before its appropriation to Colchester Abbey in 1204, may have been of twelfth-century origin. The same year, however, saw the new bishop of Lincoln, William of Blois[3], insisting on the endowment by the canons of Dunstable of a vicarage in their church of Polluxhill. The vicar was to receive the altar dues, ten acres of land, and a third of the tithes. This was a fit precedent for a diocese whose bishops throughout this century

[1] It has been suggested to me that this habit of posing legal conundrums to the Pope merely shows inefficiency in the bishop, and that Innocent III's protest was quite justified. I pass on this opinion to the reader for what it is worth, but personally it does not convince me. For a discussion of this matter of decretal letters, see Mr Z. N. Brooke's article on "The Effect of Becket's Murder", *Cambridge Hist. Journal*, II, pp. 213 *seq.* His opinion is that the preponderance of English letters among the decretal letters of Alexander III and Lucius III shows that canon law as a whole was only just being recognised as completely valid in England.

[2] Miss Henrietta Garbett, in *Vic. County Hist.* (*Herts.*), IV, p. 294.

[3] *Ann. Mon.* (R.S.), III, p. 28; see also E. L. Cutts, *Parish Priests*, p. 102.

maintained a fine tradition of efficiency in their care for the services of the parish churches. In the diocese of Coventry and Lichfield about the same time at least four more endowed vicarages came into existence. Chester Abbey gained two-thirds of the proceeds of the churches of Dodleston and Handley[1], and Tutbury Priory two-thirds of Dovebridge[2], and Marston-on-Dove, on condition that they should present suitable vicars to the residual benefices. The vicar of Marston-on-Dove was also to receive 2*s.* pension from the priory. Bishop Savaric of Bath and Wells confirmed all the garb tithes and services of the church of Somerton to Muchelney Abbey on condition that the vicar should have all the altarage, arable lands, obventions and small tithes. There were also vicarages at Carshalton[3] and Talworth[4] in Surrey and Farleigh and Ditton in Kent[5] before 1215. The vicarage of Carshalton was worth 6 marks, yet we learn that Little Brickhill in Buckinghamshire[6] had a vicarage that was worth barely 4 marks, because it was constituted "before the Council". This implies that vicarages constituted before the Council were usually below the minimum of 5 marks that came to be recognised as satisfactory. The phrase "before the Council" refers to the Lateran Council of 1215, "the Council" being always an oecumenical Council when referred to in this bald fashion. Yet it was the Council of Oxford, not of Lateran, that set the minimum value of 5 marks. However, the Lateran Council was taken as authority, quite rightly, for augmentations as well as for original ordinations of vicarages. Hugh de Welles, for example, augmented the vicarage of Skendleby[7] in 1219, between the dates of the two Councils, the abbot and convent of Bardney, as rectors, consenting. Luton[8] vicarage in 1219 was ordained "by authority of the Council", and other examples of this phrase may readily be found. The bishop, "by authority of the Council" granted a pension of 10*s.* in the church of Caldecote[9] in Huntingdonshire

[1] *Chester Chart.* I, p. 122.
[2] Cox, *Notes on the Churches of Derbyshire,* III, p. 115.
[3] Heales, *Records of Merton Priory,* p. 47.
[4] *Ibid.* p. 53.
[5] *Reg. Hethe,* pp. 12, 13.
[6] *Reg. H. de Welles,* II, p. 70.
[7] *Ibid.* I, p. 132.
[8] *Lib. Ant. Hugonis Wells,* p. 22.
[9] *Reg. H. de Welles,* I, pp. 206, 240; III, p. 42.

to William Beinvill, who already held the vicarage there. The parson of Blaby in Leicestershire was John de Hinkston, nephew of the archdeacon of Stow, and was instituted by the bishop "by the authority of the Council"[1] and received one gold piece pension there. The vicarage of Norton by Daventry was also said to have been ordained before the Council.

Pope Innocent III sent many mandates to English bishops on the subject, for instance, one for Peter, bishop of Winchester, in 1205, desiring him to compel those who had obtained parsonages to appoint vicars who would serve the churches in person[2]. Clearly the early thirteenth-century vicarages in England were the direct result of Papal authority. If that authority was afterwards seriously abused, it must yet be remembered with gratitude that Innocent III's influence was the power that ensured a reasonable service of the parish churches of medieval England.

[1] Why by that authority I do not know but there is no doubt that "the Council" was the Lateran Council.

[2] *Cal. Pap. Let.* I, p. 23; also *Opp.* ed. Migne, II, col. 723.

MILLS COLLEGE
LIBRARY

CHAPTER III

A CENTURY OF GREAT BISHOPS

IN order to understand the work of Bishop Hugh de Welles of Lincoln who formally "ordained", and set down in writing, the details of 300 vicarages in his diocese, we must first consider a few definitions of technical terms.

The portion of the church revenues that belonged most essentially to the priest serving the altar came to be called the "altarage" (*altaragium*). The often quoted phrase "he that served the altar should live of the altar"[1], while enjoining a duty of providing adequately for the servitor of the altar, had in practice a limiting effect. The canonist, John of Ayton, who, as Dr Coulton says, was not always tender to the monks, decided that the servitor of the altar must be content if he received enough for bare food and raiment. "And having food and raiment let us be therewith content," says St Paul[2], which the monks thought a good text to apply—especially to their vicars. Originally the word altarage included only the voluntary offerings made to the altar, and hence it came to mean the customary and obligatory offerings to the altar. Probably at this point there arose a confusion of ideas between altarage as altar-dues, and the portion possessed by the actual servitor of the altar. Since he often, in fact generally, had the small tithes as well as the altar-dues, these also came to be included in the term "altarage". The monks certainly tended to adopt the view that "he that served the altar should live of the altarage"[3]. The ordinations of the thirteenth century give only a general sanction to this, and no bishop ever subscribed to the view that he could not give the vicar part of the great tithes if it was necessary. It is only the broadest of generalisations that the "ordained" vicarage was endowed with altar-dues and small tithes and the rectory with the great tithes. Yet there is considerable justification for such a generalisation. For example, in 1496, in the diocese of Worms, the small tithe generally seems to have been

[1] Cp. 1 Cor. ix, 13. [2] 1 Timothy vi, 8.
[3] See the St Paul's survey quoted on p. 30.

the vicar's portion, though it is to be feared that at times he did not receive even this intact. Weiszenheim's vicar is spoken of as equivalent to the small tithes (*Plebanus sive decima minor*) but at Richardtshausen chapel "half of the small tithes nourishes the stud animals, and two laymen have them"[1]. Bishop Kennett says that the small tithes were at first a voluntary oblation, yet seeing that the Jews of old used to "tithe mint and cummin", this seems unlikely. On the other hand, we discover that the people of Chingford in the late twelfth century had never paid small tithes to anyone, a fact which may be urged in support of Kennett's statement. The word "altarage" can be given no very hard and fast meaning, although possibly local usages were sometimes quite fixed. In the documents of Hugh de Welles and his contemporaries, there are many examples of "the altarage consisting of the small tithes, etc." and of "the altarage and the small tithes" mentioned separately. The vicar of Rushden[2], Northants, in 1230 was to receive *totum altaragium et omnes minutas decimas* (the whole altarage and all the small tithes). At Aston Clinton[3], however, it was stated that the vicar should have "the altarage, except tithes of lambs and wool". Clearly in this case the small tithes were included in the altarage. At Hough in Lincolnshire[4] the vicarage consisted: *in toto altaragio exceptis decimis agnorum, lane, primo legato et excepto redditu sex solidorum de una bovata terre, et uno prato pertinente ad altaragium*; that is to say, "in the whole altarage save tithes of lambs and wool except the first legacy and except a rent of six shillings from one bovate of land, and one meadow belonging to the altarage".

The "first legacy" means either the heriot due to the lord of the manor, or more probably the more important of the mortuaries—the death offerings made to the rector *pro decimis oblitis* (for forgotten tithes)[5]. What is important about this passage is that it includes in the altarage not only the small tithes, but also mortuaries or heriots, rents from church lands, and the actual glebe or demesne of the church. Yet in spite of this wide divergence of usage the word is in constant use in the

[1] *Zeitschrift...Oberrheins*, XXVII, pp. 313, 415.
[2] *Reg. H. de Welles*, II, p. 234.
[3] *Ibid.* II, p. 90.
[4] *Ibid.* III, p. 73.
[5] See Appendix C.

most formal official documents, and there must have been many legal disputes about its meaning in particular cases that have not been recorded for posterity. Many a twelfth-century rector must have soothed his conscience with the thought that his vicar was receiving all the altarage, and should not the minister "live of the altar"? This thought is implied in the introduction to the St Paul's survey quoted above. Another difficult word that occurs in the documents about vicarages is "garb", which properly means a sheaf. This was the sheaf of corn, which was the "great tithe". Although Elizabethan lawyers[1] decided that it was possible to include hay in the term "garb", there is no medieval evidence to my knowledge to justify this, and even those lawyers declared that, since the practice varied, the word must be judged according to use. Hay, with the garb tithes, was frequently reserved to the appropriators, and so may be considered akin to the great tithe, and it was sometimes even called great tithe but more generally it was expressly included in the small tithes.

Nearly 300 vicarages in the diocese of Lincoln were definitely founded at the instigation of Hugh de Welles, and it is only in a very small minority of cases that we are told that the vicarage was ordained "long before". Of these some required augmentation, such as Skendleby, already mentioned, and Duns Tew, "which is said to be insufficient, and it is not known by whom it was ordained". It consisted of the altarage and the small tithes, two and a half virgates of land, and a manse, and the rectory belonged to Merton Priory.

In 1219 Richard, bishop of Salisbury, William, abbot of Westminster, and Richard, abbot of Waltham, gave a decision in an ecclesiastical suit between St Albans Abbey and the bishop of Lincoln. It is a mistake to exaggerate this case, as some have done[2], into a formal test case, after the modern manner, of the bishop's right to ordain vicarages in the appropriated churches of monasteries. It was not the first time that the bishop had attempted to do this, nor, I think, would even the abbot of St Albans have claimed his case as representative. Dunstable

[1] Barsdale *v.* Smith in *Croke Reports* (*Elizabethae*), I, p. 633, ed. London, 1669.

[2] Rev. J. C. Cox, in *Vic. County Hist.* (*Northants.*), II, p. 18; (*Hants.*), II, p. 21: also *Gesta Abbatum Mon. St Albani* (R.S.), I, p. 276.

Priory[1] had submitted to similar treatment at the hands of his predecessor, William of Blois, in the case of the vicarage of Polluxhill. The fact is simply that it was now the great abbey of St Albans, privileged above all others in England with Papal exemptions and Royal favours, that was challenged by the bishop. The Papal commissioners, above mentioned as the judges, were representative both of episcopal and abbatial dignities. The verdict seems to have been given on a just and unbiased consideration of the canon law, as it applied to the one case of St Albans Abbey. A former verdict of the abbot of Sibton was confirmed and the vicarage was declared to be ordained as follows:

> The perpetual vicar was to have all obventions and small tithes of the church and of all its chapels and a manse in which he could live. He was not to have the garb tithes or the church lands, but he was to bear all ordinary burdens, namely the parochial, the sinodal (the dues of the cathedral church), and the archidiaconal. The vicar was to be presented to the Bishop for institution and the Bishop was to have full jurisdiction in the church and the custody of the vicarage when vacant.

Another great point in dispute in the same case was the position of the cells of the monastery at Belvoir, Hertford and Beaulieu. On this matter the judges decided for the abbot, to whom they adjudged the cure of souls. He might place his monks in them or remove them without hindrance by the bishop. These cells were obviously of the *prioratus curatus* type, and this adverse decision was not much less of a blow to the bishop than the other decision was to the monastery. Yet, nevertheless, it was a great day when Hugh de Welles could feel certain of his power of insisting on the ordination of fit vicarages in all churches in which the monasteries did not possess definitely episcopal rights. Although not a test case necessary to the commencement of his work, the defeat of the abbey of St Albans on the first issue may well be regarded as his hardest and greatest victory, without which his work would have remained imperfect. From the great chronicler of St Albans, Matthew Paris[2], such acts as this

[1] Hearne, *Chronicon sive Annales Prioratus de Dunstablia* (Oxford, 1733), I, p. 49.

[2] Matthew Paris, *Chron. Maj.* (R.S.), III, p. 306.

gained for Hugh the title of "persecutor of the monks, and the hammer of canons and all religious". The *Liber Antiquus*, which was compiled about this date, contains the record of nearly 300 vicarage ordinations in the churches of monasteries and of absentee rectors. Even this did not complete the work, for in October 1220, when Hugh visited Dunstable Priory[1], he ordained vicarages in five of their churches, after holding inquisition into the values of the churches and their vicarages. The values of these were as follows:

	Vicarage	Whole church
Studham	6 marks	20 marks
Totternhoe	5 ,,	12 ,,
Chalgrave	5½ ,,	15 ,,
Segenhoe	5½ ,,	15 ,,
Husborne Crawley	5 ,, 4*s*.	12 ,,

The prior was to sustain all burdens as to the hospitality to the archdeacon and sustentation in books, chancels, vestments, utensils and tallages for his portion. The vicar was to bear all other burdens.

In 1222 it was expressly stated in a Papal mandate[2] to the bishop that he should appoint resident vicars who should be advanced to the priesthood as their cures required. Probably this was in reply to a request by Bishop Hugh for further guidance and powers.

In 1222 was held the Council of Oxford[3] under Archbishop Stephen Langton, which took up the cause of the parish priests and made rules, for the maintenance of which future bishops were to wage a long and, on the whole, a very successful struggle. Where the church had been divided between two or more rectors, the portions were to be consolidated on the death of any of them and in future there was to be no more than one vicarage founded in a church. Long-standing custom, however, was respected in this enactment, and those churches that had been so divided of old were excepted from the general rule. No one was to be admitted to a vicarage unless he was willing to minister personally and proceed to priestly orders within a short time. Any who would not conform to these conditions should be

[1] *Ann. Dunstab.* (ed. Thos. Hearne), I, p. 95; *Ann. Mon.* (R.S.), III, p. 59.
[2] *Cal. Pap. Let.* I, p. 85.
[3] Wilkins, *Concilia*, I, p. 587, caps. xiii–xvi.

deprived of their vicarages. It was also forbidden to the rector to make himself a vicar and dispose of the rectory to anyone else. The most important rule of the Council, however, was that which defined a suitable value for a vicarage in terms of money.

But since very often the luxury of worldly goods shuts off and draws away certain from the office committed to them, to the immoderate scandal of the people; and since poverty of the same things compels others to beg miserably to the shame of our order: it behoves us in either case, having the temper of moderation, to consult the rule of the churches, therefore we have determined that there be assigned to a perpetual vicar at least five marks of the returns, that is to say, as much as can be given to farm for five marks, unless, perhaps, it be in those parts of Wales, where on account of the slenderness of the churches vicars are content with a smaller stipend. Let the diocesan bishop also weigh the competence of the church and determine whether the vicar ought to bear the burdens of the church, or the parson, or both between them, provided however, that the archdeacon of the place either from both or one of them, shall receive his due fees. Let him, however, be content with one payment of fees.

Hugh de Welles made a determined effort to make the vicarages in his diocese conform to these rules, and had begun to do so even before the Council of Oxford definitely formulated them.

In 134 vicarages mentioned in the *Liber Antiquus*, where the values are given, 50 are assessed at less than 5 marks, 63 at between 5 and 6 marks, and 21 over 6 marks. They range from 3 marks to £11. 1*s*. 6*d*. in the case of St John the Baptist at Peterborough. These, however, were only assessed values, and were, therefore, according to the usual custom, lower than the actual values. Evidence from the Rolls of Bishop Hugh, where assessments given are often higher, confirms this view. The following instances are picked out from the *Liber Antiquus* and the Rolls. The whole church, *totalis ecclesia*, was the church before the subtraction of the vicarage.

Reference	Name	Vicarage	Whole church
L.A. p. 71	Alkborough	6 marks	40 marks
R. I, p. 213	,,	6 ,,	11 ,,
L.A. p. 55 *R.* III, p. 78	Ancaster	5 ,,	20 ,,
L.A. p. 3 *R.* I, p. 183	Aston, North	5 ,,	100*s*.
L.A. p. 24	Barford, Great	8 ,,	20 marks

Reference	Name	Vicarage		Whole church
L.A. p. 56 *R.* III, p. 79	Bracebridge	6 marks (nearly)		20 marks
L.A. p. 58 *R.* III, p. 83	Bullington	3½ ,,		100*s*.
L.A. p. 23	Cardington	5 ,,		10 marks
R. III, p. 18	,,	8 ,,		24 ,,
L.A. p. 60 *R.* III, p. 85	Cockerington, South	3 ,,	and more	100*s*.
L.A. p. 61 *R.* III, p. 87	Grimoldby	4 ,,		12 marks
R. I, p. 185	Haynes	4 ,,		12 ,,
L.A. p. 22	Stotfold	5 ,,		15 ,,
R. III, p. 77	Stow-Birthorpe	4 ,,		15 ,,

L.A. = *Liber Antiquus*. *R.* = Rolls or Register (Cant. and York. Soc.).

I have given two cases in which the assessments were very widely different for no very apparent reason. There is not the slightest evidence, to my knowledge, of a change in the ordination of Cardington, for instance, yet not merely the values but the proportions between rectory and vicarage differ.

It is, as a matter of fact, an instance that shows the difficulty of judging values that were simply assessed values, for values given within a few years often show a marked discrepancy probably for no other reason than different standards taken by the assessors.

These figures indicate how frequently was the proportion of rectory to vicarage as two to one[1]. Dr Coulton has added together[2] the valuations of the 39 cases in the *Liber Antiquus*, where both church and vicarage are given for comparison. The total of the churches (that is, rectory and vicarage together) comes to £343. 6*s*. 8*d*. and that of the vicarages to £123. 1*s*. 3*d*. It is probable that Hugh had in mind the old Gelasian division of the tithes, and considered that the monasteries only had a right to the portion of the poor and of the church fabric. If the vicar had been regarded as quit of the duties of feeding the poor and of repairing the church fabric, this division would have been fair enough. Regarding the various special oblations and the produce of the church lands as amply compensating for the

[1] In 1216 the bishop of Arras had granted to the vicar of the church of Camblain a portion amounting to one-third of the church. The vicar sued for one-half, but the archdeacons of Arras and Ostevant, who acted as arbiters, decided for the bishop. *Arras Chartulary*, No. 75. Other examples of the one-third vicarage are found in my Appendixes A and B. It was very common.

[2] *Hist. Teach. Misc.* III, p. 181.

natural tendency to give short weight and measure in tithes, it would have required a parish of only 15 tithe-payers to make a resident rector quite as rich as his average parishioner, making a very large allowance for dilapidations. If a vicar received one-third of a church, he would have been as rich as an average parishioner in a parish of 45 tithe-payers. This would represent, perhaps, a village of 150 souls. In a village of this size, if there were any destitute poor, they ought not to be allowed to starve; the vicar would have been relieved of the moral obligation to feed them, and the monastery would, in all probability, be too far away to do so. Clearly, then, either there must be a local endowment set apart by the monastery, or else the monastery must incur the charge of having robbed either the poor or the vicar who fed them. Such a local endowment is very seldom found, although in later times the charity of individuals often made some attempt at supplying this lack. As far as the vicar was concerned, the one-third rule was no great injustice, save when he had any considerable share of the burdens of the church to bear. For his own personal use, he was, by ancient custom, entitled only to one-third. If it be granted, as it readily may be, that the other two-thirds was an excessive amount to set apart for the church burdens, one may easily condone the acquisition by the monks of a part of these two-thirds. The monasteries gave many fine churches to the world, many a poor man went to them and found help and food, and a well-ruled monastery was worth much in example, in learning, and often even in economic value to the world. It is not attacking any system, any doctrine, any faith, to declare that the monasteries displayed inordinate greed. While not insisting that tithes contributed by parishioners need necessarily be spent entirely within the parish, for no one would claim that to-day for the civil taxes paid by a parish, we must protest that it was grossly unfair for a monastery to take two-thirds of the tithes, and leave the vicar the other third plus most of the burdens. Among Hugh de Welles' ordinations such an arrangement is, indeed, rare. Generally the vicar had to pay only the sinodal dues, as for example, at Bonby[1] in Lincolnshire, where the vicarage was worth 5 (and even 7 marks according to a little later assessment[2])

[1] *Reg. H. de Welles*, III, p. 61. [2] *Ibid.* III, p. 178.

and at Chalgrave[1] where, as stated above, the vicarage was worth 5½ marks, and the whole church 15. At Burreth[2], in Lincolnshire, where the vicarage was calculated at only 3½ marks, Tupholme Abbey undertook all the burdens, finding even books and ornaments. Barthorp[3] vicarage was assessed at 4 marks, and Sempringham Priory undertook all the burdens, ordinary and extraordinary. At Billingborough[4], whose vicarage was of 5½ marks as against a 14 marks assessment of the whole church, the same priory bore all the burdens, while Catley Priory did the same at Billinghay[5] (vicarage nearly 5 marks, whole church 16 marks). At Chalfont St Peter, in Buckinghamshire, the vicar was to receive the altarage and certain lands with the buildings on them. Missenden Abbey probably received about two-thirds of the profits (cp. *Taxatio Papae Nicholai*, Record Commission, p. 33 *a*). The burdens[6] were divided so that the vicar paid sinodals, and the abbey entertained the archdeacon when he visited the church and all other burdens were to be borne proportionately. The vicar of All Saints, Hertford[7], had to bear all the ordinary burdens, although he received only the obventions of the altar and the small tithes. The value of the vicarage is not stated, as there was a litigious claim of a pension by the abbey of 23 marks, so it is impossible to say whether it was exceptionally large. At Timberland[8], the vicar received only one-third of the church, yet had to bear all the burdens. The vicarage was worth 6 marks or more, according to one entry, and 10 marks according to another a few years later. At Turville[9], a church of St Albans Abbey, the vicar had to bear all the ordinary due and customary burdens save that of entertaining the archdeacon. The vicar of Willingham[10] was to bear all the "ordinary burdens", by which phrase is meant those occurring regularly every year. These are distinctly exceptional cases in the diocese under Hugh de Welles; it was nearly always the monastery that had to bear all the

1 *Reg. H. de Welles*, III, p. 3.
2 *Lib. Ant.* p. 63.
3 *Ibid.* p. 54.
4 *Reg. H. de Welles*, III, p. 78; *Lib. Ant.* p. 55.
5 *Lib. Ant.* p. 55.
6 *Reg. H. de Welles*, II, p. 64.
7 *Ibid.* III, p. 46; *Lib. Ant.* p. 29.
8 *Reg. H. de Welles*, III, pp. 75, 215.
9 *Ibid.* I, p. 197.
10 *Lib. Ant.* pp. 94, 95.

burdens save sinodals, which the vicar very frequently had to pay. So far the division was as fair as could possibly be expected, considering what a great improvement these conditions must have been on those of the twelfth century.

A typical simple vicarage *ordination* in a church belonging to a monastery is that of Burgh-on-Bain[1], where the vicar received all the altarage, save the tithes of lamb and wool, and also a toft, which was presumably a piece of ground for a house. He was to pay sinodals only, and his vicarage was worth 60*s*. This was rather a small one. The vicar of Tallington[2] received the altarage and a toft, and although he had to pay back 24*s*. to Belvoir Priory, and to pay sinodals, this vicarage was worth 5 marks. The altarage and manse that comprised the endowment of the vicarage of Alkborough[3] ordained according to the statutes of the Council, were worth 6 marks. Bitchfield[4], in Lincolnshire, was appropriated in the sixth year of Hugh de Welles' pontificate (1216) and the vicarage, worth only 3½ marks, was endowed in the altarage, a toft, and in three quarters of wheat, one of manure, and one of hay, to be paid yearly by Bourne Abbey, which had to sustain all episcopal and archidiaconal burdens. The vicarage of the Templars' church of Bradwell[5] was worth 10 marks, but the duties were correspondingly severe. The vicar was bound to officiate daily at the mother church and at the chapel of Kelmstock, and thrice a week and on feast days at the chapel of Holywell. He received the altarage, the small tithes (mentioned separately here), the third sheaf of the demesne, with the small tithes, and tithes of crofts at Bradwell. Three chaplains were necessary in the church, but by whom they were to be paid is not definitely stated. Possibly the vicar had to pay them himself, although they probably were not all full-time workers in the parish.

A more complex ordination is that of Burley-on-the-Hill[6] in Rutland, where the vicar received all the altarage, save the tithe of lambs, and the altar oblations of 15 days in the two feasts of Holy Cross; and the tithes of hay and a mill which the last vicar

[1] *Reg. H. de Welles*, III, p. 60; *Lib. Ant.* p. 44.
[2] *Reg. H. de Welles*, III, pp. 91, 203.
[3] *Ibid.* I, p. 213.
[4] *Ibid.* III, p. 88.
[5] *Ibid.* I, p. 183; *Lib. Ant.* p. 3.
[6] *Reg. H. de Welles*, II, p. 166.

had obtained from the lord of the manor and from the parishioners. He received, moreover, a portion of wood and pasture worth 10*s.* yearly, the church demesne land with all its belongings, save a barn used by the nuns for storing their garb tithes, and a manse. He was to pay sinodals only, and the rectors, the nuns of Nuneaton, were to entertain the archdeacon on his visitation. For the service of the chapel of Alesthorpe three days in the week there was an endowment of half a bovate of land, which the nuns kept, and they paid to the vicar 3*s.* a year for it.

The vicarages of Oseney Abbey[1] in the diocese were all ordained by Bishop Hugh according to a pattern. They were situated at Oxford (St Mary Magdalene), Cowley, Foresthill, Kidlington, Hampton-Gay, Weston, Watlington, Hook Norton, Chastleton and Waterperry. The vicarages of Barton and Sandford had already been ordained and so did not come within the scope of this act. The vicar of each of the other churches was to have 2 marks a year for his clothes; any mortuary (*i.e.* legacy made at death to the Church to compensate for tithes that had been forgotten or mislaid in the payment of tithes during the dead man's lifetime), should belong to the vicar up to the value of 6*d.*, and a half of anything beyond that should also be his. The mortuary is here called the second legacy (*secundum legatum*), the first being, I believe, reckoned, in this context, as the heriot that was due to the overlord. Whenever the vicar celebrated mass, he was to receive a mass penny and the offerings of the faithful reasonably made to him. He was to be fed at the table of the canons, or else to receive food sent from that monastery. If necessary, he was to be provided with a horse, for such purposes as visiting the sick and attending councils. If he himself was not a canon he was to have the key to the abbey, and be undisturbed in his cure and receive a sufficiency of food. There was to be also a clerk for the church and a boy to wait on the vicar, both being kept at the expense of the abbey, which was to bear all the burdens. In theory, such an ordination seems ample, but the vicar must, in practice, have been in a much more dependent position than those of his contemporaries who had a definite allotment in

[1] *Reg. H. de Welles*, I, p. 179; *Lib. Ant.* p. 1.

tithes. Independence, although it may be abused, is itself a good thing, and a vicar who could be deprived of his clothing allowance and his very food if a quarrel arose between him and the rectors, must have envied his brother vicar who could point to hay, direct from the tithe-payers. The ordination of Bishopthorpe[1], in the diocese of York, in 1269 illustrated the frequent lack of respect for the vicar's independence by decreeing that the vicar was to receive a meal on Sundays like the servants of the nuns of Clementhorpe, the rectors. If he was discontented with the meal, it was to be left for him until he receive it quietly.

Where the monastery was situated in or near the same parish as the appropriated church, the vicar was reduced to a position of even greater subservience. The vicar then usually had to take his meals with the monks, as at Breedon-on-the-Hill[2], where the ordination was similar to the Oseney type of vicarage. At Northampton[3] the bishop ordered a diligent enquiry as to what the vicar of All Saints ought to receive as a corrody from the priory of St Andrew's, and what was sufficient to support completely two chaplains, who should help the vicar. The result was the ordination [3] by which the vicar was allowed to take his food either in the refectory or in the chamber of the prior, at his choice, or elsewhere, if he prefer it. His servant was to have food like one of the more important servants of the convent. The vicar was also granted 30*s*. a year for wages, and a separate dwelling-house, half of the mortuaries, and 1*d*. from every Mass, and 1*d*. from every marriage. The monks were to bear all burdens and support two secular chaplains, and the clerks necessary to them, all of whom with the vicar were to take an oath of fidelity to the monastery concerning the temporalities of the church. Leicester Abbey was induced to grant similar terms to the vicars in their churches of St Nicholas, St Martin, and St Michael[4] at Leicester. At Swinford[5], the Hospitallers were required to provide a manse for the vicar so that his parishioners could have easy access to him. In the Breedon[6] ordination, also, it was expressly stated that the vicar should be provided

[1] *Reg. Giffard*, I, pp. 59 *seq*.
[2] *Reg. H. de Welles*, II, p. 275.
[3] *Ibid*. II, pp. 148, 241.
[4] *Ibid*. II, pp. 285, 300.
[5] *Ibid*. II, p. 297.
[6] *Ibid*. III, p. 87.

with dwelling-houses outside the priory. The toft of the vicar at Bourne[1] was to be within the abbey by the gate, the idea being probably to ensure both a certain freedom of access of the parishioners to the vicar, and the close supervision of the vicar by the abbey. The toft, manse or dwelling-house was obviously regarded as an essential part of a vicarage ordination, for in many cases, such as that of Hackthorn[2] belonging to Bullington Priory, it is expressly stated that a manse, not already existing, is to be found for the vicar, while in others it is noted that there is no such manse yet assigned, as at Croxton Kerrial in Leicestershire and Guilsborough[3] in Northamptonshire.

Where the rector was not a monastery but an absentee or incapacitated individual, a notably different type of vicarage prevailed. The vicar frequently received the whole products of the church, and was required to pay a pension to the rector. This was the rule at Buckminster[4] where the vicar paid 6 marks, at Covington[5] where he paid 40*s*., at Bowden[6] where he paid 20*s*., at Braybrooke[4] where he paid 2*s*., and at Launton[6] where he paid 2 marks. On the other hand, the vicar of Bulwick[7], in Northants, received a portion detailed in the same way as those of many of the vicarages in churches held by monasteries. He was to receive the altarage, the small tithes and first fruits, the whole tithe of demesne, and of a mill, the tithe of pannage of the manor, and a meadow and two messuages. He was to have a chaplain continuously ministering in the chapel of St Lawrence. Here the parson was a member of a noble family, Walter de Cantelupe, who had been presented to the rectory by William de Cantelupe. Similar detailed vicarages are to be found for Flamstead (Hunts.)[8], Brant Broughton (Lincs.)[9] and other places where there was a non-resident rector. At Whissendine[10], in Rutland, the vicar received the whole church and paid 10 marks yearly to Lindores Abbey, an instance that shows that this type of vicarage, although much more common where the triple relation of patron, rector and vicar existed, is also found in some monastic churches.

[1] *Lib. Ant.* p. 61.
[2] *Ibid.* p. 68.
[3] *Reg. H. de Welles*, II, pp. 122, 317.
[4] *Ibid.* II, pp. 170, 289.
[5] *Ibid.* III, p. 53.
[6] *Ibid.* I, p. 105.
[7] *Ibid.* II, p. 165.
[8] *Ibid.* III, p. 46.
[9] *Ibid.* I, p. 118.
[10] *Ibid.* II, p. 184.

Apart from the ordination of vicarages, Hugh de Welles appears to have been quite as energetic in enforcing other obligations enjoined by the letter and spirit of the Councils of Lateran and Oxford. Roger, a chaplain, who was parson of one mediety[1] of the church of Boddington[2], was inducted into the other mediety, which the bishop conferred on him under the authority of the Lateran Council. The vicar of one of the medieties was Hugh de Botendon (*sic*) whose right, if any, in the vicarage of the other mediety was reserved to him subject to a pension of 8 marks to Roger the parson. The need for this consolidation of divided churches is revealed strongly by the condition of Brocklesby[3] in Lincolnshire, where the vicarage was not yet ordained, probably because the bishop was waiting for a chance to consolidate the four portions. One portion was in the patronage of Newhouse Abbey, another of Tupholme Abbey, a third of one Gilbert de Kent, and a fourth of a certain other clerk. At Shenley[4] (Herts.) the rector, who was instituted at the presentation of his mother about 1222, was not sufficiently learned, and was obliged to attend the schools, but was promised the whole church if the vicar should die and he himself should be worthy. Whether the rector himself died, or resigned next year does not appear, but a new rector was then appointed saving the perpetual vicarage.

The qualifications of presentees were rigidly examined and, if insufficient, the institution was made conditionally for a time, after which they could be reviewed. When Silvester the deacon was instituted to the perpetual vicarage of Whitchurch[5] in Oxfordshire, he was required to be ordained priest at the next ordination and to serve personally. He received the whole church, paying 10 marks yearly to a non-resident rector; obviously because he was a foreigner, he was required to have with him a chaplain capable of administering confessions and other sacraments in a tongue known to the parishioners. Walter de Tonton, clerk, was given the custody of the parsonage of Kidlington[6], a vicarage worth 4 marks being reserved to M., a

[1] *Medietas* sometimes merely means "half". Sometimes, as here, it means a benefice consisting of half the church revenues.

[2] *Reg. H. de Welles*, I, p. 151.

[3] *Ibid.* III, p. 90.

[4] *Ibid.* III, pp. 37, 39.

[5] *Ibid.* I, pp. 33, 48.

[6] *Ibid.* I, p. 22.

chaplain, subject to his being re-examined in music and singing and being found sufficient. If he was not found sufficient he was to be deprived and the parson was to present another vicar. At Great Steeping[1], Thomas, a deacon, was instituted about 1219 to the custody of the vicarage at the presentation of Bardney Abbey until the next ordinations. As he was not sufficiently learned he was to attend the schools and to be examined at the next Lent ordinations, and the archdeacon of Lincoln was to see that a suitable chaplain was meanwhile provided for the church. The parson of Adstock[2] (archd. Bucks.) was under the requisite age, but was instituted by special dispensation, on condition that he should study in the schools. The canons of Leicester Abbey were to receive their due pension from the church, and a perpetual vicarage of 5 marks was to be appointed. If the vicar should die within seven years, Robert the parson was to appoint another, but if not, he need not after that appoint any vicar, but could take the whole church for himself. Lambert de Bradeham, perpetual vicar of Melton Ross[3], Lincolnshire, was to be ordained and to have with him a chaplain as a co-adjutor, because he was aged and feeble. Peter de Northamptonia, vicar of Little Houghton[4], Northants., was in 1234 deprived by sentence of the abbot of Cirencester and other lawful judges, because he would not attend any summons, nor would he reside in his cure, nor would he minister in his priestly office as his oath required. A vicar of Great Kimble[5], Bucks., had been deprived of his vicarage by sentence for incontinence, but such drastic measures were rare, and this instance, while indicative of a normal vigilance on the part of the authorities, cannot be regarded as of any great importance as evidence.

While the sacristan of Rochester Priory had been asked to enlarge the charter of the vicar of Haddenham[6], Bucks., Merton Priory was promised 5 marks, in the church of St Peter de Merton, Bedford, a larger portion[7] than the 2 marks allotted to it by Bishop Hugh, at such time as the proceeds of the vicarage there should have increased sufficiently to allow it. Lest we be tempted to regard him too much as the "hammer of the monks"

[1] *Reg. H. de Welles*, I, p. 161.
[2] *Ibid.* II, p. 52.
[3] *Ibid.* I, p. 120.
[4] *Ibid.* II, p. 270.
[5] *Ibid.* II, p. 72.
[6] *Ibid.* I, p. 71.
[7] *Ibid.* III, p. 1.

it is well to note that Hugh himself granted pensions from churches to monasteries, such as that of 12*s*. in the church of All Saints, Bedford[1] to Newenham Priory. He was also responsible for a very large number of fresh appropriations, as that of Bitchfield[2] to Bourne Abbey, Cammeringham[3] to Blanchland Abbey and Kimpton[4] to Merton Priory[5]. Obviously Hugh was not an opponent of monastic rights, as such, in churches, but only a bishop anxious to carry out the decrees of the Councils and to see that the cure of souls was adequately and canonically served. On this he was inexorable, as has already been shown by his attacks on the greatest monastery of his diocese, and as is shown by his summons to the prior of Bridlington[6] to show evidence of privileges that formed any legal impediment to the ordination of vicarages in the churches of that priory.

Bishop Robert Grosseteste was an even greater man than his predecessor, being a stern opponent of all abuses, and daring to bear witness before kings and popes and councils. He was no more to the liking of Matthew Paris than Hugh de Welles had been, and this may be taken as an eloquent testimonial to his merits. In 1250 he obtained from the Pope a mandate to strengthen him in his purpose of ordaining vicarages in all appropriated churches where they were small or non-existent. Of this Matthew Paris says: "The aforesaid bishop therefore (more as it is said and as it seems, from hate of the religious, than from zeal and furtherance of the vicars) inflicted, by the authority of this mandate, damage and grievous losses on many religious".

Grosseteste showed unusual zeal, when, beginning at home, he took away the church of Aylesbury[7], in county Buckingham, in the year 1245 from the deanery of Lincoln. This work, however, was not permanent and the church was very soon after re-appropriated. Study of his register suggests that it was not in monastic churches but in the churches of absentee rectors

[1] *Reg. H. de Welles*, III, p. 94. [2] *Lib. Ant.* p. 74.
[3] *Ibid.* p. 92.
[4] Heales, *Records of Merton Priory*, p. 65.
[5] It is very difficult to sort out the new appropriations from mere confirmations.
[6] *Reg. H. de Welles*, I, p. 116.
[7] *Chron. Maj.* (R.S.), IV, p. 425.

that Grosseteste made most of his original ordinations. Frequently the details of vicarages given there prove to be repetitions of those given in the Rolls of Hugh de Welles. The ordinations at Easton-on-the-Hill[1] and Galby (Leics.), are examples of his work in the churches of absentees. In several cases he consolidated the rectories with their vicarages, enjoining residence on the rectors, as at Drayton-Beauchamp, Whitwick and Yaxley. When Lord Ferrers presented his young son, Thomas, to the church of Rand [? Raunds], Grosseteste wrote to the legate, begging him to use his influence to secure the withdrawal of this presentation, and suggesting that if that might not be so, a vicar might be provided, a provision being made for Thomas out of the fruits of the benefice.

Opposed as he was to appropriations in general, Grosseteste made several himself. To the Augustinian abbey of Oseney[2] he gave the church of Fulwell *in proprios usus*, saving 2 marks yearly to be distributed to the poor scholars at Oxford. The abbey was to cause the church to be served by a "suitable honest secular chaplain" and was itself to sustain all due and accustomed burdens. Of course it was part of Grosseteste's routine work to perform any appropriations of churches granted by Papal authority, and perhaps he could not avoid performing this one. Certainly he is found in conflict with Westminster Abbey, when he tried to prevent their acquisition of the church of Ashwell[3], but the Indulgence of Pope Honorius sanctioning this for the sustentation of the brothers, of guests, and of the poor, forced him to accomplish the necessary formalities. The vicarage of 45 marks which he caused to be ordained in the church was a forceful expression of his feelings on the subject.

Grosseteste was in a peculiar position. While he saw and hated Papal abuses, he was hindered in his war against them by a thoroughgoing theory of the Papal power. "I know and truly know", he said in one of his letters[4], "this is to be the power of the lord Pope, and of the Holy Roman Church, that he can freely ordain, concerning all ecclesiastical benefices." It was the difficult position of the true Catholic believer in the *plenitudo*

[1] *Reg. Grosseteste*, p. 197.
[2] *Ibid.* p. 461; *Epist. Grosseteste* (R.S.), p. 151.
[3] *Reg. Grosseteste*, p. 277. [4] *Epist. Grosseteste* (R.S.), p. 145.

potestatis (fullness of power) of the Papacy, when faced with the abuses legalised by the Curia. Fight as he might against unjust provisions and appropriations, he could effect nothing before a power that caused his hand to drop nerveless. Maitland[1], as a lawyer, calls this illogical, and believes that it is. It was really perfectly logical to say that the Papacy with all its legal *plenitudo potestatis* had no moral right to abuse its authority. It is simply the attitude of one, who, placing the moral law highest, can yet recognise an ultimate legal authority that may be begged to repeal its decisions, that may even be obstructed by all constitutional means and yet must ultimately be obeyed. St Louis took this same attitude.

A few examples of his work will suffice. At Whitfield in Northamptonshire, a church belonging to Eynsham Abbey, he found that the vicarage, formerly ordained by Bishop Hugh[2] according to the Oxford Council, consisted of 30 measures of wheat, and 2 marks which the rectors had only paid "with contention". Accordingly Grosseteste re-ordained it by pontifical authority[3] and so the vicar was granted the altarage, two virgates of the church land, the tithe of mills of the parish, and all tithes, including garbs and hay, of the demesne of the church (*i.e.* the glebe or sanctuary), and a manse, for all which he had to bear all burdens save the procuration of the archdeacon. The vicarage of Winwick was augmented, by 1 mark, from 5 to 6 marks[4]. He also appears to have changed the endowment of Tilton vicarage[5], in the archdeaconry of Leicester, from a canon's corrody and 20*s*. from Launde Priory, to a full ordination of altarage, toft, and half a mark's value in certain portions. It was a most desirable change from subservience to independence, and it can only be a matter for regret that he could not, or did not, do the same for all the corrody vicarages. At Cuddesdon[6], he admitted the presentee of Abingdon Abbey to the vicarage on condition that he should come to be examined again on St Michael's Day in the next year, and that if he were not then found suitable, he should be deprived. This was continuing Hugh de Welles' laudable tradition of vigilance over

[1] F. W. Maitland, *Canon Law in the Church of England*, p. 66.
[2] *Reg. H. de Welles*, II, p. 199. [3] *Reg. Grosseteste*, p. 198.
[4] *Ibid.* p. 404. [5] *Reg. Gravesend (Linc.)*, p. 150.
[6] *Reg. Grosseteste*, p. 463.

uneducated presentees. An example of opposition to Grosseteste within his own diocese was the resistance of Dunstable Priory to the augmentation of their vicarage at Studham[1], previously ordained by Hugh de Welles, to the value of 6 marks. This augmentation was quashed in 1254 by sentence of the abbot of Westminster, as Papal delegate, probably on strictly legal grounds.

The prebendal church of Leighton Bromswold[2] had already a vicarage fully endowed in it at this time, for its details are minutely set out in his register; but at Empingham[3], another prebendal church, the bishop merely reserved to himself the right of ordaining a vicarage "when it shall seem more expedient to do so". Why it was not expedient to do so at the time does not appear, and one can only hazard a guess that there was some litigation on the matter at the time. The work of ordaining vicarages in the prebendal churches was, in fact, left to a successor, Bishop Gravesend, who performed it generously and thoroughly. Empingham vicarage[4] was ordained in 1262 for the first time in a manse and buildings and the altarage, with the exception of certain small tithes. The vicarages he ordained in the prebendal church of Asgarby[5] at 8½ marks, 3*s*. plus mortuaries; that of Gretton[6] at £16. 8*s*. 6*d*. The three churches of St Mary, St Faith, and St Andrew at Wickford[7] were all served by the same vicar under the prebendary of Gretton as rector, and an inquisition revealed his vicarage to be endowed with the whole of the churches, worth £12. 12*s*. 6*d*. plus small mortuaries and other occasional profits, saving a payment of 7 marks to the holder of the prebend. Aylesbury prebendal vicarage was ordained in 1271, but Bishop Oliver Sutton in 1294 considered it necessary to make a further and separate ordination for the four chapels of this large parish. Buckden, Brampton, St Gabriel's Binbrook, Biggleswade, and Sutton with Buckingham are a few of the other prebendal churches in which Gravesend ordained vicarages[8]. At St Margaret's, Leicester[9], he changed the ordina-

1 *Ann. Mon.* (R.S.), III, p. 105.
2 *Reg. Grosseteste*, p. 296.
3 *Ibid.* p. 224.
4 *Reg. Gravesend*, p. 102.
5 *Ibid.* p. 26.
6 *Ibid.* p. 103.
7 *Ibid.* p. 15.
8 Sister Elspeth, in *Vic. County Hist.* (*Bucks.*), I, p. 284.
9 *Reg. Gravesend*, p. 160.

tion at the instance of the vicar and prebendary, assigning to the vicar tithes of curtilages instead of 6 marks pension. Such a change from money to tithes was always an improvement, for while tithes tended to improve with improving agriculture, money maintained a steady downward trend throughout the Middle Ages. The church of Lissington belonged to the dean and chapter of York, and the vicar at that time received the whole church, paying a pension of 10 marks to the rectors. Bishop Gravesend ordered that, after this vicar's decease, the dean and chapter of York should have the church again according to the form of the Lord William, once bishop of Lincoln (William de Blois), saving a competent vicarage to be taxed and ordained. A considerable number of monastic vicarages were also ordained by Gravesend, as at Bisbrooke, belonging to Daventry Priory, and Belton, belonging to Gracedieu Priory. The number of appropriations was larger than under Grosseteste, although Papal authority seems to have been responsible for several of them. Luddington[1] had been granted in 1256 to Selby Abbey[2] by the Pope, the consent of the bishop or archdeacon not being necessary. Gravesend had to complete this in 1261, when the last rector died, and he ordained a vicarage which he estimated at £9. 3*s*. Newenham Priory already possessed a mediety of Wootton[3] in Oxford Archdeaconry, and in 1273 it finally secured the other, "by grace of the apostolic see". Middleton[4] in the same archdeaconry was appropriated in 1275 by Gravesend *auctoritate pontificali*. In the same year he granted another quarter of Thorganby[5] Church to Grimsby Abbey, which already had one-quarter *in proprios usus*, by his own authority. He declared that the canons said there ought to be only one priest in one church, and that many difficulties and quarrels arose from the presence of comportionaries, while none of the portions exceeded 5 marks in value. This policy of consolidation was certainly good, and it was probably actually better for the parish that the abbey should hold even the whole church save a vicarage, than that there should be such a chaotic division. St Mary's, Bilsby[6], was appropriated on Gravesend's

[1] *Reg. Gravesend*, p. 89.
[2] *Cal. Pap. Let.* I, p. 331.
[3] *Reg. Gravesend*, p. 233.
[4] *Ibid.* p. 202.
[5] *Ibid.* p. 66.
[6] *Ibid.* pp. 37, 42.

own authority because of the constant quarrels over the division of the riches between the rector and Markby Priory, which was the rector of Holy Trinity, Bilsby, hard by. Markby Priory now became rector of both churches, and in the following year the two vicarages were consolidated under the vicar of Holy Trinity. An interesting ordination is that made by Gravesend in the church of Great Munden[1] in Hertfordshire by consent of sir Gerard de Furnivall the patron. The rector was Master John of Maidstone, who was Gravesend's vicar-general and so could not reside. The vicar was to receive all the altarage save mortuaries, "provided that the perpetual vicarage should not be taxed": that is to say, that there was to be no question of a permanently endowed vicarage of this church, which was to revert to its former status as a residential rectory.

Bishop Oliver Sutton carried on the same tradition in the latter years of the century. There seems to have been no serious reversal of this policy throughout the century in this diocese. While not all of the bishops were opposed to appropriations, all were careful to secure good service of the parish churches and fair play for the vicars. Lincoln affords excellent chances for a survey of the system, and this detailed study of the diocese serves to introduce the reader to the intricacies of vicarage history most effectively.

[1] *Reg. Gravesend*, p. 174.

CHAPTER IV

THE BUILDING OF THE VICARAGE SYSTEM

HUGH DE WELLES was perhaps the most thorough of the English bishops in ordaining vicarages, but it is easy to gain a disproportionate opinion of his work, simply because his records are copious and accessible, and those of his contemporaries much more limited and difficult of access. Yet, in sheer magnitude, the diocese of Lincoln, which included seven counties and part of an eighth, is bound to assume most importance in considering how widely any system was spread. Thus two good reasons, the plentifulness of its records and its immense size, exist for giving the diocese the prior and lengthy treatment here accorded it. Perhaps it is difficult, and even almost impossible, to prevent one's view of the system being distorted by preconceived ideas gained in long study of its working in the diocese of Lincoln, yet there is ample evidence that the same features were appearing in most of the other dioceses of England.

For York there is a mass of evidence provided by the register of Archbishop Walter Gray, who showed no lack of energy in ordaining vicarages similar in most important respects to those of Hugh de Welles. Indeed, two of the most important monasteries of the diocese, namely, St Mary's Abbey, York[1], in 1165, and St Oswald's, Nostell[2], in 1216, acquired Papal bulls that exempted them from these proceedings. Notwithstanding these exceptionally privileged houses, the archbishops did their utmost to set an example. Geoffrey Plantagenet[3], the archbishop, in 1205, allowed the canons of Dereham to appropriate the church of Kirkby Malhamdale on condition that they set up a perpetual vicarage worth 10 marks. Archbishop Gray inherited this policy, and acquired the experience and learnt the lessons of the Councils of Lateran and Oxford. He was not an opponent of appropriations, as is shown by the confirmation of the

[1] Rev. James Wilson, M.A., in *Vic. County Hist.* (*Cumb.*), II, p. 185 *b*.
[2] *Reg. Hon.* III, i, p. 30 *b*.
[3] *Reg. Giffard*, I, p. 255.

churches belonging to the archbishop[1] by Innocent III in 1216, among these being St Oswald's of Gloucester and St Wilfred's of Ripon. In 1221 he granted Hornby Church[2] to the common fund of the church of York, and in 1227 Acomb[3] to the treasurer and his successors. In 1228 he appropriated six churches to Aumâle Abbey[4], three of them expressly because the oppressions of patrons had caused vicars to be appointed who did not reside in them as they should, but he also acquired for himself six other churches from the patronage of the abbey. It was a bargain, and a good hard one, although we may allow the archbishop the credit of an honest belief in the advisability of securing, by appropriation, both a substantial income for his cathedral church and archiepiscopal dignity and an adequate supervision of the parish churches. Two years later[5] he divided the spoils, Mappleton going to the archdeacon of the East Riding, Withernwick to the prebendary of Holme, Waune or Waghen to the chancellor of York, Tunstal to the succentor of York. Plenary jurisdiction over the parishioners was reserved to the archbishop. This systematic bargaining over appropriations, of which there is no evidence in the diocese of Lincoln, nor much evidence anywhere else, was probably in the long run quite a good thing for the churches. Scandals were rather less likely in churches belonging to the high offices of the diocese, save when these were occupied by courtier pluralists, as later was very frequent, than in those belonging to a monastery that prided itself on freedom from episcopal interference. Furness Abbey[6] was treated similarly in the same year, 1228, as Aumâle Abbey. It gained two and a half churches *in proprios usus*, while the archbishop took one and a half. In the divided church a vicarage of 15 marks was to be ordained by the bishop. Similarly St Oswald's, Nostell[7], gained nearly all the churches of its patronage *in proprios usus* while the archbishop took Weaverthorp and Bolton, lest this should be to the harm of the church of York. The perpetual priest-vicar in the mother church of Weaverthorp, for himself and his companion priest, was to have a vicarage worth 24 marks, while the priest-vicar of Helperthorp

[1] *Reg. Gray*, pp. 125, 126, App. to Pt I.
[2] *Ibid.* p. 139.
[3] *Ibid.* p. 17.
[4] *Ibid.* p. 22.
[5] *Ibid.* p. 52.
[6] *Ibid.* p. 160.
[7] *Ibid.* p. 205.

chapel was to receive the equivalent of 10 marks a year for the maintenance of himself and of his clerks. The separate ordination of the chapel was on account of its distance from the mother church. While the vicars were thus generously treated, the canon of York, who was the prebendary, was to receive only 6 marks. It is clear, however, that the parish, like many others in this diocese, was of immense size, and perhaps the archbishop's assessments in any case had a tendency to look larger in terms of money than those of Bishop Hugh of Lincoln. The chancellor of York Minster[1] gained the church of Acklam, which had been renounced by Thornton Abbey, when Archbishop Gray appropriated to that abbey its two churches of Humbleton and Garton. Honorius III confirmed the grant of Acklam, because the chancellorship was so slender and scanty that its revenues did not exceed the sum of 100*s*. yearly. From Fountains Abbey, in 1217, Gray acquired Kirkby Ousebourne, which he added to the endowment of the precentorship of his cathedral five years later[2], and Pope Honorius confirmed this also. When Finchale Priory, a daughter of Durham Priory, applied for the appropriation of Giggleswick[3] it was granted, but the priory had to surrender Weighton which the archbishop claimed as having been anciently a prebend of York but since then illegally acquired by the priory. From one Richard de Umfranvill[4], Gray acquired the church of Tockerington in Northumberland, in 1222, in recompense of the damage done by Richard when he violated the peace at Hexham. The bishop of Durham confirmed this grant.

A similar policy to that of the archbishop of York is revealed by a document of 1350 relating to the diocese of Constance. The bishop, Ulric, on appropriating the church of Weitzen to the abbey of Schaffhausen, reserved to himself one-quarter of the church in lieu of first-fruits, as well as appointing a perpetual vicarage. This quarter, with one-fifth of the churches of Riegel and Rothweil am Kaiserstuhl (possibly acquired in the same way), he gave in the following year to the prebendaries of his cathedral church[5].

[1] *Reg. Gray*, pp. 143–4.
[2] *Ibid.* pp. 131, 141.
[3] *Ibid.* pp. 49, 50.
[4] *Ibid.* pp. 146 *seq.*
[5] *Zeitschrift...Oberrheins*, XXVII, pp. 490, 491.

The work was continued by the other archbishops of York of the thirteenth century, both as far as appropriations and as far as vicarage ordinations are concerned. Giffard's register shows a normal but not excessive energy. This archbishop in 1269 appropriated the church of Bishopthorpe to the nuns of Clementhorpe, saying that "care must be taken that the goods of the poor are so dispensed that the labourer receives his nourishment: wherefore, we, pitying your poverty, appropriate to you this church, given to you by the King, together with the presentation to the same". The vicar was assigned the altarage and 2 marks from the *camera* of the nuns, and one meal every Sunday "like your servants". He was also to have a house with garden. Giffard received from the Pope a letter asking him to provide Master John de Moseley, a poor clerk, to the vicarage *modicae et exili* of Warmfield[1] in 1268–9. Whereupon he ordered the archdeacon to provide this man to the vicarage "notwithstanding that he is not constituted in the sacred order[2], since he promises and is willing" to be promoted "to all holy orders forthwith, and because this appears to be very much according to the will of the lord Pope". This case throws light on the troubles of conscientious bishops from the provisions and licences of popes.

Although Archbishop Wickwane in 1281 augmented the vicarage of Blyth, in 1297 another dispute between the priory and the vicar is mentioned. The prior of Thurgarton, in 1292, probably as collector, had to be ordered by Archbishop Romeyn not to compel the vicar of Marnham to contribute to a tenth, obviously the result of the famous taxation of Pope Nicholas in 1291. The rector of Marnham[3] in 1291 had been ordered not to oppress his vicar by bringing an action against him, who, as a poor man, could not bear it:

For indeed it is not right for so great a pillar of strength to oppress such a poor member of the clergy, who, not sparing hospitality, receives those who come liberally, and aids the poor, according to the measure of his means.

Nec tantam siquidem decet columpnam talem pauperem in clero opprimere, qui, hospitalitati vacando, venientes liberaliter recipit et fovet pauperes pro modico facultatum.

[1] *Reg. Giffard*, p. 29. [2] *in ordine sacro constitutus.*
[3] *Reg. Romeyn*, I, p. 301.

The parishioners of Warter[1], in 1294, complained to the archbishop that the prior there had compelled them to make an oblation on All Saints' Day contrary to a decree of Archbishop Ludham. The consequent inquisition revealed that while Archbishop Ludham was not responsible for the decree, the oblation was a voluntary one and the parishioners should not be compelled to give it. At South Leverton[2] in 1299 the vicar and the parishioners were in dispute concerning the right claimed by the latter to shoot and play games in the churchyard on one plot (*unam placeam*) for which and its herbage the vicar paid them 12*d*. a year. These disputes may be taken as typical of many such that kept cropping up, being matters of curious interest rather than a substantial body of evidence to prove any thesis. Similarly curious is the information of 1292, that the vicar of Hucknall Torkard[3] in Nottinghamshire had gone off to the Holy Land without leave, and that his vicarage fruits were consequently sequestrated. He had gained no such recognition for his adventure as that of Eudo, vicar of Wing[4] in Hugh de Welles' time and diocese, who was "to serve personally unless he set out on a crusade".

Archbishop Romeyn, if he did not disapprove of appropriations, did, at least in theory, disapprove of non-resident rectors who served their cures by vicars. To the rector of Appleton-le-Street[5] in December 1294 he wrote praising those who laudably give themselves to the cure of souls, and those who serve their churches not by vicars but by themselves in the order that their cure required, and threatening the rector with punishment if he did not reside according to the provisions of the consolidation of vicarage with rectory that the archbishop then made.

Even after all the work of Gray, Giffard and Wickwane, Romeyn and Newark found it necessary to conduct wholesale enquiries and proceedings of *Quo Warranto* against monasteries for their churches, especially those where there were no vicarages ordained. In 1298 Newark[6] petitioned for a special licence from the Pope, that "we may make ordinations for benefices which Religious are holding for their own use without sufficient

[1] *Reg. Romeyn*, I, p. 235.
[2] *Reg. Newark*, p. 280.
[3] *Reg. Romeyn*, I, p. 306.
[4] *Reg. H. de Welles*, I, p. 100.
[5] *Reg. Romeyn*, I, p. 181.
[6] *Ibid.* II, p. 306.

title, for he [the archbishop] has power to do this by the ordinary law". St Mary's Abbey, York, was cited because there were no vicarages ordained in four of its churches, Bridlington Priory for two churches, and six other houses for one each. These houses were required to state by what authority they had appropriated the churches, and why no vicars were instituted. Probably Papal bulls were produced in answer to these enquiries in most cases. An enquiry of 1286 concerning the licence by which Sawley Abbey had appropriated Tadcaster[1] elicited the information that there were letters of appropriation from the Apostolic See, and in 1290, the Official of York was ordered to tax the vicarage. Hexham Priory[2], in the diocese of Durham, was cited about 1294 by the archbishop for not having vicars in its churches, but they doubtless proved their right, for in 1255 they had had a Papal bull granted them to the effect that they should not be compelled by the ordinary or even by Papal authority to institute a secular vicar in their conventual church of Hexham, unless special mention be thereafter made in Papal letters of this indult[3]. Newburgh Priory was not to be proceeded against by the archbishop's commissaries for having no vicarages ordained in its churches or on their right of appropriation, because the trial of their rights was reserved to the archbishop's special examination. This priory[4] had in 1259 obtained an indult from the Pope granting that their churches might be served "as heretofore" by their chaplains, and that vicarages should not be taxed, nor perpetual vicars instituted against the will of the priory, notwithstanding any Papal indult granted to the archbishop or any other in regard to the taxation of vicarages and appointment of vicars. Newburgh was an Augustinian priory and so were Hexham and Bridlington, but St Mary's of York was a Benedictine abbey, and the privileges of this house stand out as the most exceptional of all. In 1240 they had been allowed to appropriate[5] the church of Kirkby Lonsdale and serve it by a chaplain, *i.e.* a removable stipendiary. This was in consideration of their having had to make provision of 12 Roman clerks to churches of their patronage by order of the Pope, Gregory IX, and of his predecessor, Honorius, which had so

[1] *Reg. Romeyn*, I, pp. 59, 101. [2] *Ibid.* II, p. 79; Addenda, p. xlv.
[3] *Cal. Pap. Let.* I, p. 320. [4] *Ibid.* I, p. 365. [5] *Ibid.* I, p. 190.

impoverished them that persons wishing to join their monastery had been compelled to buy their own habits. This permission to serve churches by stipendiaries which had been granted to them generally in 1165, and was in 1240 repeated for Kirkby Lonsdale, shows the exceptional favour shown this powerful monastery.

Romeyn took the curious step, in 1289, of enquiring of the Earl of Warenne[1] whether he still approved of the appropriation of Cantley to the poor nuns of Wallingwells made at his request by Archbishop Giffard, as he did not wish to carry it into effect against his wishes. He was probably prompted by a cautious desire to prevent any future quarrel arising from any claim on the patronage by the earl or his successors. The death of the last rector, or his resignation, raised the question of bringing about the necessity of the actual induction of the priory. It was probably not due to any objection to appropriations as such, for he made Bilton in the Ainsty[2] a prebend of his cathedral and "taxed" a perpetual vicarage in it, and gave the church of Brayton[3] temporarily to the archdeacon of York, William of Hambleton, "because those who are in greater offices frequently have greater burdens which they cannot support". His successor, Archbishop Newark[4], instructed his representative at Rome, Sir Roger de Mar, to ask for the appropriation to the archiepiscopal *mensa* (literally "table" but really personal income) of the church of Bolton worth 60 marks, of Wheldrake worth 30 marks and of Misterton worth 35 marks, to compensate for the destruction of the archbishop's manors of Hexham and Alwinton by the Scottish invaders. Clearly, whatever views they might officially express, the thirteenth-century archbishops of York were not averse to making fresh appropriations as often as it suited them.

Throughout England, wherever there is evidence, one finds the bishops adopting cheerfully as their policy, or at least bearing with resignation, the decrees of the Councils. Archbishop Gray with his thorough but bargaining system, Richard Poore[5] and William of Blois with apparent conscientiousness,

[1] *Reg. Romeyn*, I, p. 88.
[2] *Ibid.* I, p. 145.
[3] *Ibid.* I, p. 123.
[4] *Reg. Newark*, p. 305.
[5] *Sarum Cart. and Doc.* (R.S.), p. 162.

and most of their contemporaries, can be found creating, with varying degrees of effectiveness, the same system as that with which Hugh de Welles permeated his diocese of Lincoln. This evidence is reviewed by me in my Appendix B. Behind all the bishops stood the Papal Curia, like a fickle divinity, now encouraging, now marring the work. The laws of the Church were good, but the lawyers made them of no effect by their tradition. Honorius III issued mandates to the archbishop of York[1], to the bishop of Worcester[2], to the bishop of London[3], and the bishop of Salisbury[4] between 1220 and 1226 against non-resident vicars, parsons who succeeded their fathers in their benefices, and vicars and rectors who did not proceed to orders, and similar parochial offenders. On the other hand, confirmations of appropriations were scattered broadcast[5], as the registers reveal. Pandulf, the elect of Norwich, might even take two years' revenues from all the churches, not conventual or belonging to religious, in his diocese that fell vacant within two years from 1220. Glastonbury Abbey[6] might retain to their own uses from 1219 onwards for six years all those churches of their advowson that fell vacant, provided they appointed fit vicars, as a compensation for their loss by the dissolution of the union with Bath as a second capitular church. The 1216 licence to the canons of St Oswald's, Nostell, by which they were allowed to turn their appropriated churches into *prioratus curati*, is more definitely a breach of the policy of ordaining vicarages. Such cases prove that the Curia was open to influences which turned a just consideration for particular difficulties of bishops and monasteries into a definite reversal of the policy declared by Innocent III against appropriations and against monks serving in churches. The net results were checks imposed by the necessity of elaborate formalities, a consequent large revenue from lawsuits at the Curia, and the abolition of many local practices that were flagrantly anomalous. At least a system did come out of chaos.

Two famous cardinals, Otto and Ottobon, were responsible for constitutions regulating the customs of the English Church

[1] *Cal. Pap. Let.* I, p. 84; also in *Reg. Hon.* III, ii, pp. 54, 401.
[2] *Cal. Pap. Let.* I, p. 86.
[3] *Ibid.* I, p. 90.
[4] *Ibid.* I, p. 105.
[5] *Reg. Hon.* III, i, p. 375 *a*.
[6] *Cal. Pap. Let.* I, p. 67.

on this matter of vicarages. Cardinal Otto[1], about 1237, declared that all vicars must be deacons at least on their institution and that within a year they must proceed to priestly orders. Cardinal Ottobon[2], in the Council of London in 1268, declared against

> some who...greedily swallow up all that comes to them from an appropriated church, and leave it destitute of a vicar; or if by chance they institute a vicar, then they leave him so small a portion of the fruits that he cannot maintain himself, and bear the archidiaconal procurations and other burdens incumbent upon him: so that what was provided for alms is sucked into the thirst of greed, and turns into robbery.

All religious houses holding appropriated churches were to present vicars with competent endowment within six months, and if they failed the bishop was to do so instead. Competent houses were to be built by the monks for their vicars in which these could live honourably and receive visitors. Appropriation of churches should not be made at all unless the monastery was so oppressed by the burden of poverty, or unless some other legitimate reason should occur to make the appropriation not so much contrary to law as consonant to piety. These constitutions were regarded as exceedingly important by the bishops to whom the phrase "according to the constitutions of Cardinals Otto and Ottobon" became almost common form in the same way as "according to the late Council of Lateran" had been earlier in the century. For example, even in 1397, a vicar of "Llandeilo-vaur"[3] was instituted, taking an oath of residence "according to the constitutions of Otto and Ottobon".

Yet legislation itself does not cure evils, and it is the administrative power that must be responsible for their cure. While we have seen that many bishops were thoroughly conscientious, a Papal mandate of 1261 from Alexander IV[4] to the bishops of Worcester, Lincoln, Salisbury, Coventry and Lichfield and Llandaff reveals that there was still much to be deplored. The mandate complained of the cupidity of the religious in getting churches appropriated to them, to the extinction in

[1] Wilkins, *Concilia*, I, p. 651.
[2] *Ibid.* II, pp. 10, 11; also *Lyndwood Provinciale* (1679), Appendix, p. 119, as transl. by Coulton, *Hist. Teach. Misc.* III, p. 180, Dec. 1925.
[3] *Reg. St David's*, I, p. 23.
[4] *Cal. Pap. Let.* I, p. 375.

such churches of divine worship, the loss of episcopal rights and the closing of the doors of promotion against poor and proficient clerks, the religious in some cases boasting that they had bought such churches. The bishops had been ordered to make particular enquiry into the scandals before, and this had led to confession of simony in some cases. They were now required to make more general enquiry. Bishop Gravesend[1] of Lincoln certainly obeyed this and held the enquiry. It was to be discovered what was the motive of such appropriations, whether they were made under pretext of poverty, how many benefices had been annexed to bishops' *mensae* and to the uses of secular chapters, and whether vicarages with sufficient stipends were instituted in appropriated churches, and how many vicarages were served by the religious themselves. One-eighth or one-tenth of appropriated churches was to be set aside for alms to the poor parishioners, when the churches were four or five miles away from the monasteries. There is no evidence to my knowledge of any adequate performance of this last command. Bishops were to apply fit remedies in all those matters and the provincial of the Friars Preachers and the minister of the Friars Minor in England were appointed Papal delegates to report on the number of appropriated churches, and how they were served, and to augment vicarages with assent of the bishops. The delegates were to have reported to the Pope, but his death a few months later doubtless put an end to this good work. Yet next year, 1262, Master Leonard[2], the Papal nuncio, was required to inspect documents concerning appropriations and pluralities and to cancel all forged ones, punish forgers and send doubtful ones to Rome. Probably Gravesend's ordinations of the prebendal vicarages of Lincoln directly resulted from the mandate of Alexander IV. Clearly there had been some very shady proceedings on which not even bishops might wish to throw any more light than they were compelled to do. Alexander's attention to the English parishes probably gave a shock to many interested parties, and perhaps induced them to be more careful for some time after.

[1] *Ann. Mon.* (R.S.), IV, pp. 132–3: *Hac occasione quamplures confirmationes datae fuerunt ab episcopo et capitulo Lincolniensi viris religiosis.*
[2] *Cal. Pap. Let.* I, p. 384.

To turn to France, Lalore's collection of chartularies for the diocese of Troyes is a gold-mine of early examples of appropriations, of vicars, and of vicarage ordinations. The document of 991, already quoted, by which the abbey of Montiérender was granted three "altars" by Bishop Manasses, stipulated that there should be three vicars, who were in fact perpetual, even if they were not called that. One of these "altars", that of St Leger-sous-Brienne, in 1035 by request of Gautier, Count of Brienne, and of his mother, Petronilla, was freed by the bishop from all dues save a payment to the bishop of 2*s*. yearly on the feast of St Leger. Between 1072 and 1081 Bishop Hugh conceded eight more altars to the same abbey on condition that they should be served by vicars on the death of whom others, presented by the monks, should be admitted without any payment. These vicars should pay the sinodal dues and attend the synods of the diocese.

The beginning of the thirteenth century shows a certain increase of energy in ordaining vicarages as a result of the Lateran Council. In 1220, for example, the abbey of Montiéramey[1], in the diocese of Troyes, had to submit to the augmentation of the *porciones congrue* in all their churches "according to the statutes of the General Council". The priest of Rouilly-Sacey, for instance, gained 5 sextaries of wheat and five of *tremesium*[2], according to the measure of Troyes. Similar augmentations of grain were granted in their other churches of Courteranges, Chappes, and St Aventin. In 1222 the bishop granted an application made by the curé of St Aubin[3], a church of the abbey of Montier-la-Celle, for augmentation "according to the statutes of the General Council". In 1232 the vicarage of the church of Epothément[4] in the same diocese was augmented by the abbey of Montiérender, at the suit of the priest before the bishop. Even before the Council there is evidence that the vicarages in some parts were being augmented at the instance of Popes and bishops. For instance, in February 1211 Pope Innocent III asked the bishop of Thérouanne[5] and the chapter of St Omer to augment the *porciones congrue* of the priests serving the parishes

[1] Lalore, *Cart. du diocèse de Troyes*, VII, p. 300.
[2] Corn cut after three months' growth.
[3] Lalore, *Cart. du diocèse de Troyes*, VI, p. 307.
[4] *Ibid.* IV, p. 227.
[5] *Thérouanne Reg.* I, p. 209.

of the abbey of St Bertin. These parishes when they had been given in alms to the abbey had been poor but now they were notably increased in value. In 1214 again, before the Lateran Council was yet in session, Adam, bishop of Thérouanne[1], notified an augmentation in grain of the portion of the curé of St Hilaire at Trévent, a parish belonging to the monks of Cercamp.

Yet while evidence of this is necessarily scanty owing to the absence of those richly detailed episcopal registers that we have in England, the scattered nature of such evidence as may be gleaned from piles of volumes of monastic and episcopal chartularies indicates that there was no sudden appearance of hundreds of ordained vicarages such as we have found in England. The vicarage system in France was a much earlier growth, but one sooner permeated with much more deadly germs of decay. It is as might easily be expected from the character of the political institutions. In a country where feudal anarchy and civil war were only varied by local despotism, it was simply to be expected that the work would be less complete and lasting than in England, where ecclesiastical and lay power grew up together both quickly and sturdily. The French bishop seldom possessed such complete control as the English bishop over the monasteries of his diocese. On the other hand, since the twelfth-century monasteries in France were much stronger than in England, where, as in the diocese of Troyes, the bishop was strong, he saw the danger and met it much earlier. Not always, as in this diocese, could a French bishop venture on a wholesale attack on the monasteries and force them to do systematic justice in their churches. We may well imagine the French bishop as lying in wait for opportunities to weaken his powerful rivals, the monasteries, and seizing upon the duty of vicarage ordination as a powerful weapon that increased his prestige as much as it reduced the income of the monasteries. In England the work begun by the Lateran Council and the Council of Oxford was much easier.

The very documents in France reveal how piecemeal was the work there compared with that in England. Whereas the English bishops early developed a well-defined "diplomatic", assigning churches to monasteries, *in proprios usus*, to their sustentation

[1] *Thérouanne Reg.* I, p. 213.

and to the increase of divine worship (*ad divini cultus augmentum*), saving to the vicar a *porcio congrua*, the Continental bishops wandered in mazes of ill-defined sentences. The rector and vicar are much more carefully distinguished in English documents, and there are many less synonyms in general use for such words as "procurations" and "sinodals". The French bishop's "intuition of piety", and "consideration of his own humility", and general introspectiveness, frequently take up twice the normal space of an English bishop's and vary much more in detail. This is certainly true of the twelfth-century documents, which naturally would be less of "common form" than the typical English document of the lawyer-like thirteenth century, but it remains fairly true at a much later date. "Common form" always indicates system, and lack of it lack of system. By the end of the thirteenth century England had overtaken France and progressed far beyond it in its standardisation of ecclesiastical functions, and this is eloquently revealed by the standardised official documents.

Rare as the word *vicarius* is in all the French documents, the incumbent was actually a vicar in our English sense, though Continental bishops prefer to call him *sacerdos*, *presbiter capellanus* or *persona*. In a document of Thierry[1], archbishop of Trèves, in 1232, he is called "pastor"—"if by the will of God it shall chance that the pastor of the said church shall go the way of all flesh, the abbot of Orval should choose a person (*personam*)...". Yet in the same document the word *vicarius* is used a number of times. The divergence from the English custom was already appearing, that led to the French parish priest being called a "curé" (*curatus*, *i.e.* one who has the cure of souls, whether rector or vicar) and his assistant a "vicaire"[2]. It is the assistant whom we call a "curate", although he has not the personal responsibility for the cure of souls.

Yet although many vicarages were being ordained, many exemptions were also being granted, especially as will be seen in the churches of Augustinian and Premonstratensian houses. There was certainly no general uniformity of practice.

[1] *Cart. Orval*, p. 227.

[2] *Pastor* in the 1496 Worms' visitation records means "rector" while the vicar is *plebanus*, although I think this term may at times be used to denote any resident parish priest, whether vicar or rector.

While definite ordination deeds are rare in the French chartularies, there are many documents revealing how parish priests sought to have their portions defined in the ecclesiastical courts. The curé of Vitry-le-Croisé[1] (dioc. Troyes), for instance, sued the abbey of Basse-Fontaine in 1223 for an entire third of the receipt of the tithes, and two-thirds of the corn tithes, and all small tithes and tithes of wine and all tithes of *novalia* (*i.e.* assarts or land recently brought into cultivation). As a result he was granted by the abbey one-third of the whole tithes and all of the vegetable tithe. In 1228 the priest of Ormes[2], a church of Andécy Priory, sued the appropriators and gained augmentation from the bishop. In 1239 Herbert, priest of Barbuise[3], was engaged in litigation with the famous nunnery of the Paraclete, and was adjudged one-fifth of the tithes of assarts and all the small tithes save one-quarter of the wine. The priest of Ronchamp (dioc. Paris)[4], in 1218, sued the abbey of St Magloire, because his portion was insufficient, "according to the last Lateran Council". His portion was raised to one-third of the proceeds of the church and a considerable quantity of hay and grain. In 1234 a judgement was given in a similar[5] case between the curé of St Bartholomew of Paris and the abbey of St Magloire, defining the duties and rights of each very minutely. In 1258 Jan de Laon, a canon of Thérouanne, pronounced judgement in a suit between the curé of Notre Dame of Calais and the abbey of St Bertin[6].

In the chartulary of St Evroul there is a discussion of the legal position in the matter of assart tithes. An assart, it states, is land which has never before been known to be cultivated[7]. It is not enough that land has been idle for even 40 years but there must be no memory of its cultivation. There are some parishes where the religious once had the cure of souls themselves but have since given this up, and presented perpetual vicars to the bishop

[1] Lalore, *Cart. du diocèse de Troyes*, III, p. 119.
[2] *Ibid.* IV, p. 270.
[3] *Ibid.* II, p. 209.
[4] MS. Paris, lat. 5413, p. 303.
[5] *Ibid.* p. 80 or fol. 43 *b*.
[6] Haigneré, *Ch. de St Bertin*, II, nos. 1059–60.
[7] MS. Paris, lat. 11056, I, fol. 208 *b*; *Sext. Decret.* p. 104, col. 2. Commentator adds that if there are signs of cultivation, *e.g.* furrows, and yet no actual cultivation within the memory of man, then it is called "assart" notwithstanding the furrows.

for the cure. In those parishes the religious are the true original curates who base their claim on common right (*qui fundant intencionem suam de Jure communi*). The incumbents are only vicars who ought to be content with the portion assigned to them. In such parishes, though the religious only hold a third or a half of the tithes, they ought to receive all the assart tithes. Consequently in such parishes there is no need of any privilege (Papal or episcopal grant), but if there is any doubt it should be removed by a privilege. The authority quoted for this opinion is Guillaume de Mont Lezun.

There are other churches, continues this discussion, in which the religious have been accustomed to receive the old tithes by privilege or special donation of princes or others, but in which they never had the cure. There is more doubt about the assart tithes of these. Although the law seems to restrict the claim of religious to half of the assart tithes, however much larger the portion they had in the old tithes, yet the privileges of St Evroul's allow the abbey the assart tithes in proportion to their old tithes. Nothing is to be understood by this to prevent the incumbent receiving from the remainder enough to support him competently and to enable him to pay episcopal dues. "Saving a better judgment" is cautiously inserted two or three times.

The law[1] referred to emanated from Alexander IV, and part may be translated here as being of considerable importance.

> By a perpetual statute we declare that that Apostolic indult (which is conceded to some) that they may have the right to receive tithes of assarts in the same proportion as that in which the old belong to them, in no wise extends to those assart tithes, which, in that time when this indult was acquired or obtained, others possessed, when no mention is made in it of this: nor to others [assart tithes] unless it be only in those places where the impetrators themselves held the old then (when the said indult was obtained) and for that portion only in which they receive the old in the time of this impetration.

The commentator of the *Sextus Decretalium liber* (Venice, 1572) calls attention to the words "we declare" because Alexander IV was not promulgating a new law, but declaring the old. The important restriction to half of the assart tithes follows:

[1] *Sext. Decret.* lib. III, tit. XIII, cap. 2: *de decimis primitiis et oblationibus.*

Moreover, we determine that the same indult, obtained by those who at the time of its impetration received the whole of the old tithes, shall in no wise extend beyond half of the assart tithes: because it is not likely, if concerning the full and integral receipt of the old, that it should have been expressed that the Apostolic See equally and similarly would have granted the tithes of assarts, at so great an expense to the parish churches: and that by reason of such an indult either obtained already or to be obtained thereafter it may not be possible in assarts (which are made henceforward) to vindicate and acquire, or receive, more than half of the tithes of those assarts: even if more is held in the old, since it may not be called harsh but rather pious and benign, if (as may happen from the retraction of this sort of indult) the burdening of parish churches in the matter of the tithes of future assarts be prevented.

The Cistercians and Carthusians, however, are exempted from this:

But where, through such concessions of tithes, it happens that the parish churches are so burdened that the rectors of them cannot be suitably sustained by their returns and pay full episcopal dues, it shall be provided by the Ordinaries of the place and ordained so that there be left to the same rectors enough of the proceeds of them for them to have competent sustentation and be able to pay episcopal dues and support other due burdens.

Hence the first kind of churches discussed in the St Evroul document were the appropriated ones. The second kind, dealt with in Alexander IV's decree, were not appropriated but were under obligation of paying "pensions" to the religious. It is surprising to find that a pension might exceed even half the church even where the church was not, strictly speaking, appropriated, and this quite apart from the pension often exacted by the bishop himself. The difference lies in the history of the parish. Pensions were acquired by lay or occasionally ecclesiastical grants approved by the bishop or higher authorities, while an appropriation involved a formal induction of the monastery to the whole rectory with exactly the same ceremony, *mutatis mutandis*, as any other induction. From the rectory was then carved a vicarage. Yet a rectory, it seems, might be quite as small a proportion of the tithes, after subtraction of the pensions, as a vicarage, but the incumbent still remained a rector. He would be in a worse position than a vicar with a similar proportion of tithes, since he would have to bear all burdens not especially assigned to the pensioners. The vicar, on the other hand, only had to bear such burdens as were deliberately imposed on him, since he was not the "true original curate". At any rate such is the logical position.

In England the rectory that was such a small proportion of the whole church proceeds was rare, but in France it was common and in Germany more common still.

The greater part of the tithes of assarts or *novalia* certainly went to the abbeys. Often, as to the abbey of Hautmont[1] in 1200 or to that of Rheims[2] in 1220, the Pope granted the entire noval tithes in their parishes as they had held the old tithes. The abbey of St Hubert-en-Ardenne[3] gained a similar privilege from Innocent IV in 1244, which stated expressly that these tithes should be taken in the same proportion as the old. This was different entirely from the privilege granted to the abbey in 1178 by which no one else had the right to demand tithes from the assarts belonging to the abbey[4], or the similar ones granted to Whitby Abbey[5] about 1224 and to St Nicholas-des-Prés Abbey at Tournai[6] about 1260. These merely prevented the ground reclaimed by the enterprise of the monasteries from being subjected to tithes by others in whose parishes such ground might lie, while the other kind of privilege entitled the monasteries to claim tithes of their parishioners for their newly reclaimed lands. As early as about 1080 the curé of Feschaux[7] contested the rights of the abbey of St Hubert-en-Ardenne to the noval tithes there, but lost his case before the bishop of Liège. In 1186 the bishop of Cambrai adjudged great tithes of assarts of the court of St Peter of Hautmont[8] in the parish of St Martin-D'Élouges to the abbey of St Ghislain, because it possessed the parsonage of the altar of St Martin. In 1239 Bourbourg Abbey won by a lawsuit two-thirds of the noval tithes due from the common at Raches, against their vicar there, but sold them to him for £20 of Flanders money. In 1260 the

[1] L. Devillers, *Cart. du Hainaut*, III, p. 123.
[2] *Reg. Hon.* III, I, p. 423.
[3] *Cart. St Hubert-en-Ardenne*, I, p. 299.
[4] *Ibid.* I, p. 133.
[5] *Whitby Chart.* (Surtees Soc.), I, p. 120.
[6] *Soc. Hist. et Lit. de Tournai Mémoires*, t. 12, p. 324.
[7] *Cart. St Hubert-en-Ardenne*, I, p. 45.
[8] L. Devillers, *Cart. du Hainaut*, III, p. 171.

same abbey won a suit for two-thirds of the noval tithes of Merkinghem and the vicar was ordered to pay 38 garbs or 7*s*. of the money of Paris for their value. In 1239 the abbey of St Magloire[1] was adjudged two-thirds of the great tithes of assarts of the parish known as "the King's assarts"; while the vicar was to receive the other third, and the whole altarage and small tithes of the assarts. More fortunate was the curé of Courgivaux[2], who by virtue, one may suppose, of the rule of the half expressed in Alexander IV's decree, won against his rectors, the nuns of the Paraclete, who claimed two parts, half the large tithes and all the small ones of the assarts of the parish, in 1255.

A Swiss document may be noticed here to illustrate how general were the same conditions already described for England and France. In 1252, when a dispute arose between the abbey of Hauterive and its vicars, the bishop of Lausanne appointed Prior Aymon of the Dominicans of Lausanne to tax the portions[3]. In two churches Aymon allowed the vicar roughly half of the income. In the case of Cugy, one of these two churches, the vicar was to have the right of buying the other half of the proceeds if he wished, but otherwise the religious might sell their part to whomever they wished. The tithes of their own assarts in the parish need not be divided by the monks with the vicar but should be theirs freely and without contradiction. The vicar of Lentigny was to receive all such dues as first-fruits, oblations and mass pennies, but tithes only in certain parts and then only when these parts were not tilled by or at the expense of the monks. The vicar of Écuvillens was to receive such a portion as sir Aldricus, his predecessor, had. In fact these decisions do not seem to be original ordinations, but judicial decisions explanatory of prescriptive custom or of previous ordinations, but they reveal quite definitely enough the same processes as in England and France.

Archbishop Odo Rigaldi of Rouen kept a register of his visitations that reveals very clearly the besetting sins of the parochial system. His worst trouble was with monks and canons actually serving parish churches. This will be dealt with later.

[1] MS. Paris, lat. 5413, p. 316.
[2] Lalore, *Cart. du diocèse de Troyes*, II, p. 230.
[3] MS. Paris, Coll. Moreau, t. 905, fol. 207 *b*.

The parish priest of Neufmarché[1] was accustomed, like so many English vicars, to have his food at the priory table. Since he said that he had no clerk for his necessities in visiting the sick and other duties, the priory was ordered to find one. Two years later this order was repeated, the priory having quietly ignored it, and continued in the bad old way. Another year later and the vicar himself was an absentee, having gone to the Holy Land, and on many days the church services were insufficiently performed. The worst evil of all, however, was that about which Odo complained to the bishop of Seés in 1250: "We have found that in the parish churches they have vicars not bound to the cure[2], wherefore there is imminent danger of souls; nor have they been presented to you"[3].

This indicates the prevalence of the practice of serving churches by temporary stipendiary chaplains which was condemned by the Council of Arles in 1260, whose decrees stated that the greater part of the churches of that province belonged to monasteries[4]: "Moreover, the rule of the Lord's sheep shall not be committed to mercenaries unless they are good and experienced and then only temporarily and with cause. For the Gospel truth, promulgated from the mouth of the chief Shepherd, grievously detests that the Lord's flock should be committed to mercenaries". This same *enormis consuetudo* had already been condemned in Germany by the Council of Mainz[5] in 1225.

The Council of Salzbourg of 1274 (canon 8) decreed that all priests having cure of souls should observe personal residence from Candlemas next and no longer have "mercenaries"[6] as substitutes for a given time, under pain of deprivation. As for benefices capable of being served by vicars (canon 10), suitable men were to be presented to perpetual vicarages there within three months[7]. These canons were aimed against "mercenaries" both of secular non-residents and of religious. Such a "mercenary" is found at the church of St Pierre of Lille in 1241,

[1] *Reg. Regaldi*, pp. 413, 467, 499.

[2] *Vicarios non curatos.*

[3] *Reg. Rigaldi*, p. 81.

[4] Mansi, t. 24, col. 105.

[5] Cap. 12. Hefelé, *Conciles*, v, 2, p. 1449.

[6] "Mercenary" here simply means an amovable stipendiary chaplain, who had no "perpetual" benefice in the church.

[7] Hefelé, *Conciles*, vi, 1, p. 223.

where the Provost claimed that the vicarage belonged to himself and that the parish had never been collated to any priest for his life, nor had such a priest ever been instituted by the bishop or attended the synod as a parish priest[1]. Another is found as late as 1496 in the church of Wies-Oppenheim in the diocese of Worms[2]. The rector in this case was a commendatary, not a monastery.

The Council of Vienne[3] in 1267 even considered it necessary to prohibit the alienation of the goods of benefices by their patrons, under penalty of forfeiture of the right of patronage. This prohibition reveals how hard even quite primitive abuses died.

Finally, in 1274, the second General Council of Lyons stated precisely the essential rules for the incumbent of a parish church. He must be 25 years of age as required by a canon of Alexander III, suitable in knowledge and character, and must reside personally. The Ordinary, however, might for some reasonable cause allow him to be non-resident for a time. All parochial benefices were to be filled up within the space of six months or the collation should devolve on the bishop. Every presentee was to proceed to the order of the priesthood within a year, under pain of deprivation without warning. Such was the law, but the struggle to enforce its operation was long and bitter, and never quite successful. These rules, now so definitely formulated, represent another phase of the struggle to secure the adequate service of the churches. Vicarages being now ordained, it was necessary to secure the speedy presentation of suitable vicars. The King of England (Edward I)[4] was little more contemptuous than some other powerful patrons when he said that the decrees of the Council of Lyons did not touch the royal dignity.

[1] *Cart. St Pierre de Lille*, I, p. 269.
[2] *Zeitschrift...Oberrheins*, XXVII, p. 242.
[3] Hefelé, *Conciles*, VI, I, p. 136.
[4] *Reg. Swinfield* (Heref.), p. 6: *non supponimus se extendere ad regiam dignitatem.*

CHAPTER V

OPINIONS AND STATISTICS

BISHOP ROBERT GROSSETESTE in 1250 preached a sermon before the General Council of Lyons in which he condemned the appropriation of churches most uncompromisingly, and all absentee rectors whether they were monks or seculars were lashed by his words.

"Let not anyone say that the Curia does such things for the common usefulness of the Church", he cried[1],... "Woe unto those who say 'Let us do evil that good may come', for their damnation is just. Neither let anyone say that these, such as are aforesaid, shall save the flock by mediators, for there are many mercenaries who when they see the wolf coming, leave their sheep and flee, and the wolf seizes and scatters the sheep. Moreover the work of pastoral cure consists not only in the administration of the Sacraments and the saying of canonical hours and celebration of masses, which works, indeed, mercenaries rarely do as they should: but also in the veracious doctrine of a life of truth, in terrific condemnation of vices, in hard and in rigid chastisement of vices when it is necessary. Although they may chance to know this, which rarely happens, mercenaries seldom dare to practise it. It consists also in the feeding of the hungry, in giving drink to the thirsty, in clothing the naked, in receiving guests, in visitation of the sick, and prisoners, and especially of one's own parishioners to whom belong the temporal goods of the churches. The people should be instructed and informed by the examples of these works in the holy exercises of an active life, but to do these works is not within the power of this kind of mediator and mercenary. How by them, who hardly receive enough from the goods of the churches for them to sustain their own lives, the aids (*adminicula*) and organs of office, rule and government, being separated and drawn away from the acts of ruling and government, shall the acts of office be fulfilled? Yet when these are incomplete, is not the salvation of those who are ruled and governed manifestly endangered? Although these evils dealt with above, however, and other similar ones proceeding from the collation of pastoral cure to seculars who do not do the work, are subject for inconsolable mourning and grief, such mourning and grief is susceptible of one particle of consolation, for to these men may succeed others who may perform the works of pastoral cure. But when there is an appropriation of parish churches to religious, it is a confirmation and perpetuation of these aforesaid evils."

[1] Browne, *Fasc. Rerum*, II, p. 253.

So preached Grosseteste, a veritable thorn in the side of the Papal Curia.

Pope Alexander IV himself (according to Kennett, see *Case of Impropriations*, pp. 77, 78—but I have been unable to discover Kennett's reference)[1] complained

that the covetous Humour of the Religious had by false suggestions obtained from the See of Rome the appropriation of many parochial churches within the Kingdom of England, and the Poison of it had infected, as it were, the whole nation, while by this means the worship of God was much impaired, Hospitality intermitted, Episcopal Rights were detracted, the Doors of Charity were shut against the Poor, and the Encouragement of young Clerks and Students was defeated, by cutting off their hopes of a future Provision; with many other Losses and Scandals arising from the said appropriation of Churches.

Bishop Oliver Sutton[2], of Lincoln, while appropriating the church of Corby to the nuns of Stamford in 1284, confessed that alienations

and appropriations of parochial churches, by converting the fruits and profits of them to the use of religious persons, were absolutely odious to all the prelates of the church, and had been forbidden by a late law, nor could be tolerable save in cases of manifest poverty or other great necessity.

Archbishop Peckham[3] in 1282 likewise complained of "unlawful and unprofitable appropriation of churches".

An excellent opportunity of testing the truth of this concurrent testimony from certain aspects is afforded by the existence of the famous records of the taxation of Pope Nicholas IV, compiled about 1291. These aspects are, of course, mainly statistical and financial, for we cannot hope to see the actual conduct of parochial affairs reflected in documents of purely financial expediency. Pope Nicholas ordered a tenth to be levied on all the churches of England for a crusade to be entered upon by Edward I, who, as a matter of fact, took the money and forgot about the crusade. Consequently a new assessment was made of all the parochial and other benefices in England with a view to the levying of this tenth. There had been previous "taxations" of lower value made by various bishops, but this

[1] Probably identical with bull mentioned on p. 65.
[2] Kennett, *Paroch. Antiquities*, II, p. 44.
[3] *Epp.* (R.S.), II, p. 480.

was the first complete taxation of the whole of England and Wales. In all medieval assessments for the purposes of taxation in our modern sense, the values stated were considerably lower than the actual yearly average of receipts, there being a sort of unofficial income-tax abatement allowed. The system of taxation is a rough estimate of the lowest value at which a benefice could be farmed, but since the farmer himself always had to make a profit to induce him to take on the burden at all, it is obvious that this principle itself involves a large abatement. Miss Rose Graham has put forward evidence for this with regard to Pope Nicholas' taxation in the *English Historical Review*, XXIII, pp. 434 *seq*. Some of the figures quoted by her reveal cases where the assessment was only half of the true value, although the assessment itself was termed a *verus valor*. In fact, I doubt whether the figures often do represent more than half of the true value.

The Rev. E. L. Cutts, in his *Parish Priests*[1], has added up the figures of the *Taxatio* with the following results (the figures in brackets are my own where I cannot make mine agree with his):

Diocese	Total no. of churches	Churches under 10 marks	Chapels	Total no. of vicarages	Vicarages under 10 marks
Canterbury	221	47	15	58	28
Rochester	108	50	0	31	39 [19]
London	459	150	13	86	33
Lincoln	1738	467	76	353	279
Norwich	1165	354	17	80	35
Chichester	286	91	3	112 [114]	81
Exeter	529	344	49	139	158 [84]
Hereford	291	155	48	94	82
Salisbury	493	222	50	104	80
Bath and Wells	262	113	19	42	29
Winchester	338	84	41	53	34
Worcester	335	136	60	34 [48]	26
Coventry and Lichfield	382	154	27	28	27
Ely	135	15	3	37 [41]	35
St David's	223	124	4	0	0
Llandaff	131	72	9	9	6
St Asaph	109	47	13	63	55
Bangor	34	26	1	0	1 [0]
York	625	93	4	113	61
Durham	117	15	4	43	25
Carlisle	94	2	1	25	14
	8085	2711	457	1487 [1494] [1514]	1125 [1128] [1033]

[1] E. L. Cutts, *Parish Priests*, p. 385.

Although the *Taxatio* is not a complete record even of all the churches, for some churches like many of those of the Templars were omitted altogether as exempt from taxation, while there are others known to have existed that are omitted for no apparent reason beyond a possible exemption on their being valued below the minimum decimable value of 6 marks, yet it is plain evidence that at the very least nearly one-fifth of the parish churches of England were served by vicars, who held perpetual benefices. This in itself is not conclusive that there were as many churches as that appropriated to religious, for some of the vicarages were ordained where the rectories were held by secular clerks, but such instances are quite cancelled by the large number of appropriated churches in which no vicarages were taxed. In the archdeaconry of Suffolk there were only 22 vicarages taxed and yet there were over 60 other churches appropriated in the diocese without counting possible cases where vicarages were endowed owing to the absenteeism of secular rectors. Obviously the commissioners for the different areas interpreted their duties differently, some mentioning all cases where the churches were appropriated but taxing no vicarages, others taxing vicarages but not mentioning appropriations, and some doing neither. The archdeaconries of Coventry and Stafford, for example, have the appropriations carefully noted, but those of Derby, Shropshire, and Cheshire have not. There are only two vicarages mentioned in the archdeaconry of Chester, where there are 88 churches mentioned. In the whole diocese of Coventry and Lichfield there are only two vicarages mentioned as indecimable, that is, too small to be taxed for the tenth, and these are only mentioned because pensions in them were taxed. In 1279 Archbishop Peckham[1] authorised the bishop to institute Robert de Frodesham to the perpetual vicarage of Frodsham ordained from of old (*ordinata canonice fuerat ab antiquo*), yet in the 1291 taxation there is no mention of the vicarage. The vicarage of Rochdale was augmented in 1277 but is not mentioned in the taxation[2]. A most striking illustration of its defects is provided by comparison with the "Norwich Taxation"[3] of 1245, in which

[1] *Reg. Pecham* (Cant. and York Soc.), p. 27.
[2] *Coucher Book*, I, pp. 85, 86.
[3] *Norfolk Archaeology*, XVII, pp. 93 *seq.*

there were 114 vicarages mentioned in the diocese of Norwich, as compared with the 80 of the 1291 taxation.

While realising the limitations of the document, and discussing them more fully as they become more important, we may now turn to the definite evidence provided by it.

The figures for the diocese of Lincoln, although not complete, indicate that the work of Hugh de Welles stood firm and that there had been a number of vicarages ordained since his day. The registers of Gravesend and Grosseteste printed by the Canterbury and York Society have, each of them, copies of a considerable number of these ordinations, although nothing like the number in that of Hugh de Welles. Grosseteste performed a number of augmentations and original ordinations, while it has been seen how Gravesend's great work was the ordination of vicarages in the prebendal churches, a duty hitherto neglected or inadequately performed. In 96 cases I have been able to collate previous valuations of Lincoln vicarages with those given in the 1291 taxation with the following results:

Taxed in time of	1291 Increase	1291 Decrease	1291 Equal
Hugh de Welles, 1209–35	55	12	9
Grosseteste, 1235–54	3	5	—
Gravesend, 1258–79	3	9	—
	61	26	9

While Hugh de Welles' valuations are mainly about 5 or 6 marks, those of Grosseteste and Gravesend are often about 15 marks, while Grosseteste's valuation of Hemel Hempstead vicarage is 30 marks, and of Ashwell 45 marks. The Hemel Hempstead vicarage was re-ordained on the appropriation of the church to Hales Abbey[1] soon after 1279. Nearly all of the vicarages of which the assessment was lower in 1291 were first assessed at about 10 marks or more. It is generally the richest that appear to have decreased, although seven of the Hugh de Welles' instances are decreases in vicarages of 5 marks or less. There is no evidence of augmentation for the great majority of vicarages ordained by Bishop Hugh, certainly no such general policy of augmentation as these figures might seem to suggest. The most plausible explanations of the general increase are

[1] *Reg. Grosseteste*, pp. 282, 292.

that Hugh under-assessed his churches and vicarages as a general policy, and that the value of money had been steadily pursuing its normal medieval downward trend. Improvement of agricultural methods may also have had something to do with the matter, but these alone were not sufficiently noticeable to make all the difference. The decreases since the beginning of the century are no more than one might have expected quite naturally from local calamities, local cases of bad farming and similar genuine but transitory troubles. Normally Grosseteste seems to have been inclined to assess higher than Hugh de Welles, for no apparent reason of importance: for example, Hugh taxed Burreth vicarage at $3\frac{1}{2}$ marks[1], but Grosseteste at 4 marks[2]. Hugh taxed Saxilby vicarage at 7 marks[3], and Grosseteste at 10 marks[4], and again Hugh taxed Winwick vicarage at 4 marks[5], and Grosseteste at 5 marks[6]. There had been no recorded augmentation in between in any of these cases, although Grosseteste then added another mark to Winwick vicarage to make it worth 6 marks. Gravesend's ordinations were all made within about 30 years of the date of the taxation, so the general decrease in the assessments of the vicarages ordained by him may be readily attributed to the difference between an attempt by Gravesend to state something approaching the actual value of a vicarage and the Commissioners' policy of stating an assessed value for taxation purposes with a rebate allowed; not that any fixed rebate was thought of, but a fairly lenient standard amounted to the allowing of a rebate. Assessed values are bound to vary a great deal under any system and can never be more than a human guess at probabilities indicated by faulty evidence produced by interested parties. Every Inland Revenue official knows that from his own personal experience, and he knows that it is easier for the property holder to prove over-assessments than it is for him to prove that they have under-assessed themselves. The parish priest himself would be unlikely to guess his own income in extravagant terms and his neighbours, being farmers and farmworkers, as a rule, would not take too optimistic a view of agricultural prospects. No farmer ever does. The

[1] *Reg. H. de Welles*, III, p. 90.
[2] *Reg. Grosseteste*, p. 42.
[3] *Reg. H. de Welles*, I, p. 200.
[4] *Reg. Grosseteste*, p. 138.
[5] *Reg. H. de Welles*, I, p. 194.
[6] *Reg. Grosseteste*, p. 42.

number of Lincoln vicarages under 10 marks in the 1291 assessment is large, but not really exceptionally so, for such cases as Norwich, where they were less than half the total number mentioned, may easily be explained by a greater tendency to neglect the smallest vicarages as indecimable, or, perhaps, to assess them in with the rectory without expressly saying so. This explains the wide divergence in that diocese between the number of vicarages mentioned in the 1254 and 1291 taxations. In 1254 there were 28 Norwich vicarages taxed at less than £1, many of which do not appear at all in 1291, examples being Hainworth, Higham, Kirtling, and Knapton. The 1254 assessment was, however, very low, and it is normal to find a large increase in 1291 rising to as great an increase as that of Edwardstone in Sudbury deanery from 13*s*. 4*d*. to £4. 13*s*. 4*d*.[1] although at Eylesham, deanery of Ingworth, there is a decrease from £20 to £18. 13*s*. 4*d*.[2]

In the diocese of Worcester, Bishop Godfrey Giffard in 1271 ordained that the vicarage of Sherborne[3] was not to be less than £10 a year, and yet in 1291 it was only taxed at £5.

In the diocese of Exeter, it is possible to establish comparisons in a few cases between assessments made about 1269 and those of 1291. The vicarage of Abbotsham in 1269 was ordained in the sanctuary, altarage, and garbs up to 2 marks, but in 1291 was assessed at 1 mark. Awliscombe vicarage was found worth 7 marks, 4*s*. 1*d*. in 1269, and was restored then to its old value of 10 marks, but was assessed at £1 in the *Taxatio*. Other cases are:

	1269*	1291
Monkleigh	60*s*. +20*s*.†	10*s*. 0*d*.
Sidmouth	8 marks, 19*s*. 4*d*. and more	£2. 0*s*. 0*d*.
Aylesbeare	4 marks, 1*s*. 4*d*. and more	Not mentioned
Harpford	9 marks	”
Pinhoe	5 ”	”
Sheldon	5 ”	”

* See Bronescombe's *Register* alphabetically arranged by Hyngeston Randolph.

† 20*s*. augmentation made in 1269.

Obviously the Exeter assessors were very lenient, probably owing to the remoteness of the country and the difficulty in

[1] *Taxatio*, p. 122 *b*.
[2] *Ibid*. p. 83 *a*.
[3] *Winchcomb Landboc*, II, p. 278; *Taxatio*, p. 222 *a*.

enforcing a more rigid taxation. This explains the huge number of Exeter benefices under 10 marks, especially when considered in conjunction with the natural barrenness of Cornwall. It throws no discredit on the bishops who seem to have been as efficient as others in ordaining vicarages of which the proportion, about one in four churches, is quite high.

Bishop Peter Quinil[1] (Quivil) had, it is true, set a low standard in 1287, when he decreed that in churches of a true value of 40 marks, the vicarage was to be of 5 marks, and that as the value of the church rose so was the vicarage to increase accordingly, but ordinations made before this date do not indicate that the standard of his predecessors had been so low as this.

Canterbury, the see of the archbishop, shows no exemplary characteristics, but is fairly typical of the whole country. Chichester, a rich diocese in which were situated Lewes Priory, Battle Abbey, and many comparatively small but fat parishes, shows two vicarages to about every five parish churches, these vicarages being quite creditably but not opulently endowed. A number of them, however, were assessed higher than their rectories, examples being Battle[2] at £13. 6*s*. 8*d*. as against the £5. 6*s*. 8*d*. for the rectory appropriated to the abbey there, and Rye[3] at £10 as against the £5 of the rectory, as yet unappropriated. Rye Rectory, incidentally, was at this time occupied by Nicholas de Sprouton, one of Edward I's presentees, and presumably like very many of them an absentee rector. It is re-assuring to find that he received so small a portion of the proceeds of the church. Yet several Chichester vicarages are much less than one-third of the whole church, Lancing[4] and Grinstead[5] being less than one-fifth, and Portslade[6] about one-quarter. In this diocese the one-third rule seems to have been neglected in favour of allowing what was considered a reasonable vicarage (generally of about £5, £6 or £8) almost regardless of how rich a church might be, but taking into consideration any exceptional poverty of the rectory. In other words, if a rectory was poor the vicar shared its poverty, but if it was rich, he did not proportionately share its riches. Not that Chichester was

[1] Wilkins, *Concilia*, II, p. 147.
[2] *Taxatio*, p. 137 *a*.
[3] *Ibid*. p. 136 *b*.
[4] *Ibid*. p. 134 *a*.
[5] *Ibid*. p. 136 *a*.
[6] *Ibid*. p. 135 *b*.

unique in this; for Lincoln, Rochester, Lichfield, and even more, the northern diocese of Durham, add convincing proof that the practice was common. The rectory of Gainford[1] was valued at £100 and its vicarage at £10, that of Corbridge[2] at £75, and its vicarage at £9. 16*s*. and that of Tynemouth[3] at £71. 12*s*. 10*d*. and its vicarage at £6. 1*s*. 2*d*. The bishop of Carlisle received £38. 13*s*. 4*d*. including a pension of 14 marks, from the church of St Nicholas, Newcastle[4], his cathedral priory received another £38. 13*s*. 4*d*. and Tynemouth Priory £8, yet the vicarage was only taxed at £20. 5*s*. or less than one-fifth of the church. These Durham examples are extreme cases of the general practice with regard to wealthy churches. In those churches whose total value including both rectory and vicarage was less than about £20, the old custom of assigning the vicar about one-third of the proceeds was still very widespread. This conclusion is strengthened if we suppose that the assessors had the same sense of justice as has led to our graded income-tax, and were stricter in their assessment of rich benefices than of poor ones. This may account for the fact that, though in 1262 we are told that the religious held two out of three parts of Docking in the diocese of Norwich to their uses, the 1254 taxation[5] assessed the rectory at £26. 13*s*. 4*d*. and the vicarage at £10 and the 1291 taxation assessed the rectory at £30. 13*s*. 4*d*. and the vicarage at £10. It is an attractive hypothesis, but no more than a hypothesis.

A striking feature of the northern dioceses is the fewness of rectories valued at less than 10 marks, and the smallness of the number of chapels separately taxed. The north always has been a country of large parishes and many chapels, so it is obvious that the large assessments represented rectories or vicarages with many subordinate chapels and many duties. The number of vicarages is well up to the normal, in spite of the depreciation of values in the border warfare of these days. The bishops were obviously quite normally efficient in ordaining vicarages, and there is no such evidence of chaos as southerners sometimes seem to expect in the wild north. Durham and Carlisle dioceses

1 *Taxatio*, p. 315 *b*.
2 *Ibid*. p. 316 *b*.
3 *Ibid*. p. 316 *a*.
4 *Cal. Pap. Let.* I, p. 382.
5 *Norfolk Archaeology*, XVII, p. 117.

certainly reveal an exceptional number of appropriations, but fewer are represented in the York Taxation than might have been expected from the study of episcopal registers.

The smallest proportion of vicarages apart from Norwich, St David's and Bangor, is found in Coventry and Lichfield, in which diocese the registers, as I am told, reveal a quite exceptionally large number of appropriations. The bishop was mentioned in Alexander IV's mandate[1] on the subject in 1261. Archbishop Peckham[2], also, found it necessary to write to the dean and chapter in 1282, reprimanding them for appropriations made in their diocese, whereby the health of souls was perpetually wounded, and the Statutes of the Holy Fathers broken, and a Legatine Constitution recently made by Cardinal Ottobon was infringed. Such intervention as Peckham's[3] in 1284, when he complained that the bishop of Rochester, appropriator of Coleshill, had neglected to accomplish his ordination about setting up a perpetual vicarage there, and that of Winchelsey[4] in 1296, when he augmented the vicarage of Tutbury, indicate that the bishops of the diocese were particularly remiss, but do not justify the 1291 figures being taken at their face value. Winchelsey[5] had issued a commission to his official, William de Staundone, to enquire into the value of certain poor vicarages in this diocese and the burdens imposed upon them. Many of the vicarages were so slenderly endowed that the vicars could not bear these burdens. Perhaps the results of the 1291 taxation had been brought to the archbishop's notice, and had directly led to this move. Certainly the augmentation of Tutbury vicarage was one of the fruits of this enquiry.

The fewness of the vicarages mentioned in the Welsh dioceses of St David's, Llandaff and Bangor call to mind the exception made by the Council of Oxford in 1222, of those parts of Wales, where "on account of the poverty of the churches, vicars are content with a small stipend". Giraldus Cambrensis in the late twelfth century, said:

> All the Welsh monasteries are entangled in common in one and the same fault, which springs from a root of evil covetousness. For,

[1] *Cal. Pap. Let.* I, p. 375. See pp. 65, 78.
[2] Kennett, *Impropriations*, pp. 68–9.
[3] *Reg. Peckham* (R.S.), II, p. 720.
[4] *Reg. Winchelsey*, p. 108.
[5] *Ibid.* p. 86.

as they grow accustomed to take possession of the parishes of mother churches and baptismal churches [as distinguished from chapels of ease] and either shockingly to mutilate them of the greater part [of their revenue] or even to take them completely for themselves, driving forth the parishioners and leaving the churches empty or even ruined and destroyed[1].

Obviously, then, Wales did not lack appropriating monasteries and yet these three dioceses have only nine vicarages mentioned between them in the *Taxatio*. The inference to be drawn from this is that vicarages had not been properly ordained and that the great majority of the vicars were miserably poor. St Asaph's diocese shows a total of 63 vicarages in 109 churches; 55 of these vicarages were assessed at less than 10 marks, and of these a large proportion were too poor to pay the tenth. The chief difference between this and the other three Welsh dioceses is that the small indecimable vicarages were here assessed but were not in the others. Giraldus also[2] had affirmed that the powerful men of the country so abused their rights as patrons and defenders of the parish churches that often they usurped the whole rights, leaving only the altars with their tithes and obventions (*i.e.* the altarage including small tithes) to the clergy and even these rights they assigned to their clerical sons and relatives. The statement would not of course be illustrated in the *Taxatio*, but it reveals a country where primitive abuses had, anyhow till quite recently, flourished. Probably the abuse was destroyed mainly by the influence of King Edward I, who seized the advowsons of the Welsh "rebels" who resisted him, giving some to the bishops and retaining some in the royal hands. To the episcopal *mensa* of St David's he assigned no less than 34 confiscated churches by one grant. The wonder really is that in these difficult transitional times the record of the Welsh dioceses is anywhere near so complete as it is.

In about 1320 a similar taxation[3] was made of the Irish diocese of Ossory by mandate from the king. Here the total was 34 vicarages in 102 parish churches, a proportion of exactly one in three, of which vicarages 14 were assessed at "nothing on account of their burdens". The largest vicarage mentioned is

[1] *Opera* (R.S.), IV, p. 177.
[2] *Girald. Cambr. Itin. Camb.* lib. I, cap. 2; *Opera* (R.S.), VI, pp. 21, 22.
[3] *Hist. MSS. Comm. Rep.* x, Pt v, pp. 234 *seq.*

that of the church of *Callan cum membris* being £8, as against a rectory of 50 marks. It is less than one-fifth of the whole church and the words *cum membris* suggest that there were heavy burdens in the shape of stipends to clerks serving chapels, a large proportion of which might be thrown on to the vicar. Another case where these words are employed is that of Fiddown, where the rectory *cum membris* was worth £6 and the vicarage 60*s*. This is the two to one proportion that had been regarded as an ideal, but it only occurs in four out of the 34 cases. The one case where the vicarage is assessed higher than the rectory is that of St Martin's in the deanery of Claragh, where the prebendary's rectory was assessed at 20*s*. and the vicarage at 60*s*. The taxation is one of very low figures, and there is little doubt that the assessments were made on a much smaller scale than those of the English dioceses in 1291. Indecimable churches were taxed at nothing, and the vicarage of Dunmore, taxed at only 10*s*., and the church of Rathbeath at 10*s*., and the chapel of Kilmenhan at 20*s*., were all regarded as liable for the tenth. Probably, then, the valuations given only represent the surplus over a maximum indecimable value and are a very rough representation even of that. What they do certainly represent, however, is just ten times as much as the king could hope to get from the benefices of the diocese for his tenth. The king's assessors would content themselves with as good an assessment as they could hope to enforce. Innocent IV, in 1250, had ordered[1] the bishop of this diocese to force perpetual vicars to reside in their churches, and be ordained priests, by withdrawing their incomes. In 1320 Richard Ledrede, the bishop who made this taxation, was informed, in reply to a question to the Pope[2], that no one who held a benefice with cure of souls ought to hold also a prebendal church in which there was no perpetual vicarage ordained. In other words, a prebendary must serve his church personally, or have a perpetual vicarage ordained in it. The synod of the diocese[3] about the same time declared:

We order that no one shall be admitted to a perpetual vicarage having the cure of souls unless he is already ordained to the priest-

[1] *Cal. Pap. Let.* I, p. 260. [2] *Ibid.* II, p. 207.
[3] *Hist. MSS. Comm. Rep.* x, pt v, p. 229.

hood, or at least a deacon, or a subdeacon, who shall be ordained within the next four seasons. He shall renounce other benefices if he has any, and swear to make continual and corporal residence in the same as he shall take oath, otherwise we decree that his institution shall be null and void, and his vicarage given to another according to the sanctions of the Holy Fathers.

Hence it is clear that the bishops of Ossory, from the middle of the thirteenth century, had not altogether neglected the fight to maintain a reasonable standard of living for the parish priests, and reasonable service for the parish churches. The results, as seen by the 1320 taxation, are not exemplary, but are slightly better than one might have feared of the "distressful country". Twenty vicarages were sufficiently well endowed to pay the king's tenth, and 14 others at least existed. There must have been a larger number of absentee rectors, whether monastic or secular, than in the English dioceses, judging from the frequency of provisions to Irish benefices, as shown by the *Calendars of Papal Petitions and Letters* when Irish documents become at all frequently mentioned there. One might have feared much worse things from the complaints of simony, immorality, pluralism, maladministration, and lawlessness that there appear. "Better than feared" however need be no commendation.

CHAPTER VI

SCOTLAND

EVEN Scotland, that country situated on the edge of the world, was not outside the power of the reforming Popes, and a reasonably efficient vicarage system seems to have grown up there. This, of course, is speaking in comparative terms, and making all allowances for its lack of firm government and its decentralised condition. The same phenomena were appearing here as elsewhere when Pope Lucius[1] (*c.* 1181–5) wrote to Bishop Jocelyn of Glasgow declaring "that it is unlawful for the religious, dwelling in your diocese to hold any parish church in their hand when it falls vacant or to institute perpetual vicars in any such without your consent". They were also forbidden to impose any new pensions on churches or augment old ones. Such persons as should be presented by them to churches should seek episcopal institution and pay the *cathedraticum* (sinodals) and other dues canonically required of them. Obviously the same tendencies were showing themselves, and the same abuses scandalising the canonists here as in other parts of Europe. Scotland was not so cut off from the rest of the world that it could not copy from it, but in this there was little need to copy. Appropriation of churches was so obvious a solution of essential difficulties that it would have appeared in Japan or South America had the same ecclesiastical institutions flourished there. Of its nature a monastery was an institution that demanded a permanent endowment, for it never (after its very earliest days) set out to be self-supporting. In the Middle Ages, when money was scarce and commercial investment was "usury" and a sin, permanent endowment could only take one form and that form was land or a direct charge on land. The founders of monasteries usually granted lands to them, but seldom more than enough to provide a yearly existence for them without guarding against a growth in the size of the monastery or a sudden catastrophe. The tendency to acquire more and

[1] *Reg. Glasguense*, I, p. 53.

more lands was checked by lay jealousy and was subject to mortmain legislation. Moreover, land holding and farming was a distraction from the holy calling, and hence a simple rent or charge on land was preferable to land ownership. Mr Snape, in his book on *English Monastic Finances*, has forcibly shown that medieval monasteries seldom saved. It is difficult to see how they could have done so in days when money was scarce and when one blade of grass grew where several grow now. Doubtless the monastery often added to the material welfare of the country by improvements on its lands, but it did not stand or fall by any attempt to justify its existence economically. Frankly, it claimed a right to live by the sweat of other men's brows, that other men might, by the sweat of the monks' brows, find spiritual life. While the first monks claimed merely subsistence, their successors claimed comfort, and an excellent case can be made in justification of this. Yet even comfort in those days was a very great luxury, and meant quite disproportionate riches and large endowments. The tithe was the most satisfactory form of a perpetual charge on land then existing, for it was fairly regularly paid, being enforced by all the thunders of the Church, and from the twelfth century onwards its spiritual nature was a reasonable protection from the aggression of laymen. What was more natural than for a poor monastery to be granted relief out of the revenues of a rich church, for both existed for the same work? Even more natural was it for a rich and powerful monastery to make an excuse of a temporary straitening of circumstances to rob a poor and defenceless parish. Since the tithe was the best possible endowment, we need not be surprised to find the same struggle for its possession proceeding in France, Scotland, Denmark, the Holy Land, or anywhere else where tithes were collected.

The struggle was clearly being fiercely waged when in 1198 the bishop of St Andrew's[1] obtained from Innocent III a mandate to restrain monks and canons regular from appropriating to their own uses churches to which they had the presentation, unless such churches were exempt from his jurisdiction. In 1201 the bishop of Glasgow[2] confirmed all the appropriations of the churches mentioned in the deeds of Bishop

[1] *Cal. Pap. Let.* I, p. 5. [2] *Reg. Glasguense*, I, pp. 80, 82.

Roger of St Andrew's and Bishop Jocelyn of Glasgow concerning Kelso Abbey, and demanded that there should be perpetual vicars in them who should answer to the bishop for his dues, and for procurations as contained in the decrees of the Lateran Council (III) and acknowledge themselves well satisfied. This deed was confirmed by John, cardinal-priest of St Stephen's in Caelio, showing thus the immediate contact between the policy of the Scottish prelate and that of the central government of the catholic church at Rome. A little later in the century (1208–32) the abbey signed an agreement that the bishop should have custody of the churches after the death or cession of the vicars until vicarages should be ordained, and in each case the abbey was to set apart "a certain and reasonable portion" (*certam et rationabilem porcionem*). If it did not do this, the bishop should supply the defect. About the same time the cathedral chapter of Spynie[1] was founded "according to the example of the church of Lincoln", and an elaborate deed of Bishop Bricius, signed by eight parochial vicars and thirteen rectors, endowed the prebends of eight canons with parish churches. The dean, the cantor, the treasurer, the chancellor, the archdeacon and three other canons were assigned an average of about two churches each. No example could illustrate more aptly than this the remarks above made about the value of the tithe as a perpetual endowment. This cost the bishop nothing, created a chapter on a sound financial basis, and reduced the parish priests to subservience. In 1222 Pope Honorius confirmed five churches to the episcopal *mensa* itself and two more churches were soon after given to the cathedral for another prebend, another for the cathedral fabric, and two others conceded to the sustentation of the lights of the cathedral. It may well be wondered how many churches there were left outside the power of the bishop and his cathedral. The cathedral canons of Holy Trinity, Elgin[2], had nine, and Aberbrothoc Abbey[3] at least two in the first half of the thirteenth century.

The Scottish Provincial Council[4] of 1224 followed the example of the Council of Oxford, and it set as the minimum

[1] *Reg. Moravense*, pp. xvii, 46, 63, 66, 70.
[2] *Ibid.* p. 35. [3] *Ibid.* pp. 276, 277.
[4] Wilkins, *Concilia*, I, p. 609.

value of a vicarage 10 marks, if the church could bear it. The editor of *Statutes of the Scottish Church*[1] remarks that the Scottish mark was at this time equal to the English, and he may probably be right, but unfortunately this high minimum was often neglected. In the diocese of Moray[2] as late as about 1350 there were vicarages as follows, according to a taxation that was probably an underestimate, as all such taxations were, but that indicates a serious falling below this level:

6 were too small to be taxed	1 of 6 marks
1 of 2 marks	1 of 8 ,,
3 of 3 ,,	1 of 10 ,,
6 of 4 ,,	1 of 20 ,,

By 1350 the Scottish coinage had progressed far along the normal medieval road of depreciation.

In the churches of Holyrood Abbey in his diocese, Bishop Walter of Glasgow[3] in 1228 ordained two vicarages assessed at 100*s*., one of 6 marks, and one of 5, each vicarage being between one-half and one-third of the value of the whole church. These figures are not quite conclusive, since assessed values might possibly have not been more than half of the actual values, but in the 1275 assessment of the diocese no vicarage[4] was assessed at more than 10 marks, three were described as indecimable, and 28 were taxed at 4 marks each.

Other thirteenth-century Scottish canons provided that a vicarage manse[5] was to be built by the parson and vicar proportionately and fit to house the bishop and archdeacon on their visitation, and that repairs were to be paid for by the vicar. "Farming"[6] of churches to laymen was forbidden and was not allowed to churchmen for more than five years[7], at the end of which time it was not to be renewed to the same people. A definition was made on the subject of the tithes of gardens[8], a constant source of dispute as we find from our records of the diocese of Exeter[9]. In the cities all the tithes of gardens were to go to the vicar, but in the country the rector was to receive the

[1] *Statutes of the Scottish Church*, p. 11, n. 2.
[2] *Reg. Moravense*, pp. 362–3.
[3] *Reg. Glasguense*, 1, p. 122.
[4] *Ibid.* 1, pp. lxiii *seq.*
[5] *Statutes of the Scottish Church*, p. 12.
[6] *Ibid.* p. 13.
[7] *Ibid.* p. 14.
[8] *Ibid.* p. 21.
[9] The expression usually is "land cultivated with the spade" (*cum vanga*).

corn and the vicar the rest. Flax, wherever it was grown, was always to be regarded as the vicar's.

The details of the vicarage ordinations made by the Scottish vicars are very similar to those of their English contemporaries. In 1238 Bishop Andrew of Moray[1] assigned to the vicar of St Peter, Duffus, all the altarage, while all the great tithes were reserved to the absentee prebendary, Hugh of Duffus. The vicar was to pay all episcopal dues and find a cathedral vicar for the prebendary. This latter provision was not usual in England. The vicarage of Inverness[2], founded in 1248, consisted in the whole profits of the church, save garbs, tithes of mills, the church land and 3 marks in other portions, while the abbey of Aberbrothoc had to pay all the episcopal dues. The bishop of Brechin[3] in the same year taxed the vicarages of three churches of this abbey at £10 each, the vicars being required to pay the episcopal and archidiaconal fees, while in a fourth church of less value the vicar was to have the altarage, plus sufficient to make it up to the same value. If the altarage at any time exceed £10, the excess was to be paid over by the vicar to the abbey. Pope Alexander IV[4], who in 1258 sent a bull to the bishop of Glasgow commanding him to tax the churches of religious of his diocese for the sustentation of the ministers, considered it necessary to send a special demand to the abbey of Aberbrothoc concerning their churches in the diocese of Aberdeen[5]. He complained that the abbey had appealed unnecessarily to the Pope against ordinations made by authority of Pope Innocent III, and according to the rules of the Lateran Council, and ordered the bishop to assign the fit portions for the vicars notwithstanding any obstacle of appeal that might be raised. Consequently in 1250 the bishop ordained vicarages in all their churches in his diocese, and at the same time in all those of the abbey of Lindores, which had apparently joined Aberbrothoc in its appeal to Rome. The details are very similar in every case: the vicar usually was granted the altarage and a house, and a fairly large quantity of garb tithes. The values at which the vicarages were taxed sound very large even considering the

[1] *Reg. Moravense*, p. 274.
[2] *Ibid.* p. 276.
[3] *Reg. Episcopatus Brechin.* II, p. 264.
[4] *Reg. Glasguense*, I, p. 167.
[5] *Reg. Aberdonense*, I, pp. 18–32.

burdens, that of Banff being 30 marks, Inverurie 33 marks, and Fgwin (*sic*) 33 marks. The smallest of them was 100*s*. Each vicar was to bear all the ordinary burdens of the church and of the fabric of the chancels, and a share of all extraordinary burdens in proportion to his share in the goods of the church. This generous treatment of the vicars does not appear to have been very general and it was probably this very generosity on the part of the authorities of this diocese that led to the prolonged suit at the Curia.

The 1275 taxation of the churches of the diocese of Glasgow[1] already mentioned reveals how thorough had been the work of the bishops of that diocese, and what a large number of the churches had vicarages endowed in them. The numbers of (*a*) vicarages, (*b*) all parish churches, there mentioned are as follows under the different deaneries:

	(*a*) Vicarages		(*b*) Parish churches	
Deanery	1275	Sixteenth century	1275	Sixteenth century
Peebles	7	4	11	9
Tevidaill	6	2	16	9
Nycht	13	6	20	13
Annandie	0	0	7	4
Ruglyn	9	8	11	10
Lennox	2	1	5	3
Lanark	6	0	17	12
Kyill and Cwyghame	14	8	14	8
Carrick	6	1	6	1

There is nothing like this proportion of vicarages to be found in any English diocese, although some French ones might run it very close, and the diocese of Lausanne in Switzerland seems to have exceeded it[2]. The figures in the second column, drawn from a sixteenth-century taxation, although obviously incomplete, indicate that the proportion of vicarages remained about the same after the thirteenth century. The increase in the number of appropriated churches after 1300 was counterbalanced by the late medieval practice of appropriating not only the church but also the vicarage, and setting a stipendiary to do the work of the parish. A similar proportion, but not quite so large, is shown by the 1350 taxation of the diocese of Moray, where just

[1] *Reg. Glasguense*, I, pp. lxiii *seq*.
[2] Cp. Lausanne visitation, quoted elsewhere.

over half the parochial benefices mentioned were vicarages. Minor points of interest shown by the register of this diocese for the thirteenth century are examples of the practice by which the donor, or the appropriating bishop, reserved the patronage of the vicarage to himself. In 1228 when the bishop taxed the vicarages of Holyrood Abbey[1] he reserved the patronage of one of the vicarages to himself, and when in 1256 the church of Peebles[2] was assigned to the archdeaconry of Glasgow, he made a similar reservation. In 1292, William of Moray gave the church of Walliston[3] to the chapter, but reserved the patronage of its vicarage to himself and his heirs. While such a reservation by the bishop was not uncommon in England, I have not myself found any examples of its being made by a layman there, although a few such cases probably do exist. In Ireland, however, it was a frequent practice, and although all my examples are of the fifteenth century, I think that is rather due to the nature of my sources than significant of any specifically fifteenth-century characteristics. In the early years of the fifteenth century, Richard de Tuyt, Kt[4], gave a number of churches to the abbey of St Mary's Granard, in the diocese of Ardagh, but reserved the advowson of the vicarages to his heirs. In 1440, the Pope confirmed the grant of the church of Ballyhay[5] to the Austin Priory of Bridgetown in the diocese of Cloyne, and also this reservation made by the lay patron. In 1435, the perpetual vicarage of Athenry[6] was mentioned as being of lay patronage, and that of Ballynacourty[7] similarly in 1447. This practice enabled the layman to encourage appropriations and gain for himself a reputation of generosity by sacrificing practically none of his own rights. The only loss to him was that instead of having the patronage of a large benefice, he had that of a much smaller and less desirable one.

The kings of Scotland had been great benefactors to the monasteries and bishops and cathedral chapters at the expense of the parishes since the twelfth century. In the last decade of that century, King William gave the bishop of Moray[8] two

[1] *Reg. Glasguense*, I, p. 122.
[2] *Ibid.* I, p. 164.
[3] *Ibid.* I, p. 203.
[4] *Cal. Pap. Let.* IX, p. 29.
[5] *Ibid.* IX, p. 74.
[6] *Ibid.* VIII, p. 547.
[7] *Ibid.* X, p. 328.
[8] *Reg. Moravense*, p. 9.

churches for him to appropriate to his own uses, and in the meantime, while waiting for death to cause vacancies in the rectories, the bishop was to receive £10 yearly from the royal burgh of Elgin. Similarly, King Robert Bruce granted the church of Ellon in Buchan to the Cistercian Abbey of Kinloss, soon after 1300, and the church of Kinross[1] to Dunfermline Abbey in 1314. King David[2], before 1350, granted a church to the bishop and chapter of Aberdeen, and in the following year wrote on behalf of Holyrood Abbey to secure a more effectual appropriation of the church of Crawford (dioc. Glasgow). In 1351, John, King of France, and Joan, Queen of Scotland, prayed the Pope to appropriate a church to Cupar Abbey[3]. Before 1461, King James II[4] gave a church to the bishop of Lismore, so that he might appropriate it, which he did, gaining Papal confirmation for it. So throughout the Middle Ages the great lay lords tried to save their souls at the expense of the parishes, for the example of the kings was followed by great vassals, like those of Moray and Douglas. Whenever a monastery wished to appropriate a new church it found a lay ally ready at hand.

Logie Buchan[5] had been appropriated to the chapter of Aberdeen, but afterwards several rectors obtained the church, and the chapter was afraid of losing its rights in it. So in 1437 a Papal confirmation was secured from Eugenius IV. About the same time, the appropriation of Ratho[6] (co. Edinburgh), to a new collegiate church, was suspended for a Papal provision to be made to the rectory.

During the fourteenth century, the bishops steadily proceeded with the ordaining of vicarages where possible, but the work became increasingly difficult owing to the flood of privileges, exemptions, and vicarage appropriations that was let loose on the country during the latter evil days of the century. Bishop William of St Andrew's, in 1317, appointed a most exceptionally large vicarage of the value of 45 marks in the church of Kinross[7] on his appropriation of it, by gift of Robert Bruce, to Dunfermline Abbey. A little later, the ordination of the

[1] *Cal. Pap. Let.* IV, p. 184.
[2] *Cal. Pap. Pet.* I, p. 202; also *Reg. Aberdon.* I, p. 79.
[3] *Cal. Pap. Let.* III, p. 397.
[4] *Ibid.* XI, pp. 604, 691.
[5] *Ibid.* VIII, p. 645.
[6] *Ibid.* VIII, p. 265.
[7] *Ibid.* IV, p. 184.

vicarage of Ellon in Aberdeenshire was of the ordinary type of the small tithes and dues. The vicarage of Buittle[1], ordained on the appropriation of the church to Sweetheart Abbey in 1347, consisted of all the altar-dues and half of the church land and common pasture and of the malt tithe; while the vicar had to bear all the ordinary dues, but none of the extraordinary. If the dean and chapter of Aberdeen had to pay all the dues of the bishop and archdeacon for their church of Logie Buchan[2] conceded to them by King David in 1361, the vicar of Philorth[3], a church conceded to them by Bishop Alexander in 1362, had to bear these burdens and all others, save episcopal and royal contributions touching the garb tithes.

An earlier, but much more detailed, document concerning the burdens of churches is that of Bishop William of Brechin[4] in 1304 in which he confirmed the arrangements made by his predecessor, John, concerning the churches of Aberbrothoc Abbey in the diocese, and amplified them himself. The vicarages in these churches were worth £10 each. The abbey was to repair the churches and provide competent ornaments for them, namely at least one satisfactory priestly vestment, and chalice and missal. Small repairs in these ought to be done by the vicars but great ones by the monks for two parts, and the vicars for the third. The bishop, however, adopted the bad policy of trying to bind his successors not to augment the vicarages beyond the value of £10 each, and the vicars were to be content with their portions, pay all the ordinary dues, but not repair the church themselves. Yet at some subsequent period, probably in 1350, when all the vicars by joint action secured augmentation from the bishop of St Andrew's, the abbey succeeded in throwing more of the burdens on to the vicarage as may be seen by a bull of 1463–4. In this, it is stated that the vicars of the abbey's churches are bound to repair their churches and to conserve them alike in chalice and ecclesiastical ornaments, as in other necessities, as shown by ordinances approved by Papal authority. Yet the vicar of Bothelny[5], and others, are neglecting to do so. The Pope appointed three commissioners authorised to summon

[1] *Cal. Pap. Let.* IV, p. 225.
[2] *Reg. Aberdon.* I, pp. 95–9.
[3] *Ibid.* I, pp. 99–101.
[4] *Reg. Ep. Brechin.* II, p. 266.
[5] *Cal. Pap. Let.* XI, pp. 667–8.

the vicars and judge the case, invoking, if necessary, the secular arm to compel the repairs. This is illustrative of a quite general tendency to make the vicars responsible for more and more of the burdens as time went on. Perhaps there had been another and more ample endowment for the vicarages of this abbey, to compensate for the increase of burdens, but it may be doubted whether the augmentation of the portion in any cases corresponded exactly to the augmentation of the burdens.

From the latter years of the thirteenth century onwards, the patrons of benefices in Scotland, as elsewhere, were very much troubled by Papal provisions to their benefices. The monasteries particularly suffered by these intrusions, which sometimes even threatened them with the loss of their rectorial rights, since Popes made mistakes at times and provided to the rectories instead of the vicarages. If they could not at once get these mistakes annulled, the monks stood a fair chance of losing the rectories. Such a case occurred at Kinnoul[1] (co. Perth), where the Papal auditor appointed to judge the protests against such a provision made by Urban V decided for the provided rector, and the abbey of Cambuskenneth was deprived of its rectorial rights. The abbey[2], however, could not allow matters to rest here, and so in 1378 obtained a bull from the anti-Pope Clement VII allowing the bishop to re-appropriate the church to them, a vicarage being reserved. At this time petitions flowed in from every country of Europe from clerks who wanted provisions and were willing to bear the expenses of a suit at the Curia. Often such clerks were already rich pluralists who were on the look-out to acquire a rectory here, a vicarage there, for themselves under a nominal, but empty, obligation to provide for adequate ministrations. Such petitioners lied and slandered and blackmailed in the most outrageous manner to achieve their ends, especially in backward countries like Scotland, and even more in Ireland. The values of churches and vicarages seemed to jump about in the most ridiculous fashion according to their petitions. The vicarage of Collessie, in Fife, was said to be worth £20 in 1414, and only £10 in 1416[3]. That of Erskine (co. Renfrew), was not exceeding £16 in 1422 and £9 in 1437.

[1] *Cal. Pap. Let.* IV, p. 237.
[2] *Cal. Pap. Pet.* I, p. 539.
[3] *Ibid.* I, p. 606.

Arbroath Vicarage, in Forfar, was £4 old sterling, in 1417, and £10 in 1418. In 1345 a petitioner[1] asked for the vicarage of Insch (co. Aberdeen), because its present holder had not been ordained priest within the due time and the patron and the Ordinary had neglected to appoint a vicar. Worse examples of "common informing" by petitioners appear in later days. An informer and petitioner for a provision in 1436, and again in 1437, stated that the perpetual vicar of St Ferchanus, in Knapdale, had dilapidated his vicarage, kept a concubine, and celebrated mass while under the consequent sentence of excommunication. To these crimes he added perjury and simony. If these things should prove to be true, the Pope ordered, let the informer be instituted to the vicarage. Similar cases[2] are frequent in Ireland at this time, as in 1440 at St Tierney's, Clones, in the diocese of Clogher, where the informer stated that the vicar, Magonius Olergassa, took the goods of his church and converted them to sinister uses and was a notorious and manifest fornicator. Yet, in 1441, we find Magonius Olergassa still in possession of his vicarage and petitioning that he might also have the vicarage of Clankelly near by, to hold both together for 20 years, since the then vicar of Clankelly was a notorious fornicator and had celebrated mass while excommunicated. William Wischiart[3], the vicar of Carnwath, in Lanarkshire, in 1447, was said to have buried a suicide in his cemetery without consulting his diocesan, and to have so neglected his parish that many of the parishioners had died without the sacraments, although he was many times asked to administer them. If these things were true, William was to be deprived and his accuser instituted in his place. Obviously the business amounted to a regular trade of blackmail at this time. We may well believe that a great number of the Irish and Scottish vicars were "notorious fornicators", for such is the great peril of a theoretically celibate clergy in times of lax discipline. Yet this dastardly trade of writing to the Pope about your neighbours' sins in order to get hold of their goods for yourself shows much worse degradation than widespread forni-

[1] *Cal. Pap. Pet.* I, p. 94.
[2] *Cal. Pap. Let.* IX, pp. 90, 91, 193.
[3] *Ibid.* X, p. 320.

cation by itself would have done. The canker of the schism had eaten through and through into the church.

Meanwhile, although the abbeys suffered from these abuses, they too made their profits from the misfortunes of the Church. While the flow of appropriation deeds was steady at the beginning of the fourteenth century, the Babylonish captivity at Avignon and the subsequent schism, with the constant need of money and yet more money, added volume to the stream. The woes of the Scottish monks might easily be greater than those of their brethren in more peaceful England, and the complaint of Cambuskenneth[1] Abbey, in 1363, that it had suffered from wars, besides fire and lightning, was justified by the normally turbulent state of Scotland. Lindores Abbey[2] in 1414 bewailed its nearness to the wild Scots. Yet the parishes suffered too, and with them their rectors, who relied on the tithes, and even if the appropriation of churches may be condoned, the wholesale appropriation of vicarages that now began cannot be regarded as anything but a most flagrant abuse. In 1329 the Pope confirmed the appropriation[3] made by Robert, the late bishop of Glasgow, of the perpetual vicarages of Kilmarnock and Beith to the abbey of Kilwinning. The vicarage of North Berwick[4] was appropriated in 1361 by the bishop of St Andrew's to the abbey there, which was allowed to appoint a stipendiary priest. Anti-Pope Clement VII confirmed this in 1384. A few years earlier he had been petitioned by the Austin Canons of Cambuskenneth Abbey to allow them to appropriate the vicarage of their church of Clackmannan, on account of their sufferings from constant wars, and the theft of their chalices, books and other altar ornaments. The belfry had been struck by lightning and the choir thereby very much damaged. This permission was granted on condition that they served the church either by one of their own canons or by a stipendiary secular priest. For a time the prior of St Andrew's acquired the vicarage of Falkland (Kilgolke)[5] *in commendam* by Papal provision, but his triumph was short-lived and came to an end when it was revealed, in 1409, that the prior's office was well-endowed already and the

[1] *Cal. Pap. Pet.* I, p. 475.
[2] *Ibid.* I, p. 601.
[3] *Cal. Pap. Let.* II, p. 310.
[4] *Ibid.* IV, p. 249.
[5] *Cal. Pap. Pet.* I, p. 594.

prior had held the vicarage for several years previously without sufficient dispensation. In 1411 a petitioner was granted the vicarage of Kilmorack in Inverness[1] "notwithstanding that the prior and convent of Beauly in the same diocese had held it unlawfully for nine years". It is open to doubt whether the parishes profited by being thus drawn out of the hands of the monks, but the struggle on either side was an ignoble and unworthy one. In 1409, James de Keth, a canon of Jedburgh, petitioned for the priory of Jedburgh notwithstanding that he already had the vicarage of Oxenham, which he did not propose surrendering, and his petition was granted[2]. Example may be added to example of these abuses by which sometimes the monks profited, and sometimes lost. There was no doubt that the church was decadent and in a foul condition, and a reformation of some sort was urgently needed.

Kings, who could be generous enough with parish endowments that cost them nothing, liked to take their own pluck of these endowments. Royal presentations of officials to benefices, even if they had some sort of practical justification in the need of good government and the lack of funds with which it could be provided, were a source of distress to the parishes. Edward I in 1296 sent a mandate to his ruling officials in Scotland[3] to present suitable persons in the king's service, or others at their discretion, provided that they were English and dwelt in the country. Clearly this was to be a cheap and useful way of governing the conquered Lowlands. The native kings themselves made the customary use of their right of presentation to provide for their own clerks, this being quite a recognised proceeding throughout the Middle Ages. Further than this, they sometimes requested patrons to institute their nominees, and this request was at times as strong as a command. A late but typical example of this is found in the Brechin register[4], dated 1451, when the king wrote to the chapter as follows:

Venerabile clerkis We gret zow weile and for alsmekile as we ar informit y^{t} ye vicarage of Cortochquhy pertenyng to zour presentacioun is vacand be ye promotioun of Schir Johne Thomsoun to ye parsonage of Inueraryte we exhort and prayis zou y^{t} ye present our loued chap-

[1] *Cal. Pap. Pet.* I, p. 596.
[2] *Ibid.* I, p. 637.
[3] *Cal. Rot. Pat.* (1292–1301), p. 205.
[4] *Reg. Ep. Brechin.* II, p. 87.

lane Schir Johne Harwar yar to as ze wile do ws singular plesans and halfe special thank of ws yarfor in tym cumynge.

This letter having been ignored, the king sent a more peremptory one. It was the royal equivalent of the Papal provision and a favourite device of that day. Of a more humble tone is an English example of about 1438, when Thomas, Lord of Clifford[1], son of the Earl of Westmorland, wrote to Durham Priory asking for the vicarage of Giggleswick in Craven for one of his father's servants, William Hacforth:

considerynge that he is on able Prest and vertuous. And this you lik to do att the contemplacion of this my writyng as y may do thyng to your pleasaunce en tym to com. And Almyghte God Gyf you right gode lyf, graciously to endure for his mercy.

The granting of such favours was a nuisance that monastic patrons had to suffer in return for the goodwill of the great lay lords, who might do them so much harm or good. The parishes had to bear the indignity of being asylums for the old age or decrepitude of trusted retainers, or even worse, of providing incomes for chaplains or servants who never intended to come near them.

While stressing the evils of the Scottish church by the beginning of the fifteenth century, it must be remembered that evidence of abuses is always more ready to hand than evidence of smooth working of normal machinery. Yet, even admitting that there is little conclusive evidence of the grievous underpayment of parish priests, one is forced to the conclusion that morality was lower, service was less efficient, and abuses more prevalent in the parishes in Scotland than in the more peaceful country of England.

[1] *Finchale Charters* (Surtees Soc.), p. 71.

CHAPTER VII

CALAMITIES OF THE FOURTEENTH CENTURY. WAR, PESTILENCE AND SCHISM

THE fourteenth century was certainly one of many calamities, but the monasteries seem to have taken advantage to the full of the opportunities that these gave of pleading poverty. Doubtless war and pestilence and cattle plague were sufficient to cause very great distress, but the monasteries could not have suffered more than their secular neighbours. Moreover, the distress would be only temporary, while the appropriation of tithes meant the securing of endowments in perpetuity. It was as if a modern government had taken advantage of every temporary set-back to impose fresh taxes that were never repealed in time of prosperity. On this system the monasteries were bound to keep on appropriating churches, for it matters not how well one may be endowed, there are almost bound to come times when the ordinary income will not pay all current expenses. Insurance in those days was unknown, and so all emergencies must be met out of savings or by new endowments. Monasteries, however, did not save, and if they borrowed they must do so at usury contrary to the law of the Church and contrary to all canons of good finance. The sorrows of Abbot Samson of Bury St Edmunds in his dealings with the Jews, as related by Jocelin de Brakelond, are enough to convince us that no one with a light heart could undertake to borrow any large sum of money in the Middle Ages. Mathama[1], abbess of Langley, in 1363, petitioned the Pope for permission to apply the fruits of her new appropriation of Dalby Parva to satisfy her creditors, who would not let her leave the place until they were paid. She said that she had incurred the expenses by carrying on a suit for her monastery for seven years, and the Pope granted the petition "if expenses were thus incurred". If the Jews had long been expelled from England, there were clearly other moneylenders as extortionate to take their place, and borrowing

[1] *Cal. Pap. Pet.* I, p. 419.

obviously was no good as a substitute for appropriation of fresh churches, if, even then, the creditors had to be paid from church revenues.

The Scottish wars were the cause of much genuine tribulation to the North, and in 1306 the bishopric of Carlisle[1] was in such a reduced state through these wars, that Bishop Halton began a long suit for the appropriation of the church of Horncastle[2] in the diocese of Lincoln to his *mensa*. The negotiations lasted 12 years and must themselves have been very costly. Even then, the church was only appropriated for as long as the Scots' occupation should continue. It was a very large rectory, being estimated in 1343 at £77. 6*s*. 8*d*. (although charges then were estimated at £40) and in 1397 as not exceeding 160 marks. In 1319 several parishes[3] had been so devastated that they were no longer able to pay the tenth and several vicarages, like that of Isell, were insufficient for supporting their ordinary burdens. Consequently the plea of tribulations due to the Scottish wars is to be found in all the petitions of Northern monasteries for appropriation about this time, and in a number right at the end of the century. Two cases, however, lead one to suspect that these troubles were quite insufficient excuse for the appropriations. St Albans Abbey[4] in 1328, 1330 and 1332, obtained Papal bulls granting them the church of Appleton in Rydale in the North Riding of Yorkshire, because the abbey was burdened with a debt of 5000 marks and its rents had been diminished by the Scottish wars. The archbishop of York, "his suffragans, and other prelates of the province" offered resistance to the proposed appropriation on the grounds that the rents of their churches were diminished by the wars between England and Scotland. Finally, in 1349, the abbey secured the church[5], valued at £46. 13*s*. 4*d*., on the totally different grounds that by a constitution of Pope Benedict XII they were bound to send at their own expense five monks to the University whose costs were £10 yearly and that the fruits of the monastery had been reduced by a quarter by reason of the Black Death. It seems clear that the archbishop and the other bishops, who could easily find out the

1 *Reg. Halton*, I, p. 240.
2 *Cal. Pap. Let.* II, p. 184.
3 *Reg. Halton*, II, pp. 183 *seq.*
4 *Cal. Pap. Let.* II, pp. 270, 316, 381.
5 *Cal. Pap. Pet.* I, pp. 171–2.

circumstances of the monastery, were not prepared to swallow its stories of poverty, but that the abbey, on the other hand, was quite determined to have the appropriation some way or other, and that the reasons did not matter much. The other instance is that of Hemingborough[1], in the West Riding, whose appropriation was sought in 1347 by Durham Priory to compensate for their losses through the Scottish wars extending over 60 years. The cells of the priory at Coldingham, Holy Island and Farne, had derived their subsistence from three churches in Scotland which were worth £300 a year, but on account of the war these monks were beggars and had been living at the mother priory which itself had suffered much from the exactions of debtors. The archbishop of York and Henry, Lord Percy, were both asked to petition Pope Clement VI on the matter. Now, although the archbishop of York assented to the appropriation and it was confirmed in the Papal Chancery[2] in 1363, yet it does not appear to have taken place at once. In 1372 the king[3] petitioned the Pope on the matter, as he had done once or twice before, and the opponents of the priory, whoever they were, showed that it had appropriated four abbeys and 13 parish churches and two priories. Yet the number of monks had decreased and the 56 remaining—less than one-third of earlier numbers—"when they go out travel with three or four horses, and spend more on their food and clothing than befits men of Religion". Pope Gregory XI commanded that, if the king persisted, enquiry was to be made how many more monks would be added to the priory, what was the value of the church, and how large a vicarage would be appointed.

St Oswald's Priory[4], Nostell, near Pontefract, in 1344, induced the bishop of Durham to ask for the appropriation of the churches of Winwick and Leamington (dioc. Coventry and Lichfield) to them, because the church of Bamburgh, in his own diocese, yielded them hardly a quarter of the former profit owing to the Scottish invasions. Byland Abbey[5], which had

[1] Raine, *Northern Regs.* (R.S.), pp. 392–4.
[2] *Cal. Pap. Pet.* I, p. 464.
[3] *Cal. Pap. Let.* IV, pp. 117–18; Snape, *Monastic Finances*, p. 148; also Coulton, in *Hist. Teach. Misc.* IV, p. 37.
[4] *Reg. Bury* (Surtees Soc.), pp. 51, 52.
[5] *Cal. Pap. Let.* III, p. 114; *Cal. Pap. Pet.* I, p. 18.

been denuded of its church ornaments and loaded with debts by the Scottish wars, acquired the church of Rillington near Malton in the same year. A vicarage of 10 marks was reserved in the church, hitherto possessed by two rectors as comporcionaries, and which was of value not exceeding 32 marks. The same abbey in 1355 applied for the appropriation of a mediety of Bubwith[1] church because they had lost possessions and rents in the wars and by the recent pestilence. The archbishop of York was ordered to send a report to Rome on the matter, and he seems to have sent an unfavourable one. However, at length in 1363, the abbey[2] secured the appropriation because the relation made by Archbishop John had proved to be "insufficient and incorrect". In 1319 Whissendine in Rutland was appropriated to Sempringham Priory to compensate for a sum of 40 marks which they used to have from the Benedictine house of Paisley, and which, by reason of the wars, had not been paid for more than 14 years. Again, as late as 1386, St Dunstan's in the West, London[3], was appropriated to Alnwick Abbey, which had suffered severely and had been burnt by the Scots.

About 1324 the monastery of Burton-on-Trent[4] acquired two churches, Tatenhill and Hanbury, formerly of the advowson of Earl Thomas of Lancaster, the "martyred" rebel, and the king asked the Pope to appropriate them to the abbey. Perhaps it was these same civil wars of Edward II's reign that were meant when Peterborough[5] Abbey asked for the appropriation of Warmington in 1316, on account of their nearness to an important highway and consequent hospitality of the wars in those parts, and of diverse oppressions, exactions and expenses. In the west of England the Welsh wars were the chief excuse, as when Chester Abbey gained in 1340 the appropriation by the bishop, prior and chapter of Worcester, and in 1345 the Papal confirmation of the appropriation of the church of Chipping Campden[6] in Gloucestershire. Chester Abbey had lost 30 carucates of lands by floods, which land was of the yearly value of £100 and certain manors in Wales by reason of the Welsh

1 *Cal. Pap. Let.* III, p. 572. 2 *Ibid.* IV, p. 32.
3 Newcourt, *Repertorium*, I, p. 335.
4 Dugdale-Caley, *Monasticon*, III, p. 46, col. 2.
5 Rev. J. C. Cox, in *Vic. County Hist.* (*Northants.*), II, p. 89.
6 *Cal. Pap. Let.* III, p. 166.

wars. These wars could be pleaded on the other side of the border also, as appears from the curious case[1] of Llanynys in Denbighshire. This church at one time had been worth 100 marks and far more and was held by 24 portionaries, called "Abbatathelaswyr"; one of them, whose portion was commonly called the portion of David the priest, having the cure of souls. In 1402 it was petitioned that by pestilence and war the fruits were diminished to barely 80 marks and the ordinary had reduced the number of portionaries to two, the Pope being asked to confirm this. This he did, stipulating that the two rectors should have the church served by a perpetual vicar.

Dr Coulton has calculated roughly[2] from vol. I of the *Calendar of Papal Petitions* the number of appropriations for six years before and six years after the first appearance of the Plague in August 1348. This was 22 before and 18 after. From vol. III of the *Calendars of Papal Letters* for the five years before these were 17, and for the five years after, 20. From the index of the last two volumes published (X and XI) he calculated 27 from 1447–55 and 31 from 1455–64. These figures, which are underestimates of the real total of appropriations that were going on, are yet a thoroughly reliable guide to proportion. They were compiled to prove one point only, that the Black Death cannot be quoted as a sufficient excuse for appropriations, since they were practically as frequent before as after. This point is proved sufficiently and I have considered it unnecessary to spend hours compiling fresh figures simply to attain a greater accuracy of actual figures which, even then, my human frailty might not put beyond the need of a fresh revision.

The Chronicler Knighton[3] says of the Black Death:

So great was the scarcity of priests that many churches were desolate, being without divine offices....Hardly could a chaplain be got under £10 or 10 marks to minister in any church and where before a chaplain could be had for 4 or 5 marks, or 2 marks with board, so numerous were priests before the pestilence, now scarce any would accept a vicarage of £20 or 20 marks. But in a short time there came crowding into orders a multitude of those whose wives

[1] *Cal. Pap. Let.* IV, p. 349.

[2] Coulton, in *Hist. Teach. Misc.* IV, p. 38.

[3] Knighton, *Leics. Chron.* (R.S.), II, p. 63 (as translated in *Linc. County Hist.* II, p. 38, by Miss M. M. C. Calthrop).

had died in the plague, of whom many were illiterate, only able to read after a fashion and not able to understand what they read.

This testimony of the scarcity of priests is supported by the petition of Thomas Abbot of Croxton[1] to the Pope, which, in 1363, secured license to dispense twelve of his Premonstratensian canons of Croxton and Cockersand, in their twenty-first year, to be ordained priests, there being, on account of the pestilence, but few priests in the monasteries and churches of their order. Walden Abbey[2] acquired the appropriation of the vicarage of the parochial church there in 1366, and permission to serve it by a secular chaplain. It is noteworthy that this Benedictine Abbey did not receive permission to serve it by a monk. Through the death of serfs and *coloni*, the lands of the abbey, it was said, lay uncultivated and the monks could not bear their burdens. Since the vicar, Thomas Freman, is found still in possession seven years later, it was some time before the monks could benefit by this transaction. In 1349 William de Newentone became vicar of Newland in the Forest of Dean, a church appropriated to the bishop of Llandaff[3] in 1305, of which the king had given him the advowson, which, doubtless, had been confiscated from some Welsh "rebel". William de Newentone was ordained acolyte on March 28th[4], subdeacon on April 11th[5], deacon on June 6th[6], and priest on September 14th[7]. The exigencies of the times were probably the cause of this hasty promotion, although other examples of hastily assumed orders are available for less disastrous times. The bishop of Lincoln[8], in 1352, quoted the Plague as one of the causes of the diminution of his rents, to compensate for which he wanted the appropriation of three or four more benefices up to the total value of 200 marks. The abbey of St Mary's, Hulton[9], in 1354, complained that its revenues had fallen to £14 since the pestilence, and from that it was bound to pay £4. 13*s*. to certain persons and places, and so gained the appropriation of the church of Audley, in Staffordshire. Seldom, as here, is the full blame thrown on the Plague, although St Guthlac's Priory[10] at Hereford was allowed

[1] *Cal. Pap. Let.* IV, p. 32.
[2] *Reg. Sudbury*, p. 118.
[3] *Cal. Rot. Pat.* (1301–7), p. 313.
[4] *Reg. Trillek*, p. 485.
[5] *Ibid.* p. 491.
[6] *Ibid.* p. 495.
[7] *Ibid.* p. 502.
[8] *Cal. Pap. Pet.* I, pp. 228, 258.
[9] *Cal. Pap. Let.* III, p. 536.
[10] *Cal. Pap. Pet.* IV, p. 390.

to serve the church by its Benedictine monks in 1391, because their revenues had been diminished by pestilence, "by which even the animals die". Pershore Abbey[1], in 1394, claimed that its rents and services had been diminished by half because of the death of their tenants and serfs in the pestilence. A commission on the proposed appropriation of Heckfield[2] (dioc. Winchester), to Merton College, Oxford, in 1383, stated that the college was meagrely endowed and that its present sources of income had been damaged by plague of men and murrain of cattle, scarcity of farm servants, floods, storms, tempests, severity of weather, wars and tumults, the tenths and taxes imposed by the king in consequence thereof, and "other events and accidents such as notoriously occur in these days oftener than they did of old". The college buildings had remained structurally incomplete from the first foundation. The bishop carried out the appropriation with the consent of his priory.

An example, however, that shows plainly that the Black Death was not always the primary motive of the appropriation, is that of Colston Basset[3] (co. Nottingham). The orginal deed of Archbishop William, dated March 28th, 1349, did not mention the Plague for the simple reason that it had not occurred in time for Worksop Priory to put it among the reasons in their petition. In the Papal confirmation of 1373 it is mentioned, indeed, though we know that, however genuine a need it may have created, it was not the original cause of the appropriation. In fact, in the latter years of the fourteenth century, the mention of the Plague seems to become something very near common form, although we may be sure that the Plague had at some time dealt a shrewd blow at most monastic finances.

The spirit of the Statute of Labourers can also be discovered at work in the monastic petitions. Easton Mauduit[4], near Bozeat, Northants., was appropriated by John, bishop of Lincoln, in 1391, to Lavenden Abbey which was situated hard by the common street and the highway. Its revenues had been diminished by pestilence and epidemics, the barrenness of its lands, the scarcity of husbandmen, the fewness of servants and their immoderate wages. It was oppressed by the unwonted exactions

[1] *Cal. Pap. Let.* v, p. 15.
[2] *Reg. Wykeham*, I, pp. 138 *seq.*
[3] *Cal. Pap. Let.* IV, p. 208.
[4] *Ibid.* v, p. 74.

imposed on ecclesiastics, especially the "religious", by its debts, by hospitality, and by the sustentation of the poor, weak and infirm. The abbey, which was Premonstratensian, was to have the cure of the church, which was not two miles away from them. Southam[1], in Warwickshire, was appropriated to Coventry Priory by the bishop of the diocese in 1452, because of the barrenness of its lands, the dearth of cultivators, and their immoderate wages. Manchester Church[2], about the same time, was appropriated to the Cistercian house of Merevale, and the excessive wages are again mentioned. In this case a vicarage of 16 marks was reserved and 3*s.* 4*d.* was to be given yearly to the poor of the parish at the discretion of vicar and churchwardens. In the thirty-sixth year of Edward III (1362–3) it was enacted by Statute[3] that no parochial chaplain (*i.e.* any stipendiary priest) should by any way or colour receive more than 6 marks a year, and other annual chaplains with cure of souls should not have more than 5 marks. If any secular man paid more than 5 marks for any annual chaplain, in pence or anything else, or, if he kept the chaplain at his table, more than 2 marks for his frock and other necessities, the table counting as 40*s.*, he should be liable to pay as much to the king as he paid in excess to the said chaplain. The statute, of course, could not be generally enforced and the Parliament of 1402 asked Henry IV to renew it. He promised that he would ordain a suitable remedy by good deliberation. The complaints about "immoderate wages", and this Statute, prove that the stipendiary chaplain was profiting by the vacancies in the profession created by the Black Death. It was an age of chantry foundation and the monasteries were receiving permission in a number of cases to serve their churches by stipendiaries, and there was a dearth of chaplains (modern "curates") for the parishes. The stipendiary, however, was not the most deserving of clerks, and contemporary moralists, including the author of *Piers Plowman*, condemn roundly "choppe-churches" and those who run after chantries, despising the cure of a country parish. Yet I have gained no evidence and have no reason to believe that the vicar profited by the changes, except, perhaps in so far as he might be in a

[1] *Cal. Pap. Let.* XI, pp. 62, 83.
[2] *Ibid.* p. 49.
[3] *Rot. Parl.* III, p. 501 *a*, *b*.

position to refuse a very bad living, and wait for a better. Selborne vicarage[1], it is true, was augmented in 1352 by agreement to avoid a lawsuit, and the perpetual vicar "on account of the pestilence and scarcity of the times" was to receive half a crown a year from the late John Bound's tenement, and the rest of the appurtenances of the vicarage there set out in full. While quite a normal number of augmentations were made in the latter part of the fourteenth century, there is certainly no general tendency to blame the Black Death for the need of them, nor is there any sign of a general re-ordination in any way comparable to the flood of vicarage ordinations with which the thirteenth century opens. If the tithes were so much affected by the Black Death, as the monastic petitioners stated, we should have expected the greater part of those vicarages that were just above subsistence level (and we have seen that there were very many such) to drop below that level suddenly and necessitate a general re-ordination. From what we know of the mortality we realise that the tithes must have suffered severely, for the sudden removal of husbandmen and labourers meant the removal of tithe-payers and the loss of tithes. The only conceivable reason for the lack of particular stress on the Plague as the reason for required appropriations, is that it was open to the damning objection that, since all the world had suffered from the Plague, there was no reason to favour one body as against any other. So, while it was included in nearly all petitions, several other reasons were also introduced to darken the picture of monastic troubles. A vicar petitioning for augmentation could also be answered that not only had everybody else suffered from the Plague, but that he himself had not so much work to do now, as there were fewer parishioners. The shortage of chaplains, too, probably meant that many vicars had that much extra for themselves since they could not pay chaplains that were unobtainable. The Hereford registers, of which we have now a complete printed set to cover the period, are less useful for our purpose than some others, for instance the Lincoln registers, since they do not devote very much space to details of vicarages. Such as they are, however, they do not produce any better evidence of the state of vicarages after the Black Death than that concerning

[1] *Selborne Charters*, I, pp. 91, 92.

Much (or Great) Cowarne and Eardisland. In 1351, the Official[1] of the archbishop told the bishop to ask the rectors, Gloucester Abbey, to provide a suitable income for the vicar of Much Cowarne, and, if they refused, to cite them to appear in the Court of Arches. In 1357 the bishop[2] in his visitation of Eardisley found the vicarage badly endowed. Owing to the confined position of his dwelling house, the vicar had no room to walk, or grow leeks, or other herbs, and so the bishop assigned him part of the glebe land, belonging to the rectors, Lyre Abbey. The vicar of Alberbury[3], in 1368, petitioned for augmentation which was to be made if the plea was well-founded. There are no details of such an augmentation set out in the register. The Exeter registers, the Bath and Wells register of Ralph Shrewsbury (1329–63) and the Winchester register of Wykeham (1367–1404) are similarly unconvincing. There is an unfortunate scarcity of printed registers for this period at present, but on the evidence to hand there seems little reason to believe that any exceptional number of augmentations took place between 1348 and 1400.

At St Laurence's, Waltham[4], in Berkshire, in 1369, the vicar had had a sentence in his favour from the commissary of the archbishop's Official augmenting the vicarage. The rectors, Hurley Priory, were said to be defrauding the vicar of the benefits of this sentence, and a Papal bull commanding its enforcement was obtained. The vicar of Wootton Wawen[5] in Warwickshire, in 1370, complained that, though the parish was large and populous, the vicarage was insufficient, and was diminished by the existence of a chapel newly built at Henley in the same parish. There is no suggestion of the Black Death about this. In 1374 the vicarage of Budbrooke[6] near Warwick (Bodebroc) (dioc. Worcester) could not be maintained on account of its poverty, and the absentee rector, Master Alexander, could not be found. The vicarage of Ashley[7] (dioc. Winton.), originally endowed in 1254, was augmented in 1385 by the commissioners of William of Wykeham. The dean and chapter of St Paul's in 1388 even petitioned the archbishop of Canterbury

[1] *Reg. Trillek*, p. 168.
[2] *Ibid.* p. 252.
[3] *Reg. L. de Charltone*, p. 48.
[4] *Cal. Pap. Let.* IV, p. 81.
[5] *Ibid.* IV, p. 86.
[6] *Reg. Sede Vacante* (Worcs.), p. 321.
[7] *Reg. Wykeham*, II, pp. 359 *seq.*

to free their church of Barnes, in the same diocese, and reconvert it to a rectory, which was accordingly done. The bishop of London in 1398 dissolved the appropriation of Willingale Spain[1] to Blackmore Priory, at the request of the prior, owing to the smallness of the vicar's income, on condition that the rector should pay 40*s*. pension to the priory. The prior of St Helen's[2] in the Isle of Wight, in 1399, was granted licence to administer the sacraments in the church there for a year and a day, the vicarage being too poor to support a vicar or curate. A petition of various parishioners in the diocese of Norwich stated that vicarages were very much diminished so that no priests or clerks could be found willing to be instituted, whereby the cure of souls was not duly exercised, hospitality was not kept, and divine worship was neglected. This produced from the Curia, even of the disreputable Pope John XXIII, in 1412, a mandate[3] to the bishop to augment, if these things were true. A return to a mandate of Archbishop Chichele concerning proposed augmentations[4] was made by Bishop Praty of Chichester about 1440 that revealed in the archdeaconry of Chichester 25 rectories and 34 vicarages not exceeding 12 marks, of which 8 rectories and 1 vicarage, although taxed and accustomed to pay tenths, were so small that there was no performance of duties. In the archdeaconry of Lewes there were 20 rectories and 5 vicarages not exceeding 12 marks in value. The prebend of Seaford and its vicarage were both unoccupied because impoverished by floods and conflagrations, as also were 4 vicarages in Hastings.

These instances, even those of voluntary renunciation of the appropriations, do not prove any general movement of augmentation, or of sympathy with the claims of the vicars. They do show the level of poverty reached by many parochial benefices at this time and encourage a suspicion that many others suffered without relief.

Abroad, similar arguments are used for appropriations as in England. The infirmary of the monastery of St James of Liège, in 1330, gained Papal approval for the appropriation of the

[1] Rev. J. C. Cox, in *Vic. County Hist.* (*Essex*), II, p. 10.
[2] *Reg. Wykeham*, II, p. 490.
[3] *Cal. Pap. Let.* VI, p. 311.
[4] *Reg. Praty*, pp. 86, 87.

church of Seraing[1], "on account of the tumults of wars, which in those parts between you (the bishop) and the citizens of Liège have lasted through many ages". It being a Benedictine house, the bull stipulated that a suitable portion for a perpetual vicar should be reserved. When Russon[2] was appropriated to Borcette Abbey of Cistercian nuns by the bishop of Liège the reasons were not only the calamity of wars and malice of the times but also the waste of the abbey goods (*ex sumptuosa plerumque suorum et monasterii sui tuitione bonorum*). The revenues were to be applied to the "pittances" (special food allowances) of the nuns who frequently, it was said, suffered penury of food and indigence in clothing. This appropriation was made by the bishop in 1319, and confirmed by the Pope in 1332. For the fourteenth century in France as a whole, however, I am forced to confess a shortage of evidence due to the fact that very few French monastic chartularies, my chief sources, have relevant documents much later than about 1300.

The Hundred Years' War brought about considerable change in the allegiance of a number of English monasteries and in the possession of a number of English appropriated churches. The policy of English kings towards aliens became harsh not so much for patriotic reasons as for financial. Alien clerks were cited and fined, as in 1346 when the vicars of Dixton and Dymock[3] in the diocese of Hereford were cited, as aliens holding benefices, to appear before the king and council in London. The alien priories were all taken into the king's hands and mulcted, and fined most deplorably, and frequently the custody of them was handed over to some courtier who took his pluck with lamentable thoroughness. Consequently, in 1347–8, the vicar of Haugham[4] in the diocese of Lincoln, was compelled to petition the king in Parliament for arrears of his vicarage of 50*s*. The priory there had been taken into the king's hands, and by him granted to the bishop of "Cardoil" (Carlisle) since when the money had never been paid. The king, in answer to the petition, ordered a brief to be sent to the bishop demanding payment, failing which he was to be summoned before the king.

1 *Reg. John XXII*, II, p. 378.
2 *Ibid.* II, p. 353.
3 *Reg. Trillek*, p. 260.
4 *Rot. Parl.* II, p. 212 *b*.

When the church of Alberbury[1] had been thus confiscated with the alien priory there Bishop Lewis de Charltone in 1369 found it necessary to inquire whether the vicar, Thomas Moneford, had been admitted simoniacally. At last the alien priories themselves sought remedy by petition in Parliament, by asking that they should be paid a reasonable farm by such custodians, lay or clerical, secular or religious, to maintain divine service and make other reasonable and due charges according to their terms of foundation. This was granted, and a little later, confirmed[2]. Yet these promises proved very unsatisfactory remedies. In the end the appropriated churches of alien monasteries were frequently confiscated and granted to other foundations. William of Wykeham's[3] foundation of St Mary's College, of Winchester, at Oxford, was in 1392 granted the churches of Isleworth, Heston, Twickenham and Hampton, belonging to the monastery of St Valery-sur-mer; Hamble, Hound, and West Worldham belonging to the priory of Hamble-le-Rice or its mother house of Holy Trinity, Tiron, in the diocese of Chartres; and Harmondsworth belonging to the priory of Mont Ste Catherine by Rouen. These churches were all together valued at 300 marks. The Papal bull announcing this stated that it was the Pope's intention to compensate, and the editor of Wykeham's *Register*[4] says that the bishop bought the churches for the purpose. When Hornchurch, alias Havering, in Essex, was in the same year appropriated to the new college, the bull stated that its former appropriators, the monastery of SS. Nicholas and Bernard of Montjoux (dioc. Sion), were to be compensated when they returned to their allegiance from the anti-Pope. A number of English appropriated churches were granted afresh in this way, the Pope breaking off their connection with foreign houses, an example being when Kirkstall Abbey, in 1397, gained possession from St Martin's Abbey, Aumâle[5], in the diocese of Rouen, and was granted seven churches in Yorkshire said to have belonged to Aumâle. These churches had yielded little or no profit to Aumâle Abbey, the inhabitants of that country being enemies of King Richard and adherents of the anti-Popes. In

[1] *Reg. L. de Charltone*, p. 52.
[2] *Rot. Parl.* III, p. 262.
[3] *Cal. Pap. Let.* IV, pp. 440, 441.
[4] *Reg. Wykeham*, II, p. 212 and note; Rymer's *Foedera* (ed. 1709), VII, p. 697.
[5] *Cal. Pap. Let.* V, p. 16.

1414 the blow fell at last in the shape of a general dissolution of alien houses, yet really the catastrophe was rather theoretical than actual. The damage had already been done, and this unconventional and arbitrary act was only perpetuating changes of ownership that had already taken place. It put an end to the harmful custodies of courtiers and eventually most of the goods of the priories found their way back into ecclesiastical hands. The priory of Ware[1], including the appropriated rectory, was given to the king's new priory in honour of Jesus of Bethlehem at Shene. The pious King Henry VI was impelled by his conscience to grant away such of the old possessions of alien priories as remained in the royal hands. For instance, All Souls College in 1441 gained with others the priory of Alberbury. In this case the college could not prove its right to the appropriated rectory of the church as part of the goods of the priory until 1521, when it promised to keep Bishop Bothe's anniversary in gratitude for his assistance in the matter[2].

In England the Great Schism did not have such disastrous effects as abroad because the king was always strong enough with his chief archbishops and bishops to enforce general recognition of one Pope at a time. More confusing were the general annulments of appropriations that had been granted but had not already taken effect because the rectors had not yet died or resigned. Urban V in 1366[3], Boniface IX in 1402[4], Innocent VII[5] and Calixtus III[6] on their accessions, all annulled formally those appropriations that had not already taken place, whether of rectories, vicarages or other benefices. These had the effect of bringing fresh suits to the Papal Curia—for exemption from these revocations—and brought fresh facts. They also put off the evil day in many cases, although there were probably few in which it was averted entirely. In 1375 the appropriation of the Yorkshire church of Whixley[7] to the minister and brethren of St Robert by Knaresborough was confirmed, notwithstanding Urban V's general revocation. In 1397 the vicarage of the church of Kimbolton[8] in Huntingdonshire was appropriated to Stoneley Priory to be served by one of their Augustinian canons.

[1] Newcourt, *Repertorium*, I, p. 901.
[2] *Reg. Bothe*, pp. 85, 86, 114.
[3] *Cal. Pap. Let.* IV, p. 180.
[4] *Ibid.* VI, pp. 4, 29, 284, 417, 468.
[5] *Ibid.* VII, p. 411.
[6] *Ibid.* XI, p. 62.
[7] *Ibid.* IV, p. 205.
[8] *Ibid.* V, p. 16.

A former appropriation of the church had been rendered null by Urban V's general revocation and a fresh one had been made by Bishop John of Lincoln under Papal mandate. The bishop allowed three canons in succession to hold the vicarage and the Pope now confirmed this by a formal appropriation of it. Kemsing[1] (dioc. Rochester), Chipping Norton[2], East Claydon[3], Hacconby[4] and Hogsthorpe[5] in Lincoln, Harlow[6] in London, Hornsea[7] in York, and Denford[8] in Coventry and Lichfield are benefices whose appropriations were exempt from the general annulment of Boniface IX. A different kind of revocation is found in 1451 only for the city and diocese of St Andrew's[9], the reason being a shortage of clerks, who could not afford to be educated unless with the help of a secular benefice. This again dealt only with those churches whose appropriations had been granted but had not yet taken effect.

The Conciliar Movement aroused hopes of a remedy in some ardent Reformers. Among the 72 heads of accusation preferred against Pope John XXIII, number 11 was that in the diocese of Bologna he had sold six parish churches to laymen who had named at their will priests to say mass. He had, it was said, committed crimes of this kind yet more serious. Another accusation, which probably amounted to the same thing in different words, was that he had transferred to laymen a great part of the tithes belonging to the episcopal *mensa* of Bologna[10]. This was the lowest depth to which a Pope could descend in this matter. In 1408 the English complaints were voiced by Richard Ullerston, Professor of Divinity in the University of Oxford, by the advice of Robert Halum, bishop of Salisbury, soon to be made a cardinal, in a statement of grievances to be reformed by a General Council. It was entitled *Petitiones Ricardi quoad Reformationem Ecclesiae Militantis*[11]. The fourth article was "against the anomalous appropriation of churches" which stated that the parishioners were defrauded equally of good curates (*i.e.* priests with cure of souls) and teaching. The divine

1 *Cal. Pap. Let.* V, p. 13.
2 *Ibid.* V, p. 599.
3 *Ibid.* VI, p. 157.
4 *Ibid.* VI, p. 4.
5 *Ibid.* VI, pp. 81, 162.
6 *Ibid.* V, p. 152.
7 *Ibid.* VI, p. 192.
8 *Ibid.* VI, p. 417.
9 *Ibid.* X, p. 176.
10 Hefelé, *Conciles*, VII, I, pp. 235, 238.
11 Kennett, *Impropriations*, App. p. 7.

worship was taken away considerably and in most cases there was no appreciable recompense.

It quoted the sermon of Robert Grosseteste which stated that "when there is Appropriation of parish churches to Religious, it is a confirmation and perpetuation of the aforementioned evils". There was a destruction of the Church and in no wise any edification. Not even an angel from heaven had power to do these things, although they might have been done by the accursed member of him who had power to hurt Job. He emphasised[1] that

by these appropriations parishioners are defrauded of good pastors and teaching, and of alms...and divine service is sensibly diminished. ...The Church experiences this everywhere, and especially the English church....This system [or rather disorder] plainly tends in no way to the edification of the Church, but to its destruction.

He pleaded that not only a future limit should be set, but that:

Prelates, clerks, and other skilled men in kingdoms, should diligently examine into the motives of appropriations and, if they find the evidences insufficient [for instance that they are invalid, either because they suggest falsehood or suppress the truth which ought necessarily to be expressed in appropriations of this kind, or that they tend to the detriment of the Church] in whatsoever cases it be thus decided by these inhabitants of the realm, who are able best and most faithfully to judge of such matters, in all such cases the appropriation should simply be quashed and the collation [of the church] should return to the original patrons.

The article ends by a dramatic appeal for a new Jerusalem and a return of the Golden Age as it was instituted from the beginning. It was, in fact, something of that nature that Ullerston was asking for, when he requested that such appropriations be undone and advowsons returned to the former patrons. Just as Queen Mary could not restore the property of the dissolved monasteries, so no Pope could possibly have defied vested interests in this manner. Whether as a result of this petition or not, a Concordat[2] was made between Pope Martin V and representatives of the English nation in the Council of Constance in 1418. The Pope promised, among other things,

[1] Van d. Hardt, *Mag. Constant. Concilium*, I (1700), col. 1140. As transl. by Dr G. G. Coulton, in *Hist. Teach. Misc.* IV, p. 4.

[2] Kennett, *Impropriations*, p. 111.

that in future no appropriations of parish churches should be made *motu proprio* (that is, direct from the Apostolic See) but that the bishops should be instructed to make enquiries first, and then, if they found the causes true and legitimate, they should proceed to perform the appropriation. Also there should be no revocation if scandal could proceed from the revocation —this clause being designed to prevent those scandals that arose at the Curia from successive contradictory sentences. Yet more important was the article declaring that:

> All unions, incorporations, appropriations and consolidations of perpetual vicarages in Parish churches made in the time of the Schism from whatever cause shall be revoked without distinction, and perpetual vicars shall be ordained for this time and instituted in them by the Ordinaries of the place. And in each of the Parish churches there shall be one perpetual vicar, who shall stand for the cure of souls, well and competently endowed to hold hospitality there and for supporting and dues: Apostolic letters and compositions of the Ordinaries, Statutes and Customs, and all other things whatsoever made to the contrary notwithstanding.

The extent to which this evil had been practised is revealed by the number of such grants of permission to appropriate that appear in the *Calendars of Papal Letters*, there being at the very least 100 for the years 1395–1400. The revocation seems to have been of very little effect, the Premonstratensians certainly continuing to hold their appropriated vicarages until the time of the Reformation.

Prague University[1] also protested to Martin V against the insufferable prejudices to Learning and Religion caused by the monastic encroachments on the maintenance of the clergy. Cardinal Peter D'Ailly, in his *Libellus de Reformatione Ecclesiae*[2] presented to the Council of Constance, suggested that the monks "should not unduly occupy the rights of prelates, churches and parish priests, either in tithes or other ecclesiastical profits".

Reforming opinion was unanimous on the subject but in the Councils all was futility. The Council of Basle itself confirmed appropriations, and vested interests were triumphant. Most of the prelates represented at the Council were themselves appropriators, and the anti-monastic section was not strong enough

[1] Kennett, *Impropriations*, pp. 91, 92.
[2] Browne, *Fasc. Rerum*, I, p. 413.

to enforce on the monasteries decrees which it would not have intended to apply to itself.

The Hundred Years' War in France left behind such a trail of misery that for the first half of the fifteenth century French monasteries were continually pleading for fresh appropriations. Dr Denifle's two volumes on *La Désolation des Églises.... Pendant la Guerre de Cent Ans* contain many petitions for appropriations, both of parish churches and of smaller monasteries. The eight chaplains of the Holy Spirit[1] in the cathedral church of Auch in 1419, "on account of the wars and plagues of mortalities, as well as of other events which from a long time since (alas) have stalked in those parts", gained three parish churches. The vicarage of the parish church of St Aubin[2] for the same reasons had in 1427 been so diminished for 18 years that the perpetual vicar could not reside in it for two years on end, whereby the parishioners daily suffered great loss. The prior sought permission to hold the vicarage *in commendam* and to perform its duties. The parish church of St Bonitus l'Enfantier[3] (dioc. Limoges) was so diminished that "hardly any priest could live in the vicarage without opprobrious mendicity", and so in 1427 petition was made for the appropriation to it of a parish church near by. The office of the pittancer of the capitular church of La Vaivre, which hitherto had been abundant, was now diminished and in 1419 it gained a parish church. The abbey of St Sauveur de la Fontaine, which had hitherto been well endowed, gained in 1439 four more churches. The episcopal *mensa* of Angoulême, in 1428, the bishop having been captured in the wars, gained a priory and several parish churches for its relief.

Many of the pleas were undoubtedly justified by the barbarity of the wars, but in one case deception was definitely proved. The chapter of St Opportune[4] at Paris in 1444 represented its income as very much deteriorated, and said that as there were no baptismal fonts at the Église des Innocents the parishioners had to go to St Opportune for the baptism of their children. Consequently the chapter gained confirmation of the appro-

[1] Denifle, *La Désolation, etc.* I, p. 195.
[2] Diocese of Bazas; Denifle, *La Désolation, etc.* I, p. 208.
[3] *Ibid.* I, p. 305.
[4] *Ibid.* I, pp. 472, 473.

priation by them of the Église des Innocents. Representatives of this church soon after in 1457, complaining that the chapter had taken off the relics, vessels, and other things legitimately belonging to the church, and neglected the service so that the church was falling into a pitiable condition, asked for the dissolution of the appropriation, which was granted. But, as Dr Coulton says[1], no ordinary village church could have secured a revocation of this kind[2].

So the whole period 1300–1450 is one of unceasing appropriations and rapid encroachment on the part of the monasteries on the parishes. Looking back on this period, records of abuse are not far to seek, and, although the excuse may readily be made that the rectors of unappropriated churches were non-resident, immoral and neglectful of both the cure of souls and the upkeep of their churches, yet these wrongs did not turn the curse of excessive appropriation into a blessing. Professor Tait declares that vicarages[3] were on the whole served better than rectories. For this he offers in evidence that he can only find one case of licence for non-residence to a vicar in Lancashire, in the registers of Coventry and Lichfield, and that was in 1309 when the vicar of Blackburn was licensed to go on pilgrimage for one year. The frequency of the names of Langton, Standish, Halsall, and le Welsch among the rectors of Wigan, Standish, Halsall and Oughton proves the use of the patronage to provide for younger sons. Licences to study were frequent, and rectors were frequently instituted when in minor orders or having received the first tonsure only. The Rev. J. C. Cox[4] makes the same kind of remarks for Berkshire, where he says that the visitation of 1393 proves that rectories were worse served. There were seven non-resident rectors, and in each case there were grave defects, as at Woolhampton, where the chancel roof was in bad condition, and the rectory house ruinous although the rector had received 18 marks for its repair. At Welford, there

[1] Coulton, in *Hist. Teach. Misc.* IV, p. 24.

[2] A revocation of the appropriation of the church at Sens (Brittany), which was a priory with cure, was secured by the duke of Brittany in 1453. It had been appropriated because the buildings of St Pierre de Rilley, near Fougères, were in bad condition and because of the war. The building was now repaired and the war had ceased. (Denifle, I, p. 490.)

[3] Professor James Tait, in *Vic. County Hist.* (*Lancs.*), II, p. 31.

[4] Rev. J. C. Cox, in *Vic. County Hist.* (*Berks.*), II, pp. 16, 17.

was a bad smell caused by jackdaws in the church. At Sutton Courtney the rector gave no alms to the poor, and the churchyard was grazed by horses and cows to the destruction of monuments to the dead. Of the appropriated churches, however, Cholsey had grave defects in the nave and roof, which were to be repaired by the parishioners by All Saints' Day next under penalty of 100*s*. for default. Thatcham had its roof in bad repair, and the vicar of Kintbury was incontinent. The worst condition was at Basildon, a church belonging to Lyre Abbey, where there had been no mattins, or vespers, or mass for a long time, no notice was given of festivals, people were married without banns and children baptised without unction. The vicar was excommunicated for incontinence.

This sort of evidence merely shows that, while there were many unappropriated churches in just as bad condition as the worst of the appropriated, and some decidedly worse, the monastic rectors were satisfied with a low level of performance which frequently fell into definite abuse. The appropriated church certainly gained by the better residence of the vicar, although a non-resident rector would always be bound to put in a vicar during his absence. Moreover, vicarages were always freer from royal and even Papal interference than rectories, usually because they were too small to make it worth while. The ordinary easy-going resident rector, who might even have a "concubine", was undoubtedly preferable to a vicar, whose poverty did not make him more spiritually minded and yet prevented him from affording much help to his neighbours. The worst offenders were undoubtedly the rich courtier pluralists, like Bogo de Clare, who would hold 25 or 40 benefices at a time and let them fall into ruin. Commendataries and provisees were also very bad offenders, as in the case of Dientesheim[1], a church of the cathedral chapter of Worms. This in 1496 was in the hands of a commendatary who did not reside, nor had a vicar there, nor a vicarage house, although there was a place where there had been a house formerly. The church throughout was ruinous. These offenders were rivalled by the monasteries only in their worst times of internal decay, but even normally the monastery was a negligent rector, regarding the service of

[1] *Zeitschrift...Oberrheins*, XXVII, p. 269.

the parish as a sheer burden rather than a divine duty. Nor were all monks blind to the inevitable evils of appropriation, for when Abbot Hugh de Leven of Meaux tried to appropriate the church of Easington, soon after 1339, he was unsuccessful for five years because many of the convent declared against the project, protesting against the enormous injuries that would from thence arise to be lamented by persons yet unborn[1]. This protest was, however, very seldom raised and even more seldom had any effect. In 1366 Sir John de Warthewyk[2] complained in forcible terms to the archbishop of York that Wetheral Priory in the diocese of Carlisle had been dealing unjustly with the churches of Wetheral and Warwick in not supplying proper ministrations. Eynsham Abbey[3], in 1434, was found in a scandalous condition, and both the abbot and the vicar were accused of incontinence with several women. Such is the precipice on the edge of which the appropriated parish trembled, and into which it quite frequently fell. There is in fact little to choose between the condition of the parish of the absentee rector, where things might only temporarily be worse, and that of the appropriated parish, where, as Grosseteste said, the evils were perpetuated. In the average diocese, at any time in the Middle Ages, abuses could be found abounding, and if the monasteries did nothing but fail to maintain in their own parishes a higher standard than was general, they might yet be considered to fail in their exceptionally high calling.

One of the advantages of vicarages over rectories was, as has been stated above, their greater freedom from Papal interference. Yet there are quite a number of cases on record of provisions to vicarages. In 1310, for instance, a Papal chaplain[4] gained the vicarage of Mundham. The bishop of Chichester took exception to this, and refused to ordain him to major orders as was necessary, and he therefore became liable to the penalties of the Constitution of Cardinal Ottobon. It was necessary for the chaplain to obtain a fresh Papal bull confirming the vicarage to him in spite of this. In 1369 one Robert de Brigham gained

[1] Kennett, *Impropriations*, p. 89.

[2] Rev. James Wilson, M.A., in *Vic. County Hist.* (*Cumberland*), II, p. 185.

[3] *Lincoln Visitations*, I, p. 63 (1420–36).

[4] *Cal. Pap. Let.* II, p. 70.

provision of the vicarage of Aston Rowant, belonging to St Albans Abbey, but petitioned the Pope for a confirmation of this, though the abbot "pretended" that the church was in the gift of the daughter house of Holy Trinity, Wallingford[1]. This may just have been a trick to make the provision of no effect. However, in 1371, the vicar[2] resigned, being probably bought out, or forced out by sheer discomfort. At Bottesford[3], in Lincolnshire, in 1398, a vicar, who was a Papal chaplain, was said to have committed fornication with his two sisters and a parishioner, and to have had offspring by each of them. Clearly, Papal favour was no guarantee of good character and certainly none of popularity, either with the parishioners, the patrons, or the bishops.

A curious case, showing how ignorant the appropriators could be of events concerning their parishes, occurred at Davidstow[4], in the diocese of Exeter. One Baldwin, it was alleged, reported the vicar to the hospital of Bridgwater as dead, and got himself instituted to the vicarage at the presentation of the hospital, as rectors. Then the real vicar died, and the hospital, discovering the fraud, presented a certain Thomas Bernarde. Both claimed the vicarage, but judgement was given in July 1386 for Bernarde, who died in possession[5] in 1408. These were riotous days, when, in 1381, a vicar of All Saints', Sudbury, was among those excepted from pardon in the Peasants' Revolt[6]: when a vicar of Abbot's Ann[7] (dioc. Winchester) had in 1391 slain a man and was wasting the goods of the church: when a chaplain carried off the goods and chattels of his vicar at Steeple Morden (dioc. Ely), "with swords, bows and arrows"[8]: when the parishioners at Burton in Kendal[9] (1398) seized part of the cemetery and used it for a public market for traffic and pleas and caused mutilations and homicides to be committed there: when a vicar of Linkinhorne in 1411 was found murdered, after quarrels with his parishioners[10]: and when, in 1412, a vicar at Kirby on the Moor[11] in Yorkshire, an Augustinian canon of Newburgh,

[1] *Cal. Pap. Let.* IV, p. 79.
[2] *Ibid.* IV, p. 166.
[3] *Ibid.* V, p. 98.
[4] *Reg. Brantingham*, p. 167.
[5] *Reg. Stafford*, p. 163.
[6] *Rot. Parl.* III, p. 111.
[7] *Reg. Wykeham*, II, p. 429.
[8] *Ely dioc. Rem.* 1899, p. 74.
[9] *Cal. Pap. Let.* V, p. 89.
[10] *Reg. Stafford*, p. 242.
[11] *Cal. Pap. Let.* VI, p. 322.

could not reside in his vicarage because threatened by robbers[1]. Some evil-doers at Sidlesham[2] in 1404, or shortly before, cut out the leaf of the old missal, on which the vicarage ordination deed was written. The bishop of Chichester demanded the submission of the miscreants within a fortnight, on pain of falling under the greater excommunication. It was a prebendal church, but it need not have been the prebendary who instigated this crime. Perhaps it was some of the parishioners who were interested in the incidence of the church burdens, or the extent of the glebe. In 1419 Thomas Donne, vicar of Alberbury[3], falsely pretending to be the bishop's commissary, commenced proceedings of divorce between certain of the flock of the bishop of St Asaph's. The vicars of Templeroan in the diocese of Cloyne in Ireland, and of Cullompton[4] in the diocese of Exeter, in 1312 and 1361, respectively, had forged Papal letters, but in 1422 a much more sensational case of forgery came to light. The perpetual vicar of St Martin in the Field[5], London, complained to the Pope that the Augustinian chapel or hospital of St Mary Rouncevall by Charing Cross, under pretext of certain pretended letters of Boniface IX, usurped and unduly detained certain tithes and oblations of the vicarage. The archbishop had the letters under arrest, suspecting them to have been forged, since their form differed from that usual in the Papal chancery. The Pope ordered them to be sent to the chancery for examination, and a sequestration to be made of the disputed fruits pending sentence. Next year the sentence was given, and letters under the names of Pope Boniface IX, Urban VI, Clement VI, Urban V and others were declared to have been forged. The forgers were to be punished, and the forgeries publicly denounced. Certain letters of Innocent VI were sent back to the archbishop with the others, and he was to keep them in his court, and prohibit the hospital from using them or copies of

[1] The vicar of Sherborne (Gloucs.) had in 1284 been unable to reside in his cure for fear of his enemies, and the bishop of Worcester had to order the rectors, Winchcombe Abbey, to appoint another priest and provide the old vicar with a livery (*Reg. Giffard* (*Worcs.*), p. 242). The vicar of Skidbrooke (Lincs.) in 1395 could not reside without danger of death owing to certain conspiracies of some of his parishioners against him (*Cal. Pap. Let.* IV, p. 526).

[2] *Reg. Rede*, I, p. 83.

[3] *Reg. Lacy* (Hereford), p. 65.

[4] *Reg. Grandisson*, III, p. 1234.

[5] *Cal. Pap. Let.* VII, pp. 238, 282.

them until they had been proved genuine and recognised by the Apostolic See. It reads like a definitely criminal attempt on the part of the hospital to rob their vicar in this parish, a depth of infamy which, it may be hoped, was very seldom reached by monastic rectors.

With this story it is fit that this depressing chapter of calamities, of violence, and of unceasing appropriations should come to an end. The thirteenth century had created the law and the system, but the fourteenth could only partially enforce these, and the growing sickness of the Church's Head crippled the members and unnerved them for the work. The fifteenth century opened in confusion but also in hope, for not until the Conciliar Movement failed was hope abandoned and the Reformation made inevitable.

CHAPTER VIII

THE DIVISION OF DUTIES AND BURDENS

In the vicarage records of Bishop Hugh de Welles, it is frequently stated that the vicar should bear the burden of sinodals only, while the rector was required to provide sufficient and becoming hospitality to the archdeacon on his visitation of the church. In these early documents it is seldom that any other burdens are mentioned at all by name. Papal bulls of appropriation always stated that a suitable portion should be assigned to the vicar wherefrom he might be able to pay all episcopal dues, and the bishop was naturally anxious to see that this provision was carried out. So it is hardly a matter for wonder that the comparatively small burden of the sinodal dues should be singled out for special mention. The "procuration" of the archdeacon, that is, his entertainment with food and lodging and stable accommodation, or its equivalent in money, when he formally "visited" the parish, would naturally also be singled out for special mention by the secular authorities who performed the appropriation and "ordained" the vicarage. These two duties comprised practically the whole of the financial burdens of the parish towards its diocesan authorities, although usually a third payment was reserved from appropriated churches for the bishop. This is usually noted as *pro sequestris*, *i.e.* for sequestrations. When a rectory fell vacant, the bishop of the diocese reserved the fruits of it during the vacancy and imposed his "sequestration" on it. Since the rectory of an appropriated church went into mortmain and never fell vacant, a pension was reserved to the bishop as a compensation for his loss. The records of Hugh de Welles do not usually record this payment, being content with a statement of who was to pay sinodals and who the archdeacon's procurations. These records which are mainly abstracts of the documents themselves probably omit provisions concerning the burdens of the churches that were actually made at the time. When, however, a full ordination document fails to mention any more burdens, it is safe to assume that the bishop meant the rectors to bear all burdens not expressly assigned to the vicars. Obviously the burdens of a church were essentially those of a rectory, for rectory and church were synonymous words. If a vicar was required to bear any of the burdens it should have meant that his portion was made especially large for that purpose. Before there was any vicarage, the whole of the burdens were incumbent on the rector, and the appointment of a vicarage was only a substitution of other burdens for the chief duty of a rector, that of residence in his parish. By his very nature a perpetual vicar was compelled to residence, and, although non-resident vicars can be found, especially in the fifteenth century, as a general rule it may be stated that a vicar was a resident priest with cure of souls. He was the burden assumed by a rector instead of the burden of residence. Hence all burdens by right were the rector's burdens, and no vicar could rightly be called upon to bear any burden that had not been expressly imposed on him. The Council of Oxford allowed the bishop wide discretionary powers as to the assignment of the burdens, and consequently the practice varied in the extreme. The difficulty of generalising about vicarages lies in the fact that very few vicarages can be found exactly alike in their emoluments and their burdens.

The scanty information usually given in Hugh de Welles' books is usually to the effect that the vicar had to bear no burdens at all, or sinodals only, or "all due and customary burdens". In the case of the vicarage of Luton[1], however, the burdens were set down as *parochialia*, *synodalia*, *archidiaconalia*, *ordinaria et consueta* (ordinary and customary parochial, sinodal and archidiaconal burdens). What were the ordinary and customary burdens of a church is difficult to say with any precision, but probably they originally included only those dues that flowed out with perfect regularity each year. The repair of the chancel, for instance, beyond very small and inexpensive items, would only occur occasionally and probably would not be included,

[1] *Gest. Abb. St Albani* (R.S.), I, p. 276.

while the washing and mending of vestments would certainly be included.

A much more serious matter was the support of the various chaplains, clerks and cleaners, whose services were regular and clearly part of the "ordinary and customary" burdens. Every church was supposed to have its deacon to act in something like the capacity of a modern "curate" and somebody to correspond to the modern verger. Besides these, the vicar himself required the services of a boy, who perhaps was the same as the *aquebajulus* or youth in the lowest of the minor orders, who performed such menial, although divine, services as carrying holy water to the parishioners. So in 1285 the church of Donington[1] in Holland was to have a vicar, a chaplain, a clerk, and an *aquebajulus*. The vicar of Westbury[2], in the diocese of Bath and Wells, about 1290, was required to find a priest and an *aquebajulus* for the church. In Aldington[3] in the diocese of Canterbury, by an ordination of Archbishop Winchelsey in 1295, the vicar was to serve in the parish church by himself or a suitable priest with an *aquebajulus* and a deacon or secondary priest sufficient in reading and singing. At Leighton Buzzard[4] in 1399, it was considered worthy of remark, on the visitation of the bishop, that there was no *aquebajulus* there. It was also stated that the stipend of the vicar was insufficient and so one may be allowed to suppose that the vicar was compelled to economise in this way. In the corrody vicarages, that is, those in which the vicars had their meals at or from the table of the monastic rectors, these boys, clerks, and chaplains were assigned corrodies for themselves suitable to their station. Where all the ordinary burdens were assigned to the vicar without further comment, it is most likely that he had to sustain all the employees of the church. So important were these burdens that they form the largest exception to the generalisation that Bishop Hugh was only interested in sinodals and procurations.

The following columns illustrate their incidence on the vicars in cases where it is expressly defined:

[1] *Buckland Chart.* p. 118.
[2] *Bruton Chart.* p. 33.
[3] *Reg. Winchelsey*, p. 118.
[4] Sister Elspeth of the Community of All Saints, in *Vic. County Hist.* (*Beds.*), I, p. 329.

Name	Reference	Dependants of vicar	Value of vicarage
Alford	*Lib. Ant.* p. 66	1 chaplain	—
Aston N.	*Lib. Ant.* p. 3	1 chaplain	5 marks
Burgh	*Reg. H. de Welles,* III, p. 84	1 chaplain	9 ,,
Burreth	*Lib. Ant.* p. 63	1 clerk	3½ ,,
Duston	*Lib. Ant.* p. 39	1 chaplain	—
Grimsby, Gt	*Lib. Ant.* p. 43	1 chaplain, 1 deacon*	10 ,,
Kirkeby cum Osgodby	*Lib. Ant.* p. 42	1 chaplain	—
Pirton (Oxon).	*Lib. Ant.* p. 10	1 chaplain	—
Rasen, Middle	*Lib. Ant.* p. 64	1 clerk	60*s.*
Stainton, Market	*Lib. Ant.* p. 63	1 clerk	4 marks
Wroxton	*Lib. Ant.* p. 7	1 chaplain, 1 clerk	10 ,,
Winwick	*Reg. Grosseteste,* p. 510	1 clerk 1236	6 ,,
Yarnton	*Reg. Grosseteste,* p. 445	1 clerk 1235	5 ,,

* Special endowment made by parishioners.

The following are from ordinations of the time of Bishop Gravesend, mainly about 1277, although that of St Peter's in the East, Oxford, is dated 1261. As very few of the values are given, I have considered it necessary to add another column giving the valuation of the vicarages in 1291. In the case of St Margaret's, Leicester, it is stated that the vicar shall not be bound to give more of the offerings to the deacon and clerk mentioned than the oblations on the double feasts, on Sundays, and for burial when oblations are made.

Name	*Reg. Gravesend*	Dependants of vicar	Value of vicarage	
				1291
Bonby	p. 54	1 clerk		£5. 6*s.* 8*d.*
Kelstern	p. 80	Other necessarii and ministri*		—
Lafford	p. 72	1 priest, 1 deacon, other ministri	20 marks;	£8
Langford	p. 232	2 priest chaplains, 1 clerk		£5
Leicester, St Margaret	p. 159	2 priests, 1 deacon, 1 clerk	6 marks plus altarage;	£9. 6*s.* 8*d.*
Liddington	p. 130	1 priest or deacon, 1 clerk, 1 priest		—
Nassington	p. 131	Chaplains and clerk and necessarii		—
Oxford St Peter in E.	p. 214	3 chaplains and suitable ministri	12 marks;	£5
Pinchbeck	p. 63	Suitable ministri		—
Rothersthorpe	p. 131	1 clerk		—
Rothley	p. 163	1 deacon, 1 clerk. Suitable clerks and chaplains in chapel		£13. 6*s.* 8*d.*
Sutton with Bucks.	p. 254	1 clerk, 1 deacon	15 marks plus altarage;	
Wootton	p. 233	1 priest and suitable ministri		—

* One three days a week.

The phrases usually employed are "he shall have with him a companion chaplain" (*capellanum socium*) or "he shall cause the churches to be served by himself and a suitable chaplain or clerk" or "he shall find a chaplain or clerk at his own expenses". Where, however, as at Bradwell, it is simply stated at the end of the vicarage ordination "There are necessary (three) clerks", the evidence cannot be taken as sufficient to show whether the vicar or the monastery had to bear the burden.

These columns illustrate how a vicar whose benefice was only of the normal low value, was yet expected to provide for his clerk who, although possibly only a part-time worker, must have been a heavy burden to a poor vicar living on the margin of poverty. The two ordinations of Bishop Grosseteste here quoted, in view of that bishop's rigid scruples on the matter, seem to add strong evidence in favour of the supposition that it was quite normal for a vicar to have to support one other person besides himself on his meagre 5 or 6 marks. The prebendal churches being fat and large required an abnormal amount of service, and consequently the large-sounding vicarages ordained by Gravesend are no evidence of his superior virtue. Here are concrete examples, in fact, of the generalisation which, as I believe, almost amounted to a rule, that where the vicarage was large the burdens were correspondingly large. If only there were more substantial evidence for the large parishes of the diocese of York, apart from several examples where the chapels were put under distinct vicars, the case might be easily proved. Instead we have to be content with such scanty notices as at Weighton[1] in 1253, where the vicar was required to have the church and chapels served at his own expense, and at Giggleswick[2] in 1259 where he was required to provide suitable *ministri*. In 1323 when Seamer was appropriated to Whitby Abbey[3], the vicar was required to provide chaplains wherever wont, and a deacon in Seamer Church, and some 50 years later this vicarage was taxed at 10 marks and the rectory at 40.

At Buckland Brewer[4] in Devonshire the vicar, as an ordination deed of 1269 states, was to have with him one chaplain on an

[1] *Reg. Gray*, p. 118.
[2] *Finchale Chart.* (Surtees Soc.), p. 66.
[3] *Whitby Chart.* (Surtees Soc.), pp. 485–93, 252.
[4] *Reg. Bronescombe*, p. 39.

income that was assessed in 1291 at £1. This, of course, merely illustrates the absurdity of expecting a true value from the *Taxatio* that had set out to be a *verus valor*. The vicar of Hartland[1] had to maintain one clerk on an income assessed in 1261 at £5, although it was ignored in 1291, apparently as being too small to tax. Harpford[2] vicarage, worth 9 marks in 1269, had to support a chaplain for its chapel at Fen Ottery, but this vicarage also was ignored in 1291. On the other hand, at Tawton[3], the dean and chapter of Exeter had to bear the cost of maintaining two chaplains, and two clerks in the two chapels, an enormous burden that could not possibly be assigned to a vicar without the creation of a vicarage of size unprecedented in this diocese. The vicarage itself was worth 10 marks. In the same year, 1269, a vicar who was instituted at Colyton[4] was required to sustain all due and customary burdens and a suitable chaplain at "Suthe" (*i.e.* Shute). That other *ministri* were included in the "due and customary burdens" is revealed in a woeful tale of 1330, when Bishop Grandisson[5] visited the church. The poor vicar was leprous and yet ministered publicly, a pathetic example of a man clinging to his work against all rules and to the imminent danger of the public. They were wont to have there from the vicarage revenues a vicar and a chaplain, and from the alms of the parishioners a deacon and two clerks, and the vicar was wont to find them. At that time they had only the leprous vicar, a chaplain, and a clerk, and the vicar refused to find any more. He was legally bound to all the burdens, to find all the books and to repair the chancel of Shute chapel. In 1291 this vicarage[6] had been assessed at £5, a considerable sum for this diocese, but one which is quite explained when we read of these heavy burdens imposed on the vicar. If this valuation represented a true value of as much as £10, the vicar is yet entitled to all our sympathies for his behaviour. The vicarage of St Probus[7] was assessed in 1291 at £1. 6*s*. 8*d*., and yet a deed only eight years before[8] had expressly stated that the vicar ought to provide two chaplains at his own cost. Consequently it is without surprise

[1] *Reg. Bronescombe* p. 101.
[2] *Ibid.* p. 102.
[3] *Ibid.* p. 28.
[4] *Ibid.* p. 126.
[5] *Reg. Grandisson*, I, p. 572.
[6] *Taxatio*, p. 156 *a*.
[7] *Ibid.* p. 147 *b*.
[8] *Reg. Quivil*, p. 330.

that we find Bishop Stapeldon[1] in 1312 commenting that the canons of the collegiate church of Glasney who lived there took such a large portion of the revenue, that an altogether insufficient income was left to the vicar of the parish. Therefore, he made a fresh ordination of the vicarage. The taxation of St Wendron's[2] vicarage in 1347 expressly included the stipends of the chaplains, as one of the ordinary burdens to be borne entirely by the vicar, also the repairs of the chancel, but not the rebuilding of the chancel when it should be necessary. At St Kew[3] the vicar in 1355 denied the assertion of the monks of Plympton Priory that he ought to find and sustain a chaplain in the church. The case was brought before Bishop Grandisson, who arranged a compromise by which the vicar had to provide the chaplain, but was granted certain great tithes to help him do so. This amounted to an augmentation of the vicarage, for by the 1283 ordination[4] the vicar had been required to bear all customary burdens. Hence the judgement was bound to go against the vicar and the grant of the great tithes is only proof of the good will of the bishop towards the parish clergy.

In 1280 Archbishop Peckham[5] had to rebuke the dean and chapter of Lichfield for their greed over the church of Bakewell that had been appropriated to them. The deacon and subdeacon of the church were found begging their bread, and the archbishop ordered that they should henceforth eat at the vicar's table. For this purpose the value of the vicarage was increased by 10 marks. The deacon was also to receive a mark, and the subdeacon 10*s*. for providing themselves with clothes, each year. As for seven parochial chapels mentioned, the dean and chapter had thrown all the burden of maintaining ministers, providing books and ornaments, and repairing the fabric, on the parishioners of the chapels. In defence it was urged that it was only as a great favour that the dean and chapter allowed them to have the chapels. Consequently it was decided that the dean and chapter were to provide suitable chaplains and pay each of them 2½ marks, the parishioners supplying the remainder of the stipends. The dean and chapter were to find books and

[1] *Reg. Stapledon*, p. 343.
[2] *Reg. Grandisson*, II, p. 1036.
[3] *Ibid.* II, p. 1141.
[4] *Reg. Quivil*, pp. 354, 372.
[5] J. C. Cox, *Notes on the Churches of Derbyshire*, II, p. 7.

ornaments, while the parishioners had to repair the naves and chancels and to find a chalice and missal for each of the chapels. These proceedings strengthen the impression that this diocese was one of the most remiss in these matters, for when a cathedral chapter was so remiss the other appropriators were probably not ideal.

In the diocese of Bath and Wells, in 1268, the vicar of "Sowy"[1] (*i.e.* Middlezoy), a church appropriated to Glastonbury Abbey, had to find three suitable resident chaplains and suitable clerks, and bear all ordinary burdens and his proportion of extraordinary. The rebuilding of the chancel, when it should be necessary, and the archdeacon's procurations were excepted, and the abbey had to be responsible for all of this. In 1291 the portions of the church received by the abbey were assessed at £35. 7*s*. while the vicarage was only assessed at £8. 13*s*. 4*d*. In any case the burdens that the vicar had to bear were quite out of all proportion to those borne by the rectors. At St Mary Magdalene's, Taunton[3], however, in 1308, the burden of sustaining three secular chaplains was transferred from the vicar to the rectory, and in 1415 the priory[4] is found to have been sentenced to support the secular priests celebrating in seven chapels of the church, and the Pope then mitigates this by allowing them to serve the chapels by canons. In the prebendal church of Yatton[5] in Somerset the vicar complained that his vicarage of 10 marks (afterwards assessed at 12 marks) was not sufficient to maintain himself and two chaplains as well. The rectory was assessed by the inquest at 100 marks, or more than eight times as much as the vicarage. This proportion cannot be regarded as anything but disgraceful, and the bishop assigned more tithes to the vicar in augmentation.

The diocese of Hereford yields evidence of a similar nature, although mainly of a later date. The church of Lindridge was appropriated in 1306[6] to Worcester Priory by Bishop Swinfield, at the king's request, very much against his will. In vain he protested against the dangers of appropriations, especially in his diocese, where the greater part of the parish churches were

[1] Dugdale-Caley, *Monasticon*, I, p. 30.
[2] *Taxatio*, p. 198 *a*.
[3] *Reg. Drokensford*, p. 69.
[4] *Cal. Pap. Let.* VI, p. 486.
[5] *Reg. Drokensford*, p. 270.
[6] *Reg. Swinfield*, pp. 421, 432, 433, 437, 455.

appropriated, as it was said, at the importune instance of various people. This was not an exaggeration, for in the *Valor Ecclesiasticus* of Henry VIII, there were 84 vicarages as against a total of 152 churches in the diocese. When the king insisted, the bishop quoted the constitutions of Cardinal Ottobon against him, but still in vain. The chapter, whose assent was asked by the king, procrastinated by declaring that they could not act, since their dean was at Rome. Reluctantly the bishop, being assured of his own compensation by the king, gave in to these royal importunities and appropriated the church, ordaining a vicarage of about 20 marks in value. The vicar was required to provide suitable priests for the two chapels, but the expense was reduced by an obligation laid on the rectors to allow these priests free house accommodation. The vicar was also bound to provide lights in the chancels of the church and chapels, to pay sinodals and procurations and any extraordinary burden not expressly mentioned. The rectors were required to keep up the chancels and provide the necessary books. Since this was an appropriation of which the bishop thoroughly disapproved, the vicarage ordination may be assumed to be a fair one to the vicar, but it nevertheless is not impressive in its generosity. Twenty marks may have been sufficient to support a vicar and two subordinate priests, yet it cannot possibly have been opulence. The vicar of Avenbury in 1321 was bound to provide a clerk for a chapel, and the vicar of Dewchurch[1] in 1367 a clerk or deacon for helping in the mother church. In 1422 John Carbonell, vicar of Bromfield[2], refused to pay three chaplains, and the subsequent lawsuit between him and the priory there, which was heard by the court of Arches in 1424, was decided by a verdict that the vicar ought to provide chaplains for all the four chapels dependent on his church. The prior of Bromfield, immediately after this sentence had been given and the bishop had given orders for its execution, publicly protested by a document entered by Bishop Spofford's registrar in the bishop's register, that he had repaired the chancel of Ashford Chapel only as an act of grace. This may have been a condition of the sentence, or other pressure may have been brought to bear on the prior, but the bishop, by allowing the

[1] *Reg. L. de Charltone*, p. 42. [2] *Reg. Spofford*, pp. 23, 49, 50.

entry of the document into his register, tacitly acknowledged that this burden should also legally be borne either by the vicar or the parishioners and that the priory was not liable. The vicar of Leominster[1], by a deed of 1433, was to have a portion of £20 and keep two chaplains at his own expense. The parishioners of Wigmore[2] in 1353 proved before Thomas Bellamy, the bishop's commissary general, that their vicar was bound to support a chaplain to celebrate at Leinthall chapel every Sunday, Wednesday and Friday and on all the chief festivals, while those of Stokesay[3] in 1317 proved a similar liability of the vicar there for the chapel of Aldon. It is probable that this sort of part-time work was more general than the fewness of express statements to that effect would suggest, and this may be taken as an explanation of duties that seem not only unfair but sometimes almost unbearable with the income of an average vicar. Yet it does not explain away the obvious fact that vicars were often exceedingly heavily burdened, especially with respect to the wage-bill of their dependents.

Apart from these regular chaplains, a vicar sometimes had to employ an emergency helper, or a coadjutor for special reasons, as, for example, when Silvester, a foreigner, was instituted to the vicarage of Whitchurch[4] in Oxfordshire, by Hugh de Welles. Provision was made that he should have with him all the days of his life, a companion chaplain, who should be able to minister to the parishioners in a language that they knew. Similarly, senile or decrepit vicars were given coadjutors to administer their affairs, and these had to be paid from the income of the benefice.

After the upkeep of chaplains and clerks, the next heaviest and most disputed burden was that of maintaining the chancel in good repair. Archbishop Walter Gray[5] in 1250 had decreed that the rector or vicar ought to repair the chancel in walls and roof and glazed windows, and desks, stools, and benches, while the parishioners had to repair the nave. Archbishop Winchelsey followed Gray's example for his own province. At Reculver, in the diocese of Canterbury, in 1296 there was a money-box kept

[1] *Reg. Spofford*, p. 160.
[2] *Reg. Trillek*. p. 194.
[3] Eyton's *Shropshire*, v, p. 28.
[4] *Reg. H. de Welles*, I, p. 33.
[5] *Cockersand Chart.* I, p. 53.

in the church for the offerings of the parishioners to the fabric of the church, and this had to be opened by two parishioners chosen by the whole parish (*electos per totam parochiam*) in the sight of the vicar. Probably this was how the fabric of the nave was usually supported. Certainly cases in which the parishioners had to repair the chancel of the parish church are very rare, although in 1331, when the church of St Perran in Zabulo[1] in Cornwall was visited, it was stated that the parishioners were bound to the sustentation of the chancel and the finding of matutinal books, for which purpose they received the tithe of the sanctuary land, glebe, or *instaurum*. Now, it was said, through their carelessness the sanctuary had fallen into a bad condition, and they said that they were willing to part with their tithes from it if the dean and chapter, who were the rectors, and the vicar, would bear these burdens. If not, they asked for leave to have a chest in the church in which they could collect alms for the purpose. It was a most unusual state of affairs, and the nearest analogies of common occurrence that offer themselves are only those cases in which the parishioners, being by an act of grace allowed to have an extra chapel, undertook to repair its chancel. Yet these were totally different matters really, and the reason of the Perran in Zabulo arrangements is undoubtedly that a dissatisfied and energetic generation of parishioners had agreed to take over the burdens with the endowment of the sanctuary tithes to support them, from a chapter that was tired of complaint, and of trying to manage parochial affairs at a distance, or a vicar who was anxious to shift the responsibility on their shoulders. Yet this instance was not quite unique, for in the visitation record of St Breward, it was expressly stated that in the time of Robert, the last vicar, such an arrangement was made. As in the case of Perran in Zabulo, the parishioners received the sanctuary tithes, and

[1] *Reg. Grandisson*, II, p. 607.

In 1496 it is stated at the visitation of Bisserheim Chapel Bez-U. Frankenthal, that the monastic rectors received tithes from the vicar from the glebe. This they arranged in "many places where they themselves confer churches, that they may receive tithes from the priests". It certainly does seem hard that the parish priests, already the poorer by about two-thirds of the tithes, should have to pay tithes themselves to the spoilers. At Guntersblum the glebe was also burdened with feudal dues (*praecaria*). See *Zeitschrift... Oberrheins*, XXVII, pp. 309, 251.

undertook the burdens of sustaining and, if necessary, rebuilding the chancel, and of finding matutinal books and similar things. At Alternon, in the same visitation, the window at the head of the chancel was found to be broken and there were defects in the walls and roof. Enquiry being made into the liability for these repairs, it was discovered that there was the same arrangements there as at Perran in Zabulo and St Breward. It is true that the parishioners of Montricher[1] and Cheseaux in the diocese of Lausanne in 1416 were also bound to repair the chancel of their churches, but such arrangements are very unusual in fourteenth-century England. In this Lausanne visitation one is surprised by the amount of the burdens imposed on the parishioners, the ornaments especially being assigned to them for upkeep to an extent quite unusual in England.

The parishioners of Crich[2], in the diocese of Coventry, and Lichfield, before Archbishop Peckham in 1280, asked that the burden of repairing the nave might be placed on the abbey there because it possessed so much property in the parish, but Peckham decided that the abbey ought only to do this in proportion to its possessions in the parish. In the 1342 Totnes visitation records, where the nave needs repairing it is always the parishioners who are warned to do it, although at Ringmore it is acknowledged that they are too poor to do it (No. 29). I have not encountered any English instance of an appropriating corporation taking on itself the duties of repairing the nave, although this was common in Germany. It is not infrequent, however, to find the parishioners bound to the duty of rebuilding a chapel chancel, as at Measham, belonging to Repton parish in the diocese of Coventry and Lichfield. There the priory was required to find the priest and keep the chancel in repair.

In the earlier Continental documents the vicar was usually required to pay the sinodal and procuration dues, as has been seen in the Troyes' examples of the churches of Montiéramey about 1143. At Puellemontier, about 1185, however, the rectors had to pay these dues, so even this generalisation must not be exalted into an absolute rule, general as it was. The chartularies printed by the Belgian Historical Commission, at a rather later

[1] *Société de la Suisse Romande, Visitation de Lausanne* (1416–17), pp. 24, 113.

[2] Cox, *Notes on the Churches of Derbyshire*, IV, p. 47.

date, show much more detailed arrangements about the burdens of the churches. In 1193 it was decided by Jean[1], archbishop of Trèves, that Orval Abbey should repair the church of Jamoigne, and pay the dues and provide the necessary things for divine worship, as they did in their other churches in the deanery of St Yved-de-Braine. The abbey of St Martin of Tournai, however, succeeded, in 1235, in obtaining from the parishioners of the church of Gaurain[2] a promise that they would be responsible for repairing the chancel. It was most elementary duty, one would have imagined, by all the rules of equity, that he who received the tithes of a parish, should, at least, maintain convenient chancels where the sacraments might be administered. Yet so firmly inrooted in the minds of the monks was the notion of absolute personal property without corresponding duties that they thought it a favour to allow the parishioners to set up fresh churches or chapels near their homes. The tithes were theirs, they did not want the chapels for their convenience, so why should they keep up the chancels? Doubtless, it was some such reason as this that made the parishioners of Gaurain responsible for the upkeep of their chancel. The abbot of St Magloire in 1234 allowed a chapel of ease to the church of St Bartholomew of Paris[3], to be set up on his lands, but the parishioners and priests had to bear all the expense. It is wonderful how an implicit faith in the divine right of property, can blind its believers so that they cannot see even the most elementary duties involved in their acceptance of the property. It is a common fault, an easy one to denounce but apparently a difficult one to see in oneself. The strictly legal right was on their side, for had not the Official of the bishop of Tournai already in 1217 absolved the abbey there from the upkeep of the chancel of Esplecin, for which they had been sued by the knights Alard and Nicholas and the parishioners?

A quarrel that arose at Simplevelt illustrates how some monasteries fought to evade the duties of the parish churches they held. The abbey of le Val Benoît[4] in 1262 obtained from the dean of the Council (*i.e.* Chapter) of the cathedral church of

[1] *Cart. Orval.* p. 109. [2] *Cart. St Martin,* I, p. 441.
[3] MS. Paris, lat. 5413, fol. 44.
[4] *Cartulaire... Val Benoît* (Belg. Royal Comm.), pp. 170, 255.

Maestricht, in the diocese of Liège, a document to the effect that, as the owner of the great tithes of Simplevelt, it was only bound to provide a small bell for the church that could be heard outside the bounds of the churchyard. If the parishioners wished to have a great bell that could be heard through the whole parish, they might provide it at their own cost. "If they wish to have such a convenience, let them pay the cost." Good churchmen to-day will sympathise with these poor parishioners who had not even erratic household clocks to tell them when they should set out for church. The church bell in those days was a prime necessity, not an ornament, or a sentimental appendage: it did much more than tell you that your watch was slow, for it was your watch. Arguing, one may suppose, from this standpoint of necessity, the Council of Maestricht in 1282 reversed the previous decision at the instance of several important parishioners, and declared that the owners of the great tithes must provide a great bell that could be heard throughout the parish. Moreover, they were to find the everyday ornaments of the altar, a missal with music, two windows of the church, and the roofing of the body of the church between the choir and the tower.

Another illustration is afforded by the church of Waha, in 1317, which belonged to St Hubert-en-Ardenne[1]. The Council of Rochefort visiting it found, besides other faults in the church and parish, several faults in the building. It at once ordered that these could be made good according to the custom of the parish under pain of excommunication. The parishioners appeared before the Council and submitted that they were in no way bound to answer for these faults. Enquiry made from the old members of the Council and the discovery of an old inquest formerly made on the matter led to the judgement that the parishioners were in no way bound and that the canons ought to pay for the repairs.

In the thirteenth century references to the chancel burdens are not numerous in the records of any English diocese, and this may possibly be attributed to a logical inclusion of them in the extraordinary burdens that were nearly always borne by the rectors. The silence seems to me to indicate that there was as

[1] *Cart. St Hubert*, II, p. 484.

yet no widespread attempt to impose the chancel burdens on the vicars, and that rectors were content to bear them for themselves. Yet, in the diocese of York, there are examples that show that this was not quite universal. The vicar of Bishopthorpe[1] in 1269 was to repair the chancel unless a new one should be required, when the rectors and the vicar should build it between them proportionately. The vicar of Whenby[2] in January 1283–4 was required not only to repair the chancel, but also to rebuild it when necessary, as part of the ordinary burdens of the church. At Silkstone[3] in 1284, however, the chancel costs were treated as extraordinary burdens and the vicar only had to bear one-third of them. The canons of Mattersey[4] in the church there which was, about 1280, newly appropriated to them, had to bear all the chancel costs. At Wisbech[5], in the diocese of Ely, these burdens were divided between the vicar and the monastic rectors in the same way as the oxtraordinary burdens. These instances are sufficient to show how greatly the practice varied, and that it was regarded as a matter for individual settlements and not for any general rule.

In the case of absentee pluralist rectors, the practice similarly varied. Where the vicar received the whole church paying only a pension to such a rector, he naturally had to bear all the burdens. These cases were most frequent, since the ordaining of vicarages with tithe endowments in the churches of absentees only tended to encourage and perpetuate the evil, and so became less frequent in the latter part of the thirteenth century. In 1283, when the absentee and courtier pluralist, Sir Giles de Audenarde[6], was presented to the rectory of Charing in Canterbury diocese, Peckham allowed him to take the church provided that he gave security for 40 marks for the repair of the chancel, thus ensuring that the burden was neither neglected nor allowed to fall on the vicar.

To return to the diocese of Exeter, where there are splendid facilities for a study of the incidence of the chancel burdens in monastic and capitular churches, the thirteenth-century instances there are very few and therefore inconclusive as to any

[1] *Reg. Giffard* (Surtees Soc.), I, p. 59.
[2] *Reg. Wickwane*, pp. 291–2.
[3] *Ibid.* p. 292.
[4] *Ibid.* p. 70.
[5] *Ely Dioc. Rem.* 1901, pp. 123–4.
[6] *Reg. Peckham* (R.S.), II, p. 630.

definite tendency. For the fourteenth century, however, I have collected from the episcopal registers as edited by Prebendary Hingeston Randolph, 22 cases in which the vicar was to bear the burden and ten in which the rectors appropriate had to bear it. There are probably more, but nevertheless these figures may safely be taken to represent something like the actual proportion of decisions made on the matter in this century. In the churches of the dean and chapter, the practice varied, for at St Merryn[1] and St Eval[2] the vicar had to repair the chancel, at St Gwennap[3] the dean and chapter and vicar together, while we have seen that at Perran in Zabulo the parishioners were responsible for it in 1331. At Mullion[4] the chapter was required by an early fourteenth-century ordination to put things in order that time, and the vicar would after that be liable to repairs. In 1331, when the church was visited[5], it was recorded that Bishop Bytton had well restored the chancel, but that other defects remained uncorrected. The vicarage was too slender "as was the common cry in those parts" and the vicar's courtyard badly enclosed. At St Eval[6] in 1322 a settlement was made by which the vicar was to have the chancel enlarged by six feet and to repair the books and ornaments, for which he should receive £10 from the executors of the late Thomas, Bishop of Exeter, for whose obit the church had been appropriated to the dean and chapter. The vicar of Up Ottery[7] in 1307 said that the defects of ornaments should be repaired, not by him but by the chapter, and in 1320 he also included books and chancel costs in his allegations, but the bishop decided that he ought to bear these burdens. The chapter, however, gave him 4 marks towards the repairs for that occasion, and without prejudice to any future occasion. At Sidbury[8], when the vicar was required to repair all the chancel defects he was also granted timber from the wood of the dean and chapter for the first repairs, to be made within two years. At the 1331 visitation it was said of the church of St Gwennap:

The chancel is badly roofed throughout, the glass windows dirty. The *legenda* is badly bound and not covered. And although in another

1 *Reg. Bronescombe*, p. 253.
2 *Reg. Bytton*, p. 430.
3 *Reg. Grandisson*, II, p. 606.
4 *Reg. Stapledon*, p. 341.
5 *Reg. Grandisson*, II, p. 607.
6 *Reg. Stapledon*, p. 329.
7 *Ibid.* p. 397.
8 *Ibid.* p. 368.

preceding Visitation it was contained that the defects of the Chancel, of Books and Ornaments ought to be repaired at the common expenses of the Dean and Chapter, and of the vicar, the vicar says that he is bound in nowise unless it be only to the episcopal and archidiaconal burdens and to the Chantry of the Chapel of the Holy Trinity, according to the Ordination of his vicarage. There is in that place a barn badly roofed, with one doorway carried away and another weak. The said barn needs repair or it will quickly fall into ruin[1].

In the cases of new appropriations or first ordinations of new vicarages in the fourteenth century generally the vicar was required to bear the chancel burdens, and often all the burdens both ordinary and extraordinary, as at Ilsington[2] in 1343, and Luppitt[3] in 1344. Exceptions are Northam[4] in 1363, where the vicar was only required to bear one-third of the chancel costs, and Rockbeare[5] in 1335, where the nuns of Canonsleigh Abbey were required to bear all the burdens. At St Madron[6] in 1309, the vicar was only required to keep the chancel windows and roof in repair, other chancel burdens being borne by the Hospitallers. Generally also the rectors were required to repair the chancel and the vicarage house and buildings, and see that there was a sufficiency of ornaments and vestments, in order to give the vicar a fair start, after which he was required to do all repairs. Such was the case in 1314, when Canonsleigh Abbey appropriated the church of Dunsford[7]. Any rebuilding usually had to be done by the rectors[8], but at St Erth, it is said:

The vicar is bound to sustain at his own cost the Chancel and the Matutinal books and the rest of the ordinary burdens: unless perhaps the Chancel should happen to fall into ruins without any blame to the vicar. Then the rebuilding shall fall on the Dean and Chapter and the vicar *proportionately*[9].

In 1383 it was found that repairs to the chancel of St Issey[10] were notoriously imminent, and a sequestration was made both of the rectory and the vicarage. However, the rectory was soon freed while the vicarage was kept under restraint, presumably

[1] *Reg. Grandisson*, II, p. 606. [2] *Ibid.* III, p. 1334.
[3] *Ibid.* III, p. 1344. [4] *Ibid.* III, p. 1308.
[5] *Ibid.* III, p. 1247. [6] *Reg. Stapledon*, p. 336. [7] *Ibid.* p. 143.
[8] The same provision is found in the diocese of Worms in 1496, see *Zeitschrift...Oberrheins*, XXVII, pp. 448, 453.
[9] My italics. *Reg. Grandisson*, II, p. 607. [10] *Reg. Brantingham*, p. 506.

after an enquiry had been held into the liability for these repairs. About the same time the vicar of Launcells[1] quarrelled with his rectors about the chancel burdens, and when they came to terms, he agreed to bear these burdens, and was granted two acres of land, for which he was to pay 12*d.* yearly. This was, doubtless, a compromise and the 12*d.* did not represent anything near the true rental value of the ground. The vicar of Bickleigh[2] in 1392 said that he was too poor to repair the chancel of his church and its windows, and so a visitation of the church was held to settle the dispute. Buckland Abbey, the rectors, were able to produce the ordination deed which gave decisive evidence against the vicar, whose plea of poverty does not appear to have led to any augmentation of the vicarage. The vicar of St Goran's in 1403 had petitioned the Pope[3] himself on the matter of the burdens, complaining that, although the provost and chapter of St Thomas the Martyr at Glasney ought to repair the chancel, they had taken the tithes and imposed this duty on the vicar. If this tale proved to be true, the prior of Launceston, as executor of the Papal mandate, was ordered to do justice.

At the beginning of the fifteenth century, there were a number of decisions on this matter by the bishops of Exeter, which show that the repair of the chancel had now become recognised as one of the "ordinary and customary" burdens of the church, to be borne by the vicar. In 1401, the vicar of Heavitree[4] was sentenced to bear the burdens of repairing and even of rebuilding the chancels of his church and of the chapels of St Sidwell and St David, as part of the ordinary burdens of his living. At Oakhampton in 1417, these vague words "ordinary and customary burdens" were interpreted to include the repairs of the chancel and the provision of books. The vicars of Burrington[5], Harberton[6] and St Constantine[7] all lost similar suits before the diocesan courts in the early years of the fifteenth century.

While the evidence from other dioceses indicated that disputes were always liable to arise on this important matter, there is no indication that the rectors everywhere succeeded in thrusting these burdens on the vicars so well as they did in the

[1] *Reg. Brantingham*, p. 460.
[2] *Reg. Grandisson*, III, p. 1441.
[3] *Cal. Pap. Let.* V, p. 535.
[4] *Reg. Stafford*, p. 126.
[5] *Ibid.* pp. 45, 267.
[6] *Reg. Lacy*, p. 557.
[7] *Ibid.* p. 517.

diocese of Exeter. It is true that Gloucestershire in the fourteenth century shows a similar tendency, and perhaps a close study of records in other parts would show the same, but in fairness to the memory of the monks, the general charge must receive a verdict of "not proven". The vicars of Thornbury and Fairford[1] in Gloucestershire had to repair their chancels, but at Tytherington and Longborough the appropriators had to do this; while at Standish with its three dependent chapels the cost was divided. During the rule of Prior William de Cheriton (1377–1401) the convent of Lanthony Secunda rebuilt the chancels of Henlow, Painswick, Haresfield and Awre. Bishop Brian of Worcester gave verdict that the vicar of Winchcombe was liable, and some 30 or 40 years later (about 1389) a vicar there lost a long lawsuit on this matter. This vicar, Thomas Power, was excommunicated by Bishop Wakefield for contumacy, and appeals to the Court of Arches and thence to the Papal Curia failed to reverse the sentence. Power was sentenced at the Curia to pay 135 florins costs. About the same time the vicar of Sherborne also lost a lawsuit against his rectors, and the vicar of Hawkesbury did likewise in 1420 against Sherborne Abbey. The vicarages ordained by Bishop Clifford (1401–7) however were not liable for the chancel burdens.

Some importance[2], but not too much, for the Papal policy was never cramped by a petty consistency, may be attached to the judgement at the Papal Curia in 1399 on the burdens of the church of Holy Trinity at Cambridge. This asigned the burdens of the chancel, choir, choir windows and even sinodals to West Dereham Abbey, the rectors. There had been no previous decision made on the matter, and so a lawsuit had arisen and an appeal to Rome ensued. This good work, however, was undone two years later by a Papal licence to the abbey to appropriate the vicarage itself, which was valued at 30 marks.

The fourteenth- and fifteenth-century registers of Hereford, Ely and Winchester, or rather, such of them as are printed, indicate no decided success of a policy of shirking burdens on the part of the rectors, and the great majority of recorded cases impose the chancel burdens on the rectors. Yet they were heavy

[1] Miss Rose Graham in *Vic. County Hist.* (*Gloucs.*), II, p. 21.
[2] *Cal. Pap. Let.* V, pp. 197, 415.

burdens and were frequently neglected, causing grief to the author of *Piers Plowman*, who complained of the greed of monks, in the sermon preached by Reason.

> Little had lordes to dow to geve landes from her heyres
> To religious that have no ruthe if it raine on her autres;
> In many places ther the persons be hemself at ease,
> Of ye pore have they no pitye and that is ther charite.

"If it raine on her autres" does not of course mean that this was general, though there were cases even of that.

In the 1342 visitation of the archdeaconry of Totnes[1] we find two such cases of rain on the altars. At Hennock (No. 8) in rainy weather, water fell through the middle of the chief window on the great altar and in the chalice while mass was being celebrated. The abbey of Torre was responsible. At Tavistock (No. 52) the vicar and his helpers were not able in rainy weather to celebrate the canonical hours in the chancel, because it was not properly roofed. The duty of roofing and doing other repairs to the value of 100*s*. was incumbent on the abbey of Tavistock. In the 1496 visitation of the diocese of Worms[2], there are three more cases of "religious that hath no ruthe if it raine on her autres" besides others where the rain falls in the church. The monks and other appropriators quite frequently neglected their duty to repair the chancel or tried to impose it on someone else. In 1280 Archbishop Peckham[3] found the chancel of Horton actually fallen down. In 1304, at Hayling Island[4], the prior and vicar joined together to try to thrust the burden on the parishioners, but an episcopal ordinance frustrated that plan, and forced them to bear it together for this occasion, the prior two-thirds and the vicar one, without prejudice to the results of a further enquiry which was to be made. In 1368 it was stated that William Inge[5], the late archdeacon of Surrey, and the prebendary of Farnham, had agreed to rebuild the three chancels in that parish, and to roof them with lead at his own expense. He had found stone to the value of £100 of the money of the day, and then died leaving 100 marks by will to finish

[1] *English Historical Review*, Jan. 1911, pp. 108 *seq*.
[2] Cp. Coulton, *Five Centuries of Religion*, II, p. 85.
[3] *Reg. Peckham* (R.S.), I, p. 129: *cancellum predictae ecclesiae funditus est prostratum*.
[4] *Reg. Pontissara*, p. 166.
[5] *Reg. Wykeham*, II, p. 67.

the work. The new rector, Archdeacon Edyndone, had converted the stone to his own use, and the 100 marks were detained by Inge's executors. The vicar was commissioned to cite the archdeacon and the executors of the late archdeacon on these grave charges thus laid against them by three of the parishioners. This shows that the monasteries were not the only rectors who succumbed to the temptation of unfair play over the church repairs. In the 1342 Totnes visitation 12 chancels in appropriated and 12 in unappropriated churches were condemned. In the appropriated churches, the monastery said to be responsible save in one case (No. 60), where it was said that either the priory or the vicar was responsible. In one case it was stated that the monastic rectors were building a new chancel. This was at Cornworthy (No. 26), where the priory of nuns was resident, a fact that slightly takes away from the altruism of even this good work. On the other hand, five secular rectors were stated to have rebuilt or to be rebuilding their chancels. In particular, Sir Ralph de Pridieux, rector of Bigbury (No. 30), came in for praise, for "he did many good things there in his time, in that he built a new and truly competent chancel, and provided the said church with good mattins books and constructed several useful and necessary buildings there in the court of the rectory and the close, and repaired the old buildings well: and he received nothing for dilapidations".

Certainly no monastic rector received or deserved praise like this. Seven of the 11 worst chancels were monastic, and yet, as Dr Coulton estimates[1], if these monasteries had but made a point of spending one year's income of their appropriated rectories in each generation not only the chancels but all other belongings of these parish churches could have been kept in good repair. The dean and chapter of Exeter were among the corporate appropriators who offended, for at Widdicombe (No. 4), the chancel was insufficient, dark and badly roofed, and about 20 marks were required to repair or rebuild it. In 1426 the great priory of Lewes is found suffering three churches and a chapel that it had only appropriated in 1391 to fall into ruins. In the fourteenth or fifteenth century, the parishioners of Willesden[2]

[1] *Five Centuries of Religion*, II, p. 84.
[2] Hist. MSS. Comm. Report 9, Pt I, App. p. 40.

complained to their rectors, the dean and chapter of St Paul's, that the chancel of their church was so ruinous that a boy might easily have overthrown the walls. Robbers had entered and carried off the ornaments, Mass could not be celebrated at the High Altar, and owls and crows were flying into the church day and night and polluting it. Things had come to a pretty pass when the dean and chapter of St Paul's were found among those who had "no ruthe if it raine on her autres". That being so we need not wonder to find in far-away wild Wales the chancel of Llanrydyan[1] in the diocese of St David's ruinous and notoriously in want of repairs. The bishop in 1400 ordered a sequestration of the rectory fruits, for the Master of the Hospitallers of Slebech, the appropriators, had been admonished after the last episcopal visitation to perform the repairs, but had neglected to do so. In this year the archbishop of Canterbury complained of the notorious defects of appropriated churches and prebends in the diocese and issued a commission of enquiry on the matter, and in 1402 the vicarage of St Cleer's was sequestrated until the defects of the chancel, of books and ornaments, and of the vicarage manse should be repaired and the glebe completed. Here apparently it was the vicar who was bound to perform these burdens, and who had been remiss. In 1447 Thomas, bishop of Bath and Wells[2], petitioned the Pope to revoke and restore to the episcopal mensae (plural because of the two dioceses) all alienations made by his predecessors. By the negligence of these said predecessors, a number of churches, chapels, houses, manors and other buildings of the said mensae were in a state of desolation, ruin and decay. It was ordered that all those by whose negligence the said churches, etc., had fallen into ruin, or who were bound to repair them, or if they were dead, their executors should make due satisfaction under pain of ecclesiastical censure. It is a disgraceful tale to tell of bishops, who should have been the guardians of the churches on this matter. So instances may be multiplied and evidence accumulated, proving that appropriators and other non-resident rectors, of whatever rank or status, were often slack in performing these duties and that their churches frequently suffered

[1] *Reg. St David's* (Society of the Cymmrodorion Rec. Ser.), I, pp. 167, 175, 269.
[2] *Cal. Pap. Let.* x, p. 311.

through lack of the personal ever-present responsibility of a resident rector.

The vicarage house, as an almost universal rule with few, if any, exceptions, had to be provided by the monastery, and kept in good repair by the vicar himself. In 1268 the house of the vicar of St Ethelred at Histon[1], in the diocese of Ely, was to be constructed by Eynsham Abbey of beams of oak, there being a hall of at least 26 feet in length, and of breadth 20 feet within one side a *dispensa* and on the other a competent chamber with the necessaries of a chamber. There was to be a kitchen (*coquina*) in a competent place with bakehouse (*pistrinum*) and brewhouse (*bracinum*). All these were to be under the same roof. The house of the abbey, situated in the parish, was sequestrated until the vicarage should be finished, presumably for the vicar's use in the meantime. The monasteries were not usually allowed to evade this duty by providing housing accommodation for the vicar within the monastery, and Bishop Brantingham of Exeter[2], in 1373, as a result of a visitation of the abbey of Tavistock, where he found this abuse prevailing, ordered a competent house to be provided for the perpetual vicar outside the sept of the monastery, so that the parishioners could have free access to him night and day, to procure the sacraments. At Chepstow, however, the bishop of Llandaff[3] had ordered a room to be assigned within the priory for the vicar, who was to be treated as one of the monks. These older arrangements, however, were made unworkable in 1394 by the removal of the monks from Chepstow and the end of the priory there. Presumably the vicar then received the old priory house, or part of it, as his own under the new arrangements made by order of the Pope at the petition of John Davy, vicar. When Richard of Thornely, chaplain of Wasseford, was presented in 1329 by Hatfield Priory to the vicarage of the church of Silverley[4], he bound himself in return for certain benefits to build a house there with a hall, chamber and kitchen. This was, however, a purely temporary expedient, involving no permanent duty, being undertaken "of his own free will".

[1] *Eynsham Cart.* I, p. 260.
[2] *Reg. Brantingham*, p. 313.
[3] *Cal. Pap. Let.* v, p. 258.
[4] *Essex Arch. Soc. Transactions*, II, Pt ii (New Series), p. 141.

In 1297 the vicar of the church of St Paul's Cathedral at Sandon[1] had a manse containing one acre with houses, garden and curtilage, and for this he paid a penny yearly to the bailiff or "farmer" of the lands belonging to the chapter there. In the 1458 visitation, the vicarage of All Saints', Walton[2], another church of St Paul's, was recorded as consisting of a hall with two chambers and, above them, solars (lofts) on the east side of the same hall. At the end of the hall were a buttery and a larder-house. The house was in good repair so far as the walls and thatched roof were concerned but the porch was badly roofed. The kitchen was in good repair, but the walls and roof of the stable needed reparation. In 1336 the vicar of West Harptree (dioc. Bath and Wells)[3] was assigned part of the rectory houses, but this was found inconvenient, and in 1344 it was ordained that he should have a manse separate from the rectory houses and nearer the church. He was assigned the whole manse of the tenant of the church opposite the gates of the Rectory with its courtyard and close adjacent. It had a hall and two solars and two cellars, and a kitchen, barn, stable for three horses and a dovecot were to be built. The vicar himself was to maintain the manse.

In 1403 when Church Broughton[4] (dioc. Coventry and Lichfield), was appropriated to Tutbury Priory, it was ordained by Bishop Burghill that a suitable house should be built by the priory consisting of a hall, two chambers, a stable and a garden, contiguous to the church. The vicar was to keep it in repair. Similar arrangements were made in the same year at Dronfield, which was appropriated to Beauchief Abbey. In 1425 the vicarage house of Bulmer[5], in the diocese of London, was to consist of a hall with two chambers annexed, a bakehouse, a kitchen, a larderhouse, and a chamber for the vicar's servants. There was also to be a hayloft and a competent garden.

Dilapidations of vicarage houses, which even now are the subject of fairly frequent complaint, owing to a higher standard of repair, were then the subject of constant remark. The early fourteenth-century visitations mentioned in the Exeter registers

1 *Visitations of St Paul's* (Camden Soc.), p. 49.
2 *Ibid.* p. 91.
3 *Reg. Salop.* pp. 298, 510.
4 J. C. Cox, *Vic. County Hist.* (*Derbyshire*), II, p. 8.
5 Newcourt, *Repertorium*, II, p. 104.

reveal this, as, for example, at St Breward[1] in 1329. At St Sancreed[2] (dioc. Exon.), in 1331, the vicar refused to acknowledge that he was bound to repair a small house (probably a shed or out-house) although he had been ordered to do so before in a previous visitation. Wherever a vicar was remiss in general matters his vicarage house was usually found in disrepair, as at Locking[3] in the diocese of Bath and Wells in 1264, where the vicar refused either to reside or proceed to orders.

In the 1342 Totnes visitation nearly all the vicarage houses needed repairs, and about eight were very bad. At Kingsteignton repairs were required to the value of 10 marks (No. 11); at Broadhempston, the vicar had repaired part, but more repairs were still required to the value of 10 marks (No. 14): in another £20 (No. 23); in another church the vicarage buildings were vile, insufficient and ruinous, and only one barn passed as satisfactory (No. 36); at Ermington repairs worth 20 marks were required (No. 43); at Walkhampton (probably), 5 marks (No. 45); at Lamerton many dilapidations (No. 53); at another place £10 (No. 80); and at other places dilapidations of smaller values. The houses of resident rectors were also bad, but slightly better on the whole than those of the vicars, there being a decidedly bigger percentage that received a clean bill. In one case, that of Buckland Monachorum (No. 48) it is noted that the vicar received 40*s*. and two quarters of oats towards his dilapidations and his building had been competently repaired by him. It was exceedingly rarely that vicars received such help, much as it was needed. The vicar of to-day frequently has to ask his parish to help him with this heavy burden, as every church councillor knows.

In the visitation of the churches of St Paul's Cathedral in 1458 the vicarage houses at Barling[4] and Navestock[5] were found in bad condition. In 1445 it was stated that £10 was not sufficient to pay for the repairs of the vicarage houses at Burham[6] in Rochester diocese, while in 1448 the vicar of Birling[7], in the same diocese, complained among other things that the vicarage buildings were so decayed through negligence of Bermondsey

[1] *Reg. Grandisson*, I, p. 514.
[2] *Ibid.* II, p. 607.
[3] *Reg. Giffard* (B. and W.), p. 2.
[4] *Visitations of St Paul's*, p. 75.
[5] *Ibid.* p. 72.
[6] Thorpe *Reg. Roffense*, p. 199.
[7] *Ibid.* p. 173.

Abbey that they could hardly be repaired with £20. This is a rare instance because in England the upkeep after the first building, nearly always fell on the incumbent.

The glimpse afforded us of the customs of the German diocese of Worms in the 1496 visitation reports[1], shows that there the vicarage house was nearly always to be kept in repair by the appropriators. This was also the case with regard to the choir, and, more remarkable still, to the nave, and very frequently to the ornaments. The churches of this diocese seem, however, to have suffered in their revenues to an extent quite unparalleled in England, owing to the appropriations and pensions of religious corporations and even of laymen. There are a number of instances where it was not known who ought to repair the vicarage house, which seems to indicate that the appropriators were loath to perform the duty when there was any chance of its being shifted on to the vicar. A close reading of the reports leaves little room for doubt that the appropriators bore most of the heavy burdens simply because the vicars were already reduced to as low a level of income as was consistent with any decency, a level considerably below the normal of the vicars of the average English parish. Nearly all the churches were appropriated, and it is very doubtful if even one could be found quite free of all pensions due from the tithes. The smallness of the vicar's portion does not explain, it must be acknowledged, the fact that the corporate rectors usually repaired the nave, a burden which in England was universally incumbent on the parishioners. Yet the parishioners did in this diocese usually have to keep up the baptistery, and the tower and sometimes some of the ornaments as well, besides the wall of the churchyard and occasional smaller duties, in all of which they were quite frequently very remiss. After all, the tower and the baptistery are a large part of the building of any church, and it simply appears never to have been established, as a general rule that the parishioners should support the whole of the nave in these parts. The state of repairs, which was at least at the normal low medieval level in this visitation, by no means indicates any particular goodwill on the part of the appropriators in the supporting of their burdens. They certainly did not volunteer

[1] *Zeitschrift...Oberrheins*, XXVII, pp. 229 *seq.*, 385 *seq.*

to undertake burdens for the sheer joy of relieving others. In these matters as in most others, the foreign visitation records reveal the English Church by comparison as quite exemplary in the thoroughness and legality of its administration.

In the diocese of Exeter there are at least three cases recorded where the duty of becoming rural dean in turn is expressly mentioned as a burden on the vicar, namely, at Bickleigh[1] in 1356, at Northam[2], in 1363, and Loddiswell[3] in 1413. This is also found in a deed relating to the vicarage of Keynsham[4] in the diocese of Bath and Wells in 1405. This is an example of those medieval offices that everyone tried to avoid, but that have now become an honour. It must have been indeed an unpopular office when the efficient rural dean incurred the hatred of his neighbours as a spy on their lesser efficiency, and when the inefficient rural dean was liable to severe reprimands from his superiors, perhaps for faults that were not always his own. Clearly the office was not regarded as a step in advancement, but as a thankless burden that did nobody any good.

Examples of various burdens may here be noticed. The vicar of Tunstall had to repair the desks of the chancel and the service books[5], pay procurations and sinodals, and collect and pay Peter's pence. The vicar of Lodeswell had to repair the chancel and windows, and the ceiling over the high altar, to provide lights for the altars, and office-books and one psalter; to collect and pay the king's tenths, and the dues to episcopal legates and Papal nuncios, to the archbishop, and their officers and commissioners, and to the archdeacon. At Grantchester[6], near Cambridge, in 1380, however, among the extraordinary dues expressly laid on the rectors, Corpus Christi College, were the royal tenths, the procurations of Papal nuncios and royal subsidies. The ordinary burdens in this case were assessed at 2*s*. 4*d*. for sinodals and 12*d*. for archidiaconal procurations,

[1] *Reg. Grandisson*, III, p. 1442.
[2] *Ibid.* III, p. 1247.
[3] *Stafford*, p. 244.
[4] *Reg. Bowet* (B. and W.), p. 46.
[5] The services books and ornaments seldom received a clean bill at visitations. The incumbent in England practically always had the duty of keeping these in repair. The Totnes and Lausanne and Worms visitation all bear eloquent witness to the general remissness in these smaller matters and sometimes even in the very cleanliness of the vestments. See also Coulton, *Five Centuries of Religion*, II, p. 84, for remarks.
[6] *Ely Dioc. Rem.* (1895), p. 139.

besides which bread and lights were to be found by the vicar whose vicarage was taxed at £4. It is unnecessary to do more than indicate by these examples the varied nature of the burdens on the vicars, and to emphasise that they differed so enormously and that no hard and fast rules can be laid down about them.

In the old Gelasian division of the tithes the services of the church and the upkeep of the fabric had each been assigned a share. An equal share had been assigned to the poor of the parish, but these fared far worse than the services or the fabric in the division of the spoils of appropriated churches. The immediate responsibility of a resident rector was a great safeguard, and the duty could be the more easily enforced by the bishop or the archdeacon. The resident rector was frequently a well-to-do man, but the vicar very seldom. While the tendency to exaggerate the benevolence of the resident rector must be firmly resisted, there can be no possible doubt that an absentee rector whether sole or corporate, would be less likely to perform these charitable duties.

A famous courtier pluralist, Bogo de Clare[1], was rebuked by Peckham in these words:

> We complain...that on visiting certain of your churches, or rather, churches held in your name, we found there by the account of many creditable people, that you did not perform the duties of rector, but rather acted as ravisher (*raptor*) because concerning the carnal goods of the poor, you minister nothing, or practically nothing to them.

Mr Giuseppi, in an article in *Archaeologia*, adds his testimony to the same effect from the household accounts of Bogo de Clare. The sums given in alms were almost negligible. There is no reason to suppose that Bogo was more than a few degrees worse than many other courtier pluralists in this respect. They drew the money from their benefices as payment for their services to the king, and probably very seldom thought of the spiritual aspect. This is no excuse, but it is an explanation.

The monasteries were little more conscientious in their provision for the parishioners of their far-away appropriated churches. There appears very seldom to have been any definition of this duty in the agreements made between the monasteries

[1] *Reg. Peckham* (R.S.), I, pp. 371–2.

and their vicars, and, doubtless, the duty frequently fell to the ground between the rectors and the vicar. Ivo of Chartres[1], about 1150 argued that the monks were the poor, and the most deserving of the poor, because they were voluntarily following the poor Christ. Consequently the monasteries always represented the appropriation as the transference from one section of the poor to another of what rightfully belonged to the poor. Every petition, as matter of common form, contained such a plea of poverty, and every deed of appropriation recited the plea. Consequently, if the "poor" in the monastery were to be fed, the poor of the parish had to go hungry. In the earlier centuries in England there is practically no evidence of any kind as to distributions to the poor by the appropriators. The bishops, even the best of them, seem to have made no organised attempt to secure the proper performance of this duty, and early vicarage ordination deeds are silent on the matter. It may be that the monasteries gave generously and perhaps even foolishly to all the destitute who came to their gates, but what of those who lived far away from any religious house? What of the poor man tied to the soil and normally solvent, who fell on bad days? Even if this system was operated with all charity and good faith by the monasteries, did it not encourage vagabondage, and leave the most deserving poor to starve? The vicar might give a little out of his own property, or refrain from taking his tithe from the blind beggar, but the monastery was far away and ignorant of the troubles of the poor parish. In the *Valor Ecclesiasticus* of Henry VIII there are not infrequent endowments attached to various parishes mentioned as having been provided by some benevolent individuals by their wills, and it may be that the very negligence of the monasteries gave rise to this private charity. Godstow Abbey in 1310 declared that it was under no obligation to distribute the customary wheat and rye mixture to the yearly value of £1. 6*s*. 8*d*. in weekly doles to the poor of their appropriated parish of Bloxham[2]. It was, in effect, a declaration that if the abbey should fall on less prosperous days, the stopping of this weekly distribution would be one of the first economies.

[1] Migne, *P.L.* ep. 192, t. 162, col. 200.
[2] *Godstow Chart.* (E.E.T.S.), 1, p. 231.

Professor Claude Jenkins, on the other hand, points out that the evidence of Odo Rigaldi's Register is decidedly favourable, on balance, to the monasteries. He shows that, out of 38 houses for which we have periodical information, 11 at one time gave alms every day, though 2 had later to restrict this; and 22 gave three times a week and most of the rest twice. Some of the last two classes gave also to lepers in addition. (See *Church Quarterly Review*, October 1925, for Professor Jenkins' full discussion of the matter.)

In England, the church, having failed to supply adequate remedy, the laity, as represented by the Commons, tried to step in an interfere. In 1365 they complained to the king[1] that appropriators had caused the impoverishment of the realm, and the cessation of alms and other works of charity. In 1391 they represented to the king[2]:

that whereas the parish churches had been endowed for the glory of God and the succour of the parishioners, nevertheless the patrons of the said benefices, and especially Religious...do mischieviously appropriate the said benefices throughout the kingdom and beat dolorously to the ground the houses and buildings thereof, and carry all away, cruelly destroying and subtracting from the poor and needy those divine services hospitality and other works of charity which were wont to be done in the said benefices.

It was answered[3]:

The King wills, that henceforward in every Licence that is to be made in the Chancery for the Appropriation of any parish Church, it be expressly contained and comprised That the Diocesan, at such Appropriation, shall ordain, according to the value of the Churches, a proper sum of money to be yearly paid and distributed from the fruits and profits of the said churches by those who have the Churches to their own use [*i.e.* the appropriators], and by their successors, to the poor Parishioners of the said Churches, in aid of their livelihood and daily sustenance: and that the Vicar also be well and properly endowed.

Shortly after this followed an Act[4] (15 Rich. II, cap. 6) which provided that:

Because divers damages and hindrances oftentimes have happened, and daily do happen to the parishioners of divers places, by the

[1] *Rot. Parl.* II, p. 284.
[2] *Ibid.* III, p. 293 *b*.
[3] *Ibid.* III, p. 468 *a*.
[4] As translated by Dr G. G. Coulton in *Hist. Teach. Misc.* (Jan. 1926, p. 3).

appropriation of benefices of the same places, it is agreed and assented that in every licence from henceforth to be made in the chancery of the appropriation of any parish-church, it shall be expressly contained and comprised, that the diocesan of the place upon the appropriation of such churches shall ordain, according to the value of such churches, a convenient sum of money to be paid and distributed yearly of the fruits and profits of the same churches by those who will have the said churches in proper use, and by their successors to the poor parishioners of the said churches, in aid of their living and sustenance for ever; and also that the vicar be well and sufficiently endowed.

These words are no stronger than those of the parishioners who succeeded in obtaining from Pope Martin V in 1426 an annulment of the appropriations of West Hoathley, Patcham, Ditchling and Wivelsfield Chapel to Lewes Priory[1]. This great priory, they alleged, had allowed the buildings to fall into ruin, divine worship to be greatly diminished, and the cure of souls very much neglected. The former hospitality shown to the poor by the rectors had been altogether withdrawn. Yet these churches had only been appropriated by Papal[2] authority in 1391. This practical example throws light on the words of the Commons, men who must have had in their minds many examples of these desolating effects. The result was the Act, a very primitive piece of Poor Law, which shows how it was assumed that the Church ought to provide for the poor. It was not until Tudor times that the State took over this duty, when it took over the Church itself. Even then it tried hard to make the Church machinery suffice for its administration. In medieval times the Church owned so much of the national wealth and controlled so much of the national administration that it was only right that it should perform the most elementary religious duties of feeding the hungry and clothing the naked[3]. It is true that many a deed of kindness leaves no record behind it, yet while tribute may well be paid to nameless monks who took the food and raiment of charity to the poor, the very absence of

[1] *Cal. Pap. Let.* VII, pp. 445–6. [2] *Ibid.* IV, p. 396.

[3] *Reg. Grandisson*, p. 730. An early case of reservation of an endowment for the poor on the appropriation of a church is at Broadwoodwidger (co. Devon) in 1333–4, when it was appropriated to Frithelstoke Priory. There 100 poor were to be supplied *in pane, potagio et campanagio* to the value of 1*d.* each on the obits of Richard and Walter who gave the advowson to the Priory for appropriation.

records is proof that there was no adequate organisation of parochial charity, such as was really necessary for a thorough performance of parochial duties. Alms at the monastery gates do not excuse unrelieved poverty in the distant appropriated parish, though they should equal them in value. The petition of the Commons is a sweeping indictment of a complete breakdown of the parish relief, by men who in this as in other matters were entitled to be a grand inquest of the nation.

The effects of the new Act begin to appear at once. In 1399 the bishop of Chichester[1] appropriated the churches of Alfriston and Fletching to Michelham Priory. The king's licence contained provision that the vicarages were to be properly endowed and 15*s*. of each church set apart in money or in fruits for distribution to the poor parishioners on Christmas day. This must have been the time of the year when the poor were poorest, for the medieval winter meant great feats of endurance, there being little to eat besides bread, fish caught in wintry seas, salt meat and such fruits and vegetables as keep during the winter. Even these must have been very dear, especially when stocks ran low at the end of the winter. From the church of Warfield[2] in Berkshire, in the same year, there was set apart 5*s*. a year to be distributed to the poor of the parish by view of the vicar and six parishioners. Next year half a mark was assigned to the poor of Cliffe Pypard in Wiltshire[3].

In 1404, when Bishop Burghill of Coventry and Lichfield[4] appropriated the church of Hathersage to Launde Priory, he stipulated that a portion should be set aside for the poor of the parish. In 1418 Minsterworth in the diocese of Hereford was appropriated to the Augustinian Priory of St Oswald at Gloucester, and half a mark was set aside for distribution at the four quarters of the year to the poor parishioners[5]. This cannot be considered a generous provision considering that the Gelasian division had assigned a quarter of all the tithes to the poor. The appropriations of Cheshunt to the Hospitallers[6] in 1433 and Fordingbridge[7] in 1447 to the college of St Mary and St

[1] *Reg. Rede*, p. 165. [2] *Cal. Pap. Let.* v, p. 246.
[3] *Ibid.* v, p. 327. [4] *Vic. County Hist.* (*Derbyshire*), II, p. 8.
[5] *Reg. Lacy* (Heref.), pp. 51 *seq.* The statute of 15 Richard II is expressly quoted here as the reason for this provision for the poor.
[6] *Rot. Parl.* IV, p. 461 *b*. [7] *Ibid.* v, pp. 132–3.

Nicholas at Cambridge, and Heanor[1] to Dale Abbey in 1473 were made under similar conditions. At Mackworth in 1509 the rectory was assigned to Darley Abbey, saving pensions of 6*s*. 8*d*. to the bishop of Coventry and Lichfield, 1*s*. to the dean and chapter of Lichfield, and 2*s*. to Coventry Priory, but only 3*s*. 4*d*. was assigned to the poor parishioners. In January 1512–13, Denny Abbey was required to pay to its vicar of St Pandonia of Eltisley[2] £8 a year, to the bishop 3*s*. 4*d*. and to the archdeacon 1*s*., while the poor were assigned only 1*s*. on Maundy Thursday. The church of Alberbury (dioc. Hereford), was appropriated to All Souls' College, Oxford, in 1521, and 5*s*. were reserved for the poor parishioners, while the bishop was to receive 53*s*. 4*d*. for his triennial Visitation dues, and the archdeacon 13*s*. 4*d*. for his annual Visitation dues, and the Commissary General 6*s*. 8*d*.[3] In the *Valor* of Henry VIII there is recorded of Glentham[4] a payment of 7*s*. given in alms yearly to the poor parishioners "for the appropriation of the church". The church had actually been appropriated about 1273, by Bishop Gravesend[5] to the dean and chapter of Lincoln. Whether or not this actually was, as it seems to be, a payment reserved in the appropriation of the church, is not clear. Gravesend's register records no such reservation, but it is quite probable that the practice enjoined by the Act of 15 Richard II, cap. 6, had already appeared before then, although very spasmodically and never as a deliberate thought-out policy. There seems little doubt, however, that whereas such sums were seldom set aside before 1391, after that date they became general, and that it was the influence of the king's chancery that procured the change. When the Reformation swept away these endowments with the others it did much harm, but clearly the existence of them must not be counted unto the monasteries for righteousness. The monasteries, chapters, colleges and bishoprics that swallowed up nearly one-third of the parochial revenues of England, had a clear duty to provide for the poor of the appropriated parishes. If they did this they were but unprofitable servants; if they did not they deserved in some large degree the word that Gascoigne,

[1] Cox, *Notes on the Churches of Derbyshire*, IV, p. 234.
[2] *Ely Dioc. Rem.* (1911), p. 136.
[3] *Reg. Bothe*, p. 96.
[4] Valor, IV, p. 9 *b*.
[5] *Reg. Gravesend* (Linc.), p. 93.

a fifteenth-century Chancellor of Oxford University, branded across their works of parochial appropriation, *furtum*—theft.

Robert Aske[1], the leader of the Pilgrimage of Grace, when examined on his trial, said "that he grudged against the Statute of suppressions, and so did all the country, because the Abbeys in the North gave great alms to poor men and laudably served God: in which parts of late days they had small comfort by ghostly teaching". This is an idealised picture, painted by partisan zeal and a love of all that was best in the old order. It was, however, only a half truth, and neither Aske nor anyone else could have proved that the monasteries did their full duty towards their parishioners. If the monasteries gave great alms, they took much greater: if they fed the poor at their gates, the poor in their parishes went hungry. The Reformation destroyed monastic charity and did not hasten to supply the void, and worse days followed than ever before. Yet if the parishes after the Reformation were scourged with scorpions, it must not be forgotten that the monasteries had scourged them with whips.

[1] Gairdner, *Letters and Papers*, XII, i, no. 901, p. 405.

CHAPTER IX

THE REGULARS AND THE CURE OF SOULS

NORMALLY since 1215, as has been seen, the churches appropriated to religious corporations were served by perpetual secular vicars. Yet in the earliest days of appropriation there were exceptions to this procedure so important that in France, at any rate, there was a positive danger to the ordinary secular rule of the Church. If Innocent III had been less firm the canon vicar might have become the rule, and the secular priest the exception. If there had been previously, as authorities tell us, a struggle between Churchmen and laymen for the *dominium* of the parish and its goods, there was now quite definitely one between secular and regular clergy, not merely for possession of tithes, but also for the cure of souls. The Lateran Councils, and especially the fourth, decided definitely for the secular clergy, but even then what could not be accomplished by the ordinary law was frequently brought about by Papal dispensation. With a little special pleading one might represent the Reformation, especially the English Reformation, as a revolution of secular clergy against the threat of "regular" domination. Without going to such an extreme, one is forced to realise that the dual allegiance of a secular vicar was a serious danger to the tradition of secular control of diocesan affairs. If this danger was less than one would expect from the extent of monastic ownership of tithes, it is because the monasteries of the later Middle Ages were quite frankly concerned primarily with appropriations as a financial expedient for their own advantage. Appropriations were indeed made *ad divini cultus augmentum*, but the divine worship that was to be augmented was that inside the monasteries, not that in the parishes. When a monastery appointed one of its own members as a vicar, it was quite frankly because the vicarage had been appropriated to the monastery. The most cursory survey of the appropriation documents leaves no possible doubt that it was the welfare of the monastery that was being considered mainly.

Whether this was justified is another matter; here let it suffice to emphasise it as an indubitable fact.

There was no doubt about the opinion of the secular clergy on regular encroachments from quite early times.

The great Archbishop Hincmar of Rheims[1], in a synod at Rheims in the year 874, declared in most emphatic terms that the religious profession and the cure of souls were incompatible.

Since not only priests of our *parochia* (diocese) by presumption that is illicit, and even pernicious to themselves and to the people committed unto them, are said to neglect their churches, and to obtain a portion in the monastery of Montfaucon, but even canons of the same monastery are said to occupy the churches of rural parishes, it behoves us not only to show what the sacred canons determine on the matter, but also to use the vigour and censure of the same sacred canons against those who contemn them, if they do not correct themselves.

The Blessed Leo says (Epist. 89 ad Nicetam):

that each one not puffed up by ambition, nor drawn away by avarice, nor depraved by the persuasion of men, should persevere where he has been ordained. For if one has not been puffed up by ambition, he will not seek to ascend from a less to a greater church; if he is not drawn away by avarice he will not seek the things that are his own, but those that are of Jesus Christ. Hence he will not desert his own people and fly as if to the safety of a monastery, or if he is a canon ordained in a monastery, he will not leave the monastic service. He will not seek, for the sake of lust of filthy lucre, on account of the proceeds of the tithe, to invade the churches of rural parishes, careless if it should happen that infants die without baptism, or the sick pass away without communion and reconciliation. It is agreed and certain that the monastic cloister and due services, and the things that are necessary to the people in rural parishes, cannot at the same time be sought by him. How, if in the silence of the dead of night, either a newborn infant should fall into danger, or a sick man ask for the fortification of the *viaticum*, should a canon go forth from the cloisters of a monastery, and reaching the village of the sick, avail to help their necessities?

So spake an authoritative voice even in such early times, but the words fell on deaf ears. Instances of the very evil foreseen by Hincmar may be found in the pages of later history. For example, at Dienheim, about 1496, there was a Cistercian monk

[1] Migne, *P.L.* t. 125, col. 795.

vicar, who lived in the court of the abbot of Eberbach[1]: "Once a certain woman was neglected at night in the matter of Church sacraments; the clerk knocked at the gate, but could not be heard by reason of the distances and the dogs barking, wherefore the neighbours beg that you, reverend Father [bishop] may weigh the perils in your mind, and impose the usual [duty of] residence upon the parson". Such misfortunes were naturally not everyday occurrences, but it must not be forgotten how terribly shocking it would be to the conscientious medieval mind that such things should ever occur. It was like throwing away souls to the devil.

Hincmar was referring to a canon regular, and from the earliest time it was an accepted doctrine that canons were fitter people to hold parish churches than monks. In origin the monk was one who renounced the world utterly, swearing to live a cloistered life of chastity, poverty and obedience. He was not necessarily in orders at all. By the spirit of his Rule, and by the express decrees of councils throughout the centuries, he was incapable of holding a cure of souls. If he came to do so, it was only with special permission or privileges, emanating from the ultimate overriding authority, the Pope. It is thought that a regular canon was originally a priest who adopted a Rule. His monasticism, if this is true, might be considered less important than his priesthood. Considering that the Augustinian Abbey devoted itself mainly to the same ends as the Benedictine, this may appear to be a worthless quibble. Yet in practice it enabled the canons much more easily to obtain dispensations to serve the cure of souls than ordinary monks.

It seems that from the first the regular canon had been recognised as a suitable person to have the cure of souls, provided that he was kept to the observance of his Rule. It is indeed said that the Augustinian canons were founded to promote the better service of the parish churches. "If this was so," says Mr Hamilton Thompson[2], "the custom was severely checked in the thirteenth century: and when in the later middle ages, the number of appropriated churches served by Austin canons

[1] Transl. in Coulton, *Five Centuries of Religion*, II, p. 456; *Zeitschrift... Oberrheins*, XXVII, p. 253.

[2] *English Monasteries*, p. 29.

considerably increased, the quire services in their monastic churches suffered to an extent that was never contemplated by their founders." Yet certainly permission was often granted to canons of both orders in the twelfth century, showing that this work was not such an essential object of the orders that it could normally be done except by special privilege but that this privilege was readily granted. Since the origins of the regular canons and their privileges fall so far out of my period, I must hesitate to be drawn into discussing them, and I have here done no more than state the generally accepted theory.

The great thirteenth-century lawyer Hostiensis (Cardinal Henry of Susa), after describing similarities between monks and canons regular, goes on to say:

> They differ in certain particulars, for, whereas it is forbidden that monks should be left alone in villages or towns (*Decret. Greg.* lib. III, tit. XXXV, c. 2) yet on that same place there is no special warning for canons. But we must take the same principle of law as applying to both, since there is the same reason for both: wherefore licence is granted even to monks, but with this difference, that a cure of souls is more easily granted to a canon regular than to a monk, and that canons regular serve a less rigid rule: for they differ with regard to flesh-eating, and dress, and in certain other matters as all men may see and know[1].

It may be that this difference between monk and canon is no more than what Hostiensis says, a difference in severity of the Rules; or the difference in the Rules may itself be due to a radically different origin of the orders, but from the point of view of this book that does not matter. It must suffice to note that even by 1200 the difference was a recognised one of considerable antiquity.

The general custom in the twelfth century was for a house of canons regular to receive Papal permission to set up in some parish church what has been called a priory-with-cure (*prioratus curatus*) in the following form, with minor variations:

> *In parochialibus vero ecclesiis vestris, liceat vobis post decessum presbyterorum qui eas tenent, quatuor vel tres ad minus de vestris canonicis ponere, quorum unus diocesano episcopo presentatur, ut ab eo curam recipiat animarum, ita quidem ut episcopo de spiritualibus, vobis autem de temporalibus respondeat.*

[1] Coulton, *Five Centuries of Religion*, II, p. 440.

In your parish churches, however, you shall be allowed after the decease of the priests who hold them, to place four or three at least of your canons, of whom one shall be presented to the diocesan bishop to receive from him the cure of souls, so that he shall answer to the bishop for spiritual matters and to you for temporal.

These canons, in effect, formed a separate priory, and lived together by rule, and in practice often established an important daughter house. The prior was the vicar. Such permission as above was granted to the abbey of Beaulieu in Aube[1] (Premonstratensian) in 1175, to the canons of St Orso at Aosta[2] in 1184, to Basse Fontaine Abbey[3] (Premonstratensian) in 1188, and to the English Augustinian Priory of St Oswald's Nostell[4] in 1216. Concerning a church of the last-named house, the rolls of Hugh de Welles record that all the goods of the church of Breedon[5] in Leicestershire ought to be spent in sustaining five resident canons and the ministers there, and showing hospitality. The chapels of Staunton and Worthington attached to it were to have resident chaplains. Similarly in 1287 in the priories-with-cure of Shap and Bampton[6] (dioc. Carlisle), we find that in each church there was to be a secular chaplain to hear confessions and do other similar duties.

In some quite early cases, however, we find no mention of a priory, but only of a canon who was to reside as vicar. In 1140 Bishop Haton[7], of Troyes, in appropriating the churches of Auzon and Longsols to the Augustinian Abbey of St Loup, simply said that the abbot, as at the church of Moulins, similarly appropriated, should choose whatever priests he wished, whether of his own order or seculars, provided only that they be of good report, and present them to the bishop for the cure of souls. Similarly in 1173, the abbot of la Chapelle aux Planches was allowed to choose one of his canons for the cure of souls at Chassericourt[8], also St Loup Abbey in 1177, for the church of Laine au Bois[9]; the Hôtel Dieu of Chalette in 1178 for Épagne[10]; and

[1] Lalore, *Cart. du diocèse de Troyes*, IV, p. 281.
[2] *Historiae Pat. Mon. Chart.* I, col. 934.
[3] Lalore, *Cart. du diocèse de Troyes*, III, p. 163.
[4] *Reg. Honorii III*, I, p. 30 *b*.
[5] *Reg. H. de Welles*, I, p. 252.
[6] *Reg. Halton*, I, p. 39.
[7] Lalore, *Cart. du diocèse de Troyes*, I, p. 23.
[8] *Ibid.* IV, p. 22.
[9] *Ibid.* I, p. 82.
[10] *Ibid.* I, p. 87.

Basse Fontaine Abbey in 1197 for Précy[1]. It is impossible to argue definitely that there was no formal priory set up at any of these places, but it seems likely that there was not. Yet unless the canons received a very unusual permission, these canon vicars were bound to have companions of their own order with them by the general canon law.

In 1190, Guillaume, cardinal-legate and archbishop of Rheims, confirmed the Papal Indulgence made to the abbey of Thenailles[2] (diocese of Laon), by which one of the canons could be instituted parish priest in each of their parishes as they fell vacant. These canons should answer to the diocesan for spiritual things, and to their abbot for the discipline of their Order. The dangers of this system of *prioratus curati* is revealed by a bull which Guillaume d'Auvergne, bishop of Paris, obtained from Pope Gregory IX, ordering the priors curate of the Order of St Victor[3] to conform entirely in food, clothes, bedding and other things to the abbey régime, if they were bound to residence. The priors were forced to submit and ask pardon for their past failings, while Bishop William gave them absolution.

These priors curate of St Victor were appointed to four churches by virtue of a concession made by the bishop of Paris to them in 1202. The abbot was allowed to present them without consulting the bishop, and to remove them without requiring his assent, so long as others were presented within 15 days of their removal. The abbot promised to remove any presentee who seemed to the bishop unsuitable and appoint another within 15 days. Such special privileges were unusual at this early date, although in later times the removable regular vicar was by no means uncommon.

There seems to have been no documentary bestowal of their right, yet canon lawyers agree that Premonstratensian canons, the reformed canons of the order founded by St Norbert[4] at

[1] Lalore, *Cart. du diocèse de Troyes*, III, p. 28.

[2] MS. Paris. lat. 5640, fol. 48 *b*.

[3] MS. Paris. lat. 5526, fol. 43.

[4] Van Espen, III, 6, col. 1, no. 26: *Asserunt canonici Praemonstratenses, se ex speciali quoque privilegio obtinere posse Ecclesiam Parochialem saeculare, uti testatur Zypaeus* (*i.e.* Franciscus van der Zype, *Omnia Opera*, 1675 Antwerp, *Consultationes Canonicae; de Institutionibus* no. 3, p. 92). Also see the special note *et Praemonstratensibus* in *Corp. Jur. Canon. Sext. Decret.* lib. III, tit. 18, Venice 1572, p. 305. Madelaine in his *Abbaye de Mondaye*, p. 87, gives further references but they are all post-medieval.

Prémontré in 1121, were, of all regulars, those most justified in accepting the cure of souls. The reason for this seems to be that from the very time of the birth of the Order it was understood that the canons would endeavour to secure parish churches for themselves and seek the privilege of serving cures of souls by their own members, thus deliberately adopting a contrary policy to that of the Cistercians.

For example, Adam Scot, the late twelfth-century Premonstratensian, wrote:

X. *Sed et locum tuum, ut ego arbitror, mutare potes, in quo professionis es vinculo ligatus, si ad alicujus fueris regimen Ecclesiae canonice electus. Et huic quidem causae tertiae nullatenus praelati, vel conventus resistere debebunt, si et electionem tuam canonicam perspexerint, et te dignum ac idoneum agnoverint, tuamque, ob majorem sanctae Ecclesiae utilitatem, absentiam admittere potuerint* (*P.L.* t. 198, col. 505).

The Order very rapidly made its encroachments into the parochial system. The modern historian of the abbey of Mondaye[1] gives the following details. St Norbert himself settled religious of his Order in ten parishes. Abbot Evermode of Magdeburg, acting on the same principles, trusted to his canons six parishes of the town and 14 rural parishes, and sent other canons as missionaries into Slavonia. On its foundation the abbey of Mondaye[2] was endowed by Jourdain du Hommet in 1215 with the parish church of Juaye. The abbey was to have it served by a canon, and this arrangement was confirmed by the dean and chapter of Lisieux in 1217. Jourdain gave the third garb of tithe, which he had held as his own property, to the monks, Raoul de Percy yielded another, and, after several years, the heirs of Philip de Vassy before judges delegated by the Pope, surrendered all their claims in the church. Until the French Revolution, the church was constantly served by a canon of the abbey.

In 1259 Foulques d'Astin[3], bishop of Lisieux, made a slightly unusual appropriation to Mondaye in the following words:

To all the faithful who shall inspect the present letters, Foulques, by divine permission, Bishop of Lisieux, salvation in the Lord. Know ye all that, for the salvation of our soul and that of our ancestors, and successors, considering the interest of our church of Lisieux,

[1] Madelaine, *Abbaye de Mondaye*, p. 86.
[2] *Ibid.* pp. 90, 91. [3] *Ibid.* p. 93.

and of the church of St Pierre d'Ellon, we have given in pure and perpetual alms, to God and the church of St Martin of Mondaye, as well as to the canons there serving, and who shall serve God there, the entire vicarage of the aforesaid church of Saint Pierre: that is to say, a third of the tithe and all the inherent rights of the vicarage, on condition always that the canons themselves serve and administer this parish. Also are expressly reserved the rights of Vincent de Pont-de-l'Arche, canon of Lisieux, rector of the aforesaid church, during his life and no longer. On the death of Vincent, all the revenues of the cure shall come to the canons freely and perpetually. The same canons, for their tithe and the revenues of the vicarage, shall have to pay, yearly, at Lisieux, for the period of the two synods, 16 pounds tournois, 8 pounds at each synod to the chaplain who shall then serve our chapel of St Paul in our manor of Lisieux: which chaplain is bound to assist at mattins and at the canonical hours in the great church. Given in the month of April in the year of our Lord 1259.

This is a donation of a church in which a canon of the cathedral church of Lisieux was rector, not the canons of Mondaye themselves; but on the death of the rector, it may be noted, the rectory was also to go to the canons.

At Silly Abbey the Premonstratensians had their canons in some of their churches as early as 1209 and 1212, although in another church in 1223 the permission was not granted[1].

Opposition was not infrequently shown to the canons in the exercise of their special privileges. In 1220 Honorius III[2] forbade archbishops and bishops to presume to retain Premonstratensian canons who were recalled to their cloister from parish churches by their abbots. Nicholas IV in 1288 issued orders[3] that when such Premonstratensian canon vicars had been recalled to their cloisters the bishops were to admit and institute other canons presented canonically by their abbots and provosts.

This does not mean that henceforth all Premonstratensian vicars were to be removable at the discretion of their regular superiors. Alfreton[4], in Derbyshire, was always served by a canon of Beauchief in the latter part of the thirteenth century, but he was irremovable. In 1478 the visitor[5] expressly reported

[1] MS. Paris, lat. 11059, fols. 125, 143 *b*, 160, 212.
[2] *Reg. Honorii III*, I, p. 424 *a*.
[3] *Reg. Nic.* IV, p. 45 *a*.
[4] Cox, *Notes on the Churches of Derbyshire*, IV, p. 442.
[5] Gasquet, *Collect. Anglo-Premonstrat.* (Camden Soc. 3rd Series).

that canons were *perpetual* vicars in the churches of a number of Premonstratensian abbeys. These visitation records leave no doubt that many of the vicarages served by canons remained perpetual, in England at any rate, although probably in practice a canon might often vacate his perpetual vicarage at the will of his monastic superior.

In the fifteenth century a Premonstratensian canon, vicar of Theberton in Suffolk, was sued in Chancery[1] by the visitors, Thomas abbot of Bayham, and William, abbot of St Radegund, for refusing to return to his cloister at the command of his superior, the abbot of Leiston. Acting on the authority of letters patent issued to them by the king, commanding "all his officeres and trewe liegemen, of this his seide Realme to favoure helpe and socoure youre seide besechers and theyre commys-saryes in the seide correccion'" of the Premonstratensian order in England, they had called on the constable of the parish to aid them, which he did. John Doonwyche, the contumacious canon, however, supported by one John Curteys and one John Sturmy of Theberton, parishioners, would not be disturbed even by the constable. Although "stonding acursyd" he still kept the cure, and administered the Sacraments. Sir John Heveningham, being given charge of the case, examined the parishioners separately. They all stated on oath that John Doonwyche had been legally admitted by the ordinary, and instituted and in-ducted, upon the presentation of the abbot of Leiston. He claimed to be exempt, and absolved from his Order. He had served the cure for a long time well and honourably. The abbot of Leiston and many others had entered the church on Ascension Day while John was celebrating Divine service, and made a brawling and arrested him. John Curteys and John Sturmy and other parishioners had rescued their vicar. The end of this interesting quarrel does not appear, but it is to be feared that the vicar was in the wrong. At any rate, in 1478 it is stated that Leiston Abbey "has five churches. Canons have the cure in certain of them but are not perpetual"[2]. About 1416 the former canon vicar of Kappelen in the diocese of Lausanne complained that he had resigned the cure against his will. On the other

[1] *Early Chanc. Proc.* (*Record Office*), Bundle 13, no. 37; Bundle 15, no. 169.
[2] *Collect. Anglo-Premonstrat.* III, p. 46.

hand, a Premonstratensian certainly resigned the perpetual vicarage of Halesowen[1] and another took his place, in the time of Bishop Ginsborough of Worcester. This may be a case where the obedience to his regular superior led a canon vicar to renounce his perfectly legal right in the vicarage. I do not know of any general complaint that canons, when made perpetual vicars, were wont to presume on that in order to free themselves from the authority of their abbots, and so am forced to the conclusion that abbots were well satisfied with their powers in appropriated parishes even where their canons were perpetual vicars.

The time of the Great Schism was particularly fruitful to the Premonstratensians. From either Pope or anti-Pope they obtained many appropriations of rectories, with permission that the churches on voidance might be served either by removable canons or removable secular priests. They also obtained the appropriation of many perpetual vicarages in their own churches, with permission to serve the churches by removable canons or removable secular priests. In 1399 the rectory of Grimston in Norfolk was appropriated to West Dereham, the church to be served by a temporary secular or religious vicar. Vicarages were appropriated to Premonstratensian houses in the churches of Mitton[2] in Lancashire in 1396, of St John the Baptist at Cambridge[3] in 1399, and of Didbrook and Pinnock in Gloucestershire[4] in 1413, to quote only a few of the frequent English examples.

In the episcopal visitation of the diocese of Lausanne in 1416–17, a number of churches are shown to be served by Premonstratensian canons. The condition of these churches was fairly satisfactory, although, as usual, repairs of certain ornaments were commanded. The character of the vicars, also, seems to have been more satisfactory than that of the secular priests of the same diocese. The parishioners, too, seem to have been satisfactory communicants. Not all of those canons held from their houses directly. The abbot of Ballaigues was patron of Perles[5], and there was a secular rector, who did not reside but

[1] *Reg. Ginsborough* (Worcs), p. 163.
[2] *Cal. Pap. Let.* v, p. 19.
[3] *Ibid.* v, p. 196. [4] *Ibid.* vi, p. 388.
[5] *Soc. de la Suisse Romande*, t. xi, p. 202.

served the church by Fr. Jean Capellani, a Premonstratensian. It is expressly stated that the church was wont to be served by a secular. Similarly, the canon of the collegiate church of Soleure, who was rector of Selzach[1], did not reside but had a Premonstratensian vicar. The parishioners of Cressier s. Morat[2] said that their church was wont to be ruled by a secular chaplain, but the two lay patrons had presented a Premonstratensian canon to the rectory. A secular was rector of Bellegarde[3] but a canon of Gottstatt (Ord. Premonstratens.) was vicar and resided for him. Jean d'Erlenbach, vicar of Mache[4], Peter, vicar of Büttenberg[5], P. Fabri, vicar of Bürglen[6], Jean Herfellis, vicar of Sutz[7], Jean Mellinguer, vicar of Kappelen[8], were all canons of Gottstatt and held directly from their abbot.

At Cressier[9] (Neuchâtel) and Meyriez[10], the canon curé from a Premonstratensian house did not reside and served by seculars.

The churches of the diocese of Worms mentioned in the 1496 visitation as being served by Premonstratensians were far from exemplary, although this must be said of all the churches in the diocese. The provost of Enkenbach enjoyed the whole proceeds of the endowment of St Catherine's Chapel at Alsenborn, but the poor parishioners, who had founded it, were defrauded of the Divine offices. At Kaiserslautern there was a Premonstratensian monastery, and the church was served by a vicar, obviously a canon who did not have to be instituted by the bishop's authority. Although this monastery was very corrupt, the church buildings were found satisfactory, but at Erfenbach, also served by a canon of Kaiserslautern, the roof of the choir and nave was broken and ruinous[11].

In the visitation records of the English Premonstratensian houses compiled by Bishop Redman in 1478 are found the following particulars concerning the cure of souls in their appropriated churches, although one must remember that canons also received permission at times to serve other than appropriated churches.

[1] *Soc. de la Suisse Romande*, t. XI, p. 204.
[2] *Ibid.* p. 211.
[3] *Ibid.* p. 232.
[4] *Ibid.* p. 201.
[5] *Ibid.* p. 202.
[6] *Ibid.* p. 206.
[7] *Ibid.* p. 207.
[8] *Ibid.* p. 208.
[9] *Ibid.* p. 193.
[10] *Ibid.* p. 212.
[11] *Zeitschrift...Oberrheins*, XXVII, pp. 315–17.

Collect. Anglo-Prem.	Abbey	No. of churches	Vicars
II, p. 3	Easby	Diverse	Canons but only 2 perpetual
II, p. 31	Barlings	5	Sometimes canons; sometimes seculars
II, p. 58	Beauchief	3	Canons perpetual
II, p. 73	Bayham	5	Certain canons perpetual; certain seculars
II, p. 82	Maldon	3	Seculars
II, p. 130	Coverham	5	Not stated but appear to be canons; see *ibid.* II, p. 129
II, p. 151	Croxton	3	Canons perpetual
II, p. 173	Dale	4	,,
II, p. 192	Durford	1	Now a secular
II, p. 210	Egglestone	Many	Canons: only 3 perpetual
II, p. 226	Hagnaby	1	Canon not perpetual
II, p. 241	Halesowen	3	Canons perpetual
III, p. 2	Langdon	3	Canons not perpetual
III, p. 14	Langley	5	In certain canons not perpetual
III, p. 34	Lavenden	4	Some canons, some seculars
III, p. 46	Leiston	5	In certain canons, but not perpetual
III, p. 58	Newbo	3	Canons perpetual
III, p. 74	Newhouse	7	2 canons perpetual
III, p. 96	St Radegunde's	6	Some canons perpetual; some seculars
III, p. 107	Welford (Sulby)	6	Seculars
III, p. 125	Titchfield	2	Canons perpetual
III, p. 141	Torre	6	1 canon
III, p. 157	Tupholme	4	Canons not perpetual
III, p. 182	Welbeck	10 and 2 chapels	5 canons perpetual
III, p. 201	Wendling	3	Some seculars; some revocable canons
III, p. 213	W. Dereham	5	Some perpetual canons; some seculars; some revocable canons

Several interesting injunctions are found in the records of Bishop Redman's visitations, as commissary of the order in England. In 1482 he strictly commanded the vicars and other brothers having cures outside the monastery of Coverham in Yorkshire to be content with the stipends assigned to them and not remain in the monastery or otherwise burden it[1]. In about 1485, on the other hand, he was forced to order the canons of Blanchland who served outside cures to return to their monasteries, and not to celebrate in the world (*in seculo*) unless in churches appropriated to the monastery[2]. There were to be always six canons at least in the abbey. This shows that the

[1] *Collect. Anglo-Premonstrat.* II, p. 133. [2] *Ibid.* II, p. 97.

canons were serving not only their own churches but also rectories or other vicarages, probably with Papal indulgences[1] for the purpose. These were quite common in this century. In such cases the abbey was not entitled to draw tithes from the parishes. In 1488[2] at Langdon Abbey John Ramsay was found to be quarrelsome, and so the bishop gave orders for the sake of peace that he was to be sent to some cure of a parish. One feels sorry for the poor parishioners, who might suffer from their vicar's bad temper, though it may be hoped that his quarrel with the brothers of Langdon was on some particular matter, and not due to an unfortunate temperament. The vicar of Wymeswold[3] in Leicestershire, Richard Holynbridge, a canon of Beauchief, was summoned to trial at Beauchief on September 3rd, 1497, on charges of speaking against his superior, incontinence and disobedience, which charges he denied. Little evidence of the personal character of these Premonstratensian vicars is to hand, and I have no reason to believe that they were often unsatisfactory. In 1500 a vicar of Mansfield[4], neglecting the fact that he was also a canon of Easby Abbey, presumed to make a will although as a canon he was incapable of so doing. If it were proved that he was a religious, and not capable of property, he was to be punished, if necessary, by excommunication, ordered Bishop Redman.

Yet, in spite of the general tendency of the abbeys to take more and more of the tithes, there was an augmentation of a vicarage at Reepham[5], as late as 1509, when the vicar was allowed ten quarters of barley and four quarters of peas, with one load of tithe hay and pasture for six beasts. He was to have additional accommodation in the rectory farm buildings for these things, subject to his keeping his part in repair. The abbey was to provide straw for thatchery. He also received a yearly stipend of 20*s*. This was a church of Barlings Abbey, whose cures in the 1478 visitation were said to be served some-

[1] For the benefit of readers who are not familiar with such technical terms it should perhaps be stated that the word "indulgence" was not only applied to the famous documents of pardon which owed their justification to the doctrine of works of supererogation, but was generally used of documents granting special privileges to particular persons.

[2] *Collect. Anglo-Premonstrat.* III, p. 6.

[3] *Ibid.* II, p. 68.

[4] *Ibid.* II, p. 14.

[5] *Lincoln Dioc. Docs.* (E.E.T.S.), p. 131.

times by canons, sometimes by seculars. It is impossible to get any very accurate idea of how these canon vicars were paid. Even when the amount is stated the statement may be open to suspicion. For example, Gilbert Makdonyl, Premonstratensian canon vicar of Kirkmaiden in Rhinns (co. Wigtown), in 1447 was said to receive only £3 a year for his cure, although his parish was very populous and about eight Italian miles round[1]. He, it must be noted, was a perpetual vicar. Yet since these statements are his own evidence in favour of his receiving by Papal indulgence another living *in commendam*, the case against the abbey for underpayment cannot be accepted as quite definitely proved. Such petitioners were very much in the habit of underestimating their incomes, as can easily be proved by comparing different petitions relating to the same livings, the estimates varying greatly. Nor can the estimates in the *Valor Ecclesiasticus* of Henry VIII be accepted as evidence of true value, especially as the incomes of removable vicars would not be assessed at all. A "regular" however, could not complain if he had sufficient to clothe and feed him, and a good roof above him, since he had voluntarily adopted a life of poverty. He had chosen his way, and we need not waste our sympathy on him. He is altogether in a different category from the secular priest who was reduced to poverty by the encroachments of religious corporations.

The Augustinian canons secured exactly similar indulgences to the Premonstratensians, although it was never technically regarded as quite so natural for them to do so. The Gilbertine canons were under the Rule of St Augustine, so there is no need of any special study of their churches. Some bishops opposed the service of churches by Augustinians. As early as 1188 Bishop Manasses de Pougy[2] was excommunicated by Pope Clement III for opposing the foundation of the priory founded by the abbey of St Loup in the church of Marigny. The foundation of the priory-with-cure stood firm, and the bishop was apparently vanquished. In the middle of the thirteenth century, Archbishop Odo Rigaldi of Rouen held particularly rigid views on the service of churches by any sort of canon.

[1] *Cal. Pap. Let.* x, p. 275.

[2] Lalore, *Cart. du diocèse de Troyes*, I, p. 131.

Odo seems to have considered it the duty of a cathedral prebendary to reside in his church, and obtained from the Pope in 1249 an ordination that in future no prebendary was to be instituted to St Eligius[1] of Rouen unless he undertook to make personal residence there. In the same year he noted with disapproval that many canons of Lisieux had parish churches, but did not reside in them, and were not compelled to do so. In this matter the archbishop was exceptionally rigid, for certainly in England by this time the non-resident prebendary had become an established institution, and the bishop of Lincoln was soon to set to work to make elaborate ordinations for all the prebendal churches of his diocese.

As in the case of the Premonstratensians, the Austin canons were practically always given the choice of serving appropriated vicarages by secular removable priests if they preferred. Austin canon vicars were not common in the thirteenth century in England but from 1300 onwards the movement towards making them general gained momentum, especially during the years of the Great Schism. Money had to be found to finance the quarrels of the Papacy, and supporters of the rival Popes had to be bribed. The practice of appropriations was very useful for this. Not that the Popes were usually guilty of simony, but the fees at the Curia were sufficient to make litigation there welcome, and Papal officials certainly received their "palm-oil"[2]. It is unnecessary to quote instances of the appropriation of vicarages to canons. The specialist student may take down the volumes of *Calendars of Papal Letters* for these years and turn over any few consecutive pages he pleases.

Observance of the rule that canons must have companions with them in the service of churches was frequently one of the first things that bishops demanded in allowing canons, especially Austin canons, to serve churches. Bishop Halton of Carlisle[3] instituted Brother William de Malton to the church of Askham in 1295 on the express condition that he should always have a fellow-canon living with him. In the first instance such canon vicars had only been appointed on condition that a small priory of four at least was to be founded. The one canon companion

[1] *Reg. Rigaldi*, p. 734. These, however, were all *secular* canons.
[2] Cp. St Bernard's *De Consideratione*. [3] *Reg. Halton*, I, p. 55.

is a relic of this and a very small guarantee that the vicar should lead his life as closely according to the rule as possible. Bishop Anthony Bek of Durham[1] allowed Guisborough Priory to have a canon vicar at Hart in 1308, and, when this was confirmed in 1311, it was expressly stated that he was to have a canon companion.

Gregory IX solemnly insisted on this rule in his statutes for monastic reform published in 1236. "Let no monk live by himself in any priory: but let one or more fellow monks be sent to keep him company, if the revenues of the house will bear this: otherwise let him be called back to the cloister." Yet, in Odo Rigaldi's register, Dr Coulton[2] finds

44 breaches of this rule 1248–57.
17 " " 1257–63.
17 " " 1263–9.

It was one of the most frequently broken of monastic rules, otherwise there would never have been such desire to secure the appropriations of vicarages as there was at the end of the fourteenth century.

The priory of Stone[3] in the diocese of Coventry and Lichfield found it necessary to protect itself in 1259. Hitherto it had been served by the religious and two secular priests appointed by them. They were not to be compelled, ran a Papal bull, by anyone to institute a vicar in the said church. By a bull of 1255 Hexham Priory[4] was not to be compelled by ordinary or Papal authority to institute a secular vicar in their church in which they reside, unless special mention of this indult be made in the Papal letters. Yet, in about 1294, Archbishop Romeyn[5] cited them for not having a vicar there. Newburgh[6] and Sempringham Priories were confirmed in similar and more general rights in their churches, notwithstanding any Papal indult granted to the archbishop or any other in regard to the taxation of vicarages and appointment of vicars. Yet again, in 1293, Archbishop Romeyn's commissaries apparently had started proceedings

[1] *Reg. Pal. Dun.* II, pp. 1137 *seq.*
[2] Coulton, *Five Centuries of Religion*, II, p. 223 and n.; see also *Reg. Rigaldi*, pp. 47, 237.
[3] *Cal. Pap. Let.* I, p. 367.
[4] *Ibid.* I, p. 320.
[5] *Reg. Romeyn.* II, pp. xlv, 79.
[6] *Cal. Pap. Let.* I, p. 365.

against the prior of Newburgh[1] which they had to drop on receiving word from the archbishop that he had reserved the case for his own hearing. It is clear that archbishop and bishops needed to be fully satisfied of the warrants of such Augustinian houses. The bishop of Kilmore, in Ireland, even instituted a number of secular priests to the vicarage of Drumlane[2], although the priory there had appropriated it. In 1409 they had to get Papal confirmation for a re-appropriation of it.

The vicar of Taunton Priory[3], by the original vicarage ordination of 1308, was bound to celebrate in the chapels of Trull, Taunton Castle and Wilton, while the priory was to provide three secular chaplains for the chapels of Stoke, Rushton, Staplegrove St James', Taunton, and Hull. In 1455 we find that the priory[4] had been sentenced to cause celebrations to be held in all these chapels which had obviously been neglected at that time. Pleading that they could not find secular priests for them, they received a Papal bull allowing them to serve these chapels by canons of the priory.

The reasons given in 1379 by the Augustinians of Cambuskenneth[5] for the appropriation of the vicarage of Clackmannan (dioc. St Andrew's) are of some interest in themselves and as a specimen of such pleas. The rectory had already been appropriated and the abbey now petitioned the anti-Pope, Clement VII, for the appropriation of the vicarage. The Abbey, it was said, had suffered from constant wars, the chalices, books and other ornaments having been stolen. The belfry had been struck by lightning, whereby the choir was greatly ruined. These border monasteries and churches must truly have suffered terribly in the constant border fighting and looting. In 1397 the Augustinian brothers of Inis Aingin[6] (*Insula Omnium Sanctorum*) (co. Antrim), secured the revenues of the church of Rathlin, and the right of serving it by one of their canons on the plea that their priory was so reduced that the canons were forced to seek a living by the labour of their own hands outside in the world.

In 1432, Bishop William of Lincoln visited the church and

[1] *Reg. Romeyn.* I, p. 177.
[2] *Cal. Pap. Let.* VI, p. 159.
[3] *Reg. Drokensford*, p. 69.
[4] *Cal. Pap. Let.* VI, p. 486.
[5] *Ibid.* IV, p. 236.
[6] *Ibid.* V, p. 12.

priory of Canons' Ashby[1]. The perpetual vicarage founded in the church by Hugh de Welles was of the usual corrody type, the vicar having food in the priory, and a manse outside. Bishop William found this perpetual secular vicarage so much decreased and attenuated that it hardly sufficed in these days for the upkeep of the vicar. The priory produced bulls giving it permission to serve its churches by removable canon or secular vicars. The bishop, "with intense desires to help the poor and oppressed", granted that the parish church be served by such removable vicar and that the fruits of the vicarage be taken by the priory. As compensation to them for the loss of dues, the priory was to pay 12*d.* yearly to the bishop of Lincoln at Easter at the cathedral, and 6*d.* to the archdeacon of Northampton at Easter at the church of All Saints, Northampton. In default of payment of these dues, the bishop and archdeacon could sequestrate the church for all arrears without legal process.

For some reason or other a fifteenth-century Augustinian prior of Holy Trinity, Ipswich[2], as parson of the church of Higham about eight miles away, did not provide a vicar there. One John Skynner of that parish obtained permission of the bishop of Norwich to sequestrate the goods of the church and provide a parish priest there. According to Skynner's complaint, the prior "of malice ageyn' troughe' and consciens hath' affermed a pleynt of trespas ayenst your seid' supplicant before the Bayles of the seid' town' of Hippeswyche Where the seid Priour is most stronge and dweller' and your supplicaunt a straunger and also nevir dide eny trespase or' offence to the seid Priour...." Consequently Skynner petitioned in Chancery the bishop of Rochester, chancellor of England, for justice against the prior of Holy Trinity and the bailiffs of Ipswich. It is probable that the priory sent out canons to perform the services at Higham, a most unsatisfactory proceeding. Even if this were so, there ought legally in such cases to be a canon instituted as vicar and dwelling in the parish. The remedy of John Skynner, however, sounds violent and equally unsatisfactory. The circumstances seem discreditable to both sides, although the facts as stated are too scanty to allow more than a

[1] *Lincoln Visitations* (Cant. and York Soc.), 1, p. 32.
[2] *Early Chan. Proc.* (*Record Office*), Bundle 47, no. 76.

glimpse of the quarrel and the methods adopted on either side.

At the 1416 visitation, the church of Avry[1], in the diocese of Lausanne, was served by Brother Nicod Sovez, canon of St Augustine at the presentation of the provost of St Bernard (*Mons Jovis*). Unhappily by the account of the parishioners, this curé was a "public concubinary", who bought a certain house for his concubine near the church, in which he openly stayed with her. The "concubine" kept a public tavern, and kept the wine she sold in the cistern of the parish church, of which the parishioners had complained. Further, they complained that the fabric of the house and grange of the church threatened to fall into ruins. The curé was warned to expel his concubine from the boundaries of the parish, and not to have any further dealings with her at all, under pain of excommunication and deprivation of benefice and of giving 10 marks of silver to be applied in alms. Also he was warned to rebuild the house and grange within two years, up to the value of £20 of the money of Lausanne, under pain of excommunication. There is no evidence that scandals of this kind were exceptionally common among the regular vicars, for this visitation reveals a large percentage of similar ones among the seculars. It is true that the curé of Lussy[2], a canon of the same monastery, was said to be of bad life, and small learning (*male vite et sciencie modice*). The provost of Daerstetten[3] himself was a "concubinary", and was warned to expel his concubine. He dwelt alone, although he ought to have had with him two religious. The church was altogether under the diocesan and no other. The provost was to find a religious to be with him before the next feast of St Mary Magdalene, and within two years to repair and rebuild the church. This peculiar house presented a secular vicar to Oberwil[4], where repairs were needed for several ornaments, and where the curé was warned for being a public concubinary in the same way as the provost.

At Erlenbach[5], where an Austin canon of Interlaken was vicar, the parishioners were warned to repair certain ornaments. (In England it was generally the custom that ornaments should

[1] *Soc. de la Suisse romande*, t. XI, p. 165. [2] *Ibid.* p. 8.
[3] *Ibid.* p. 229. [4] *Ibid.* p. 230. [5] *Ibid.* p. 229.

be repaired by one or other of the tithe-owners, generally the vicar. In this visitation, however, the parishioners are frequently, though not always, warned to perform such repairs of ornaments.) At Montprévеyres[1], an Austin canon of St Bernard's was rector but non-resident, and served the church by a secular vicar who had not to be instituted by the bishop. This vicar also was concubinary and was warned in the usual manner. Similarly at Tours Montagny[2] there was a non-resident Augustinian who appointed a secular to serve the parish. It was complained that masses and vespers were not celebrated at the due times, and the bishop told the parishioners to proceed against the curé, his vicar and the other chaplains if they did not celebrate at the proper times.

A French example of 1459 of permission to appoint an Augustinian canon to a perpetual vicarage is found in the diocese of Limoges[3]. Pope Pius II granted permission to the prior of St Mary's, Sales, to possess the priory of Grandjardin of the same order and diocese. On account of the wars, mortalities and various other disasters which had for a long time (*proch dolori*) afflicted those parts, the buildings of the priory of Sales, especially the choir, cloisters and chapter house, were on the point of collapse, and the fruits had so diminished that they did not exceed 120 small livres of Tours. The immediate predecessor of Simon Laurence, the present prior, had been wont to keep there a perpetual vicar and only one canon. Simon endeavoured to make it his business to keep himself and six canons in the priory, but could not both do that and restore the buildings. The priory of Grandjardin had been wont to serve its parochial cure by a commensal perpetual vicar, who was presented by the prior of Sales. It seems that Grandjardin was a daughter priory of Sales. The cure of Grandjardin was now to be served by a canon perpetual vicar from Sales, who was to have a suitable portion assigned to him.

The 1496 visitation of the diocese of Worms shows an instance of an Augustinian canon acting as vicar. It has been seen earlier how Archbishop Hincmar's fears about the *viaticum* had

[1] *Soc. de la Suisse romande*, t. XI, p. 137.
[2] *Ibid.* p. 177.
[3] Denifle, *La Désolation, etc.* I, p. 305.

been justified in the Cistercian parish of Dienheim. More culpable was the Augustinian vicar of Mörsch[1] who

> neglected a woman who besought him by messengers to hear her confession and give her the Venerable Sacrament, but he put off visiting her. The parson excuses himself and lays it at the sexton's door: the sexton contradicts him and brought jurats and certain of the parish who say that this was through the parson's negligence, because she lived nearly ten hours after calling for him; yet she died without confession and ecclesiastical sacraments. Alas! This is a sorry business.

In this same church the vestments and chalice cloth were most filthy, and the Host was broken into small pieces, so it appears that this particular canon was altogether a most unworthy example.

The available evidence, which is necessarily imperfect and "patchy", seems to indicate that Austin canons were less efficient in the service of churches than their reformed Premonstratensian fellows. This is suggested, rather than definitely proved, by the evidence, but it is only what one might expect, considering how much less system there was in the organisation of the houses that may be classed together as Augustinian than in the better controlled Premonstratensian houses.

Other Orders also obtained vicarages occasionally, being allowed to have other than perpetual secular vicars in their churches. The Franciscan nuns of Denny Abbey[2] obtained permission to serve their churches of Biddenham (co. Beds.) and St Andrew's, Histon, and Eltisley, Cambridgeshire, by removable secular priests in 1402. Nuns, of course, could not serve their own churches, and this was the next most profitable thing for them. The Trinitarian friars of Ingham by Hickling in 1401 obtained similar permission for the churches of Cockley Clay and Walcot in Norfolk. As early as the third General Lateran Council in 1179, canon 9 stated that the military Orders of Hospitallers and Templars were exceeding their rights in the matter of parochial churches[3]. They were accepting the gift of churches from laymen without dispensation, giving the sacraments and Christian burial to excommunicates, and

[1] Coulton, *Five Centuries of Religion*, II, p. 455; *Zeitschrift...Oberrheins*, XXVII, p. 230.

[2] *Cal. Pap. Let.* V, pp. 416, 573 (or by one of the friars).

[3] Hefelé, *Conciles*, V, 2, p. 1095.

appointing and deposing priests in their churches without the consent of the diocesan bishops. Yet the knights did receive permission to serve churches. Hospitallers were serving the churches of Montbrelloz[1] and Douanne[2] at the time of the 1416–17 visitation of the churches of Lausanne. There was also a Teutonic knight in the church of Köniz[3], a priory-with-cure. Teutonic brothers also served the church of Vaudeville[4], in the diocese of Troyes, from the thirteenth century onwards, the appropriators being the priory of Beauvoir. Also, in 1496, there were at least four vicars of the Teutonic brotherhood in the diocese of Worms.

In 1422, the priory of Nice of hermits of St Augustine[5] petitioned the Pope to allow it to appropriate the vicarage of St Martin's, Nice. By a bull of Peter de Luna, "then called Benedict XIII in his obedience", the canons were bound to serve the church by a secular priest, but this was now so burdensome that they were paying the priest more in salary than the fruits of the church were worth. The Pope allowed the cure and administration of the church with ministering of all the sacraments to be committed to the prior or a suitable canon of the convent. It was to be done with consent of the parishioners, a most exceptional instance of consideration of the wishes of those most affected in spiritual matters by these transactions.

One could probably find examples of male members of practically all religious orders and congregations serving churches, and of houses of women regulars having their churches served by removable chaplains. The Pope could overrule any Rule or article of canon law by his special authority, and medieval Popes were in no danger of incurring the penalty expressed in the words, "The letter killeth".

Another kind of removable vicar must here be noticed. In 1398 the Pope had dissolved the appropriation of a certain parish church and its chapels to a certain monastery, because the monastery was supporting the anti-Pope Clement VII. He appropriated it to St Mary's College of Winchester[6] (New

[1] *Soc. de la Suisse romande*, t. XI, p. 184.
[2] *Ibid.* p. 197.
[3] *Ibid.* p. 221.
[4] Lalore, *Cartulaires du diocèse de Troyes*, III, pp. 228–9, 239, 307.
[5] Denifle, *La Désolation, etc.* I, p. 403, no. 858.
[6] *Cal. Pap. Let.* V, p. 86.

College) Oxford, which asked, and obtained, permission to serve it by a removable vicar instead of a perpetual, as the monastery formerly served it by a removable vicar. In 1401 the church of Swannington[1] in Norfolk was appropriated to the college named Holy Trinity Hall, Cambridge, which was founded for students in canon and civil law, "and whose fruits were so slender that they cannot be conveniently sustained". The church might be served by a student or a suitable removable priest. Similarly Christ's College, Cambridge, on its foundation, secured the church of Fen Drayton, and the right of serving it by a removable scholar, priest or Fellow of the College, or any suitable removable priest. Mr Curtois in *Christ's College Magazine*, No. 105, has shown how this right has continued until the present day, the curacy of Fen Drayton even now being an exceptional, though not quite unique[2], cure in the Church of England. There have been a number of complaints as in 1552, 1561, and 1645, about the working of this system at Fen Drayton. Curates were often men without University degrees, divine service was not held at suitable times, the curates were underpaid, and their life was often scandalous and doctrine unsound. Such are some of the recurring complaints of the parishioners.

This is rather outside the scope of this book, but the reader may be referred to Mr Curtois' entertaining and instructive article. One must confess, however, that the colleges of our older Universities were, except in recent times, no kinder appropriators than the monasteries.

In the meantime provincial councils had begun trying to prevent the exercise of parochial functions by monks. The Council of Rouen[3] of 1072 (cap. 13) had forbidden monks to buy cures. Another Council at the same city two years later, insisted "that to no monk be committed the rule of a Parish". In 1076 the Council of Winchester declared, "if anyone even canonically be received as a monk he shall not be permitted publicly to serve churches". In 1078 the Council of Poitiers stated that abbots and monks could only minister penance by

[1] *Cal. Pap. Let.* v, p. 384.

[2] New College, Oxford, is patron of similar curacies at Romford, Hornchurch, Writtle and Roxwell in Essex.

[3] Thomassin, *Anc. et Nouv. Disc.* t. 1, col. 1492.

permission of the bishop and, as for cures committed to them, they could receive the revenues, but a priest must be kept there accountable to the bishop for the cure of souls. In 1100 another Council of Poitiers decreed that "no monk shall presume to exercise the Parochial ministry of priests, that is, to baptize, to preach, to give penance". Thus, even in the eleventh century, the official policy of the Church was quite definite. The Lateran Councils of the twelfth century definitely made the rule a general one for all Christendom.

In England the service of churches by monks was comparatively rare, although by the fifteenth century there were quite 50 churches served regularly by a removable monk or secular vicar, at the will of the monastery. Early dispensations, such as that in 1165 from Pope Alexander III to St Mary's Abbey, York[1] (Benedictine), simply allowed monks to have their churches served by "chaplains", that is, by removable secular vicars. Episcopal opposition to this privilege forced the abbey to secure confirmations from the Pope[2] in 1260 and 1292. An early example of Cistercian monks actually reforming parochial services is at the chapel of Weston[3] in Leicestershire, which in 1220 was served three times a week by monks of Merevale. It is an exceptional case, as this was a decaying district and by 1291, probably, the chapel was abandoned altogether. Otherwise I have had no success in my search for churches served by monks in England during the thirteenth century, and, although I should hesitate to claim that it was never done, it must have been exceedingly rare.

In 1358, Whalley Abbey[4] was allowed to serve the parochial altar there by one of its Cistercian monks[5]. The presence of

[1] *Vic. County Hist.* (*Cumberland*), II, p. 185 *b*.

[2] *Cal. Pap. Let.* I, pp. 373, 546.

[3] Sister Elspeth in *Vic. County Hist.* (*Leics.*), I, p. 360, n. 47.

[4] *Cal. Pap. Let.* III, p. 595.

[5] See *Reg. Sudbury*, p. 83. In a similar permission granted to the Cistercian monastery of St Mary of Graces by the Tower of London for the church of All Hallows, Staining, in 1368 the episcopal permission reads: ... *Ordinamus insuper et perpetuis futuris temporibus inviolabiliter volumus observari quod per unum de professis monachis dicti monasterii ad actum hujusmodi idoneum et discretum pro voluntate dictorum abbatis et conventus et libito ammovendum seu alium quemcumque presbiterum secularem ydoneum stipendiarium et mobilem ad nutum ipsorum religiosorum propter exhilitatem fructuum et emolumentorum dicti monasterii deserviatur laudabiliter et congrue ipsi ecclesie omnium sanctorum prout expedit in divinis et animarum cura parochianorum ejusdem nullatenus negligatur*;....

secular clerks, in the monastic enclosure, it was said, had been a cause of disturbance, and the bishop of Lichfield had dispensed three monks in succession to hold the vicarage there. This excuse seems to be a good one, but it was no gain to the parishioners. Nevertheless, the service by monks of the parish church in which a monastery is situated and of the parish church which it shares with the parishioners is the most pardonable infringement of the rule. The time of the Great Schism was when the rules against the service of churches by monks were most recklessly and unpardonably broken. One imagines that it should be the very last resort of a desperate church to allow monks to leave their cloisters and dwell right away where true observance of the Rule was quite impossible. Elkington and Hindworth churches[1] in 1397 were granted to the Cistercian abbey of Pipewell to be served by a monk or removable lay priest. In 1399, Dunchurch[2], in Warwickshire, was appropriated for his lifetime to the table (*mensa*) of Roger, abbot of Pipewell, and similar permission was granted. In 1399 the Cistercian abbey of Woburn[3], which had previously gained similar permission for Birchmore Green in Bedfordshire, was exempted from the clause in the previous arrangements by which the monk who served there was bound to have with him a secular priest who should administer the sacraments to the parishioners. On the other hand, when this abbey[4] found itself in 1402 with two bulls of appropriation of Whitchurch (dioc. Lincoln), dated 1398 and 1399, the less profitable one, by which the monks had to institute a perpetual vicar, was declared at the Curia to be the valid one. In 1399 Benedictine houses[5] were given permission to have removable secular or religious vicars at Wymondham, Frittenden, Spalding, Weston in the Marsh, Moulton, Pinchbeck, Kettering and Oundle. Concerning this permission in the case of Spalding as late as 1462, Pius II granted that it should hold good although it had not taken place and probably did not by itself hold good owing to general annulments of appropriations. Probably several others of these appropriations of vicarages had suffered under the general annulments by various

[1] *Cal. Pap. Let.* v, p. 77.
[2] *Ibid.* v, p. 185.
[3] *Ibid.* v, p. 200.
[4] *Ibid.* v, pp. 153, 191, 574.
[5] *Ibid.* v, pp. 192, 193, 199, 330.

Popes[1] in the early fifteenth century, but certainly the majority did not, having either taken place in time or being allowed again by other bulls. Boniface IX was the Pope who distributed such favours with the greatest freedom.

Cluniacs also received a share, for example the abbey of Polesworth for Barwell and Quinton[2] and Monk Bretton Priory for Ruston Parva[3], all in 1399. Boniface IX's successors, however, by no means all frowned on the practice, for, to take one example, Daventry Priory in 1451 was allowed to appropriate the corrody vicarage of Daventry, Holy Cross, and the vicarages of West Haddon and All Saints' Norton, and serve them by monks if it pleased[4].

Lest it be alleged that vicarages were usually appropriated on account of the shortage of secular priests, attention must be drawn to the plea of the Cistercian abbey of St Mary's, Combe[5], in 1448. The monks petitioned to be allowed to serve the church of Naseby by one of their monks instead of by a secular as heretofore, "to avoid the scandals caused by quarrels of would-be presentees". It seems that a well-endowed vicarage could find plenty of candidates, although scantily-endowed ones might search in vain. Actually, such a shortage is but seldom alleged in the petitions as a reason for appropriations of vicarages, and usually these were quite frankly to increase the incomes of the monasteries.

A repercussion of the Schism[6] was felt at Kirk Gunzeon (co. Kirkcudbright), in 1391. This church in time of peace had been served by a Cistercian from Holm Cultram Abbey in the diocese of Carlisle, but at this time Englishmen were unable to dwell in Scotland, so the church was neglected, its tithes committed to laymen, and its service being performed first by one priest and then by another. The anti-Pope Clement VII granted the provision of the church of Brother Thomas de Glenluysse for as long as the Schism lasted.

[1] Miss Rose Graham, in the *Vic. County Hist.* (*Glouc.*), II, p. 20, says that although Boniface IX allowed Winchcombe Abbey to appropriate the church of Bledington (*Cal. Pap. Let.* V, p. 497) without any vicarage being ordained, the bishop in 1402 compelled the ordination of a vicarage. This was probably on the strength of the general revocation of appropriations by Pope Boniface IX in the same year.

[2] *Cal. Pap. Let.* V, p. 199. [3] *Ibid.* V, p. 200.

[4] *Ibid.* X, pp. 97–8. [5] *Ibid.* X, p. 30. [6] *Cal. Pap. Pet.* I, p. 576.

The Cistercian abbey of Knockmoy[1] (*Collis Victoriae*) in Ireland, had served the church of Galway by a removable vicar without permission. A secular priest obtained Papal provision to a perpetual vicarage to be set up there. Consequently the archbishop of Cashel, as Papal commissioner with the bishop of Elphin, ordained a vicarage and assigned to it all the personal dues, oblations and tithe of fish and the altarages of the parish and a manse and instituted the Papal provisee to it. The archbishop of Tuam, however, favoured the abbey, in spite of two sentences obtained by the perpetual vicar in the Papal palace. Apparently the latter won, eventually, but four years later we find the abbey obtaining a Papal mandate to prevent the perpetual vicar from usurping the whole fruits of the church and not only his vicarage.

In 1496, in the diocese of Worms, there were Benedictine monk vicars from the monastery of Wadgassen in the church of Kleinbockenheim and its chapel of Kindenheim[2], and it was stated that this was likewise true of all the other benefices of the monastery. Both this church, and its chapel, were in bad condition, rain falling through the roof. A Benedictine of Glandern (Longueville) Abbey in Lorraine held the church of St Martin at Grünstadt[3]. The Cistercian vicar of Dienheim has already been noticed; there were others at Dolgesheim and Groszbockenheim[4]. The Elector Palatine had a monk serving a chapel at Hilsberg in the parish of Aschbach[5]. The churches with monk vicars in this diocese do not show up at all well compared with those with secular vicars.

Finally it must again be emphatically stated that there is no evidence that at any time was the regular vicar looked upon as a boon to the parish. If the many examples here given are considered unduly weighted against the regulars (for is not evidence of friction easier to collect than evidence of smooth running?), I must reply that I cannot find the plea even in medieval times that the parishes were to benefit, nor any evidence that the churches of regular vicars were, as a whole, better repaired, or served, than those of resident seculars, whether vicars or rectors.

[1] *Cal. Pap. Let.* v, pp. 189, 254, 511.
[2] *Zeitschrift...Oberrheins*, XXVII, p. 284.
[3] *Ibid.* p. 298.
[4] *Ibid.* pp. 253, 258, 282.
[5] *Ibid.* p. 324.

CHAPTER X

FROM GASCOIGNE TO RODERYCK MORS

THE greatest voice of the fifteenth century raised against appropriations was that of a chancellor of Oxford University, Gascoigne, the author of the *Liber Veritatum*, a man more orthodox than his opponent, Bishop Pecock, who defended many of the ecclesiastical abuses of the day.

"Some never, or rarely, reside in their cures", says Gascoigne[1], "and either he to whom the church is appropriated, or he who does not reside in it, comes once a year to the cure, or sends to the church at the end of autumn, and, having filled his purse with money and sold the tithes, goes away from his cure into the court (*a cura sua in curiam*) where he idles in gain and luxury. Whence are made true the words written by Solomon in the 7th chapter of Proverbs, 'For the goodman is not at home, he is gone a long journey. He hath taken a bag of money with him, and will come home at the day of the full moon[2]', *i.e.* in autumn when there is fullness of fruits....For now, in England, the cure of souls has perished through appropriated churches and through the non-residence of curates and prelates, and through the promotion of the unworthy and through pluralities of benefices or malefices [sic[3]] or through the disgraceful collation of the scholastic degree and concession of graces to unworthy and vicious and ignorant persons at Oxford and other universities."

"When an Abbey or a College prays for him or for them who appropriated to them a parish church, there is a thing that destroys all things: the multiplication of evils which follow from the evil appropriation of parish churches, is, that is to say, destruction of the good parson and of doctrine and of good counsel, and of example and hospitality, and of supporting the poor and the youth at the University" (*studium*—or "at study" simply).

Yet Gascoigne will have an exception made in the case of churches that have been made collegiate, that is, he says, so that certain good persons shall remain founded in them, and do their duties in the same parish, thus made collegiate. There had been a number of such colleges founded by great men of the fourteenth century. Such was the college founded at Houghton-le-Spring[4]

[1] *Loci e Libro Veritatum*, ed. J. E. T. Rogers, p. 3.
[2] *I.e.* the harvest moon. [3] *maleficia*.
[4] *Cal. Pap. Pet.* I, p. 25.

in the diocese of Durham in 1343 in the fat parish church which had previously been collated when void by bishops at the instance of kings and queens of England to courtiers, insufficient and light persons, who turned the income to lascivious and profane uses. The need of lettered men in those parts was pleaded as the chief reason for this college, which was to consist of a rector and four other prebendaries, while there was also to be a perpetual vicarage worth 70 marks. Gascoigne excuses this sort of appropriation, but not the appropriation of churches to colleges founded elsewhere. The king's free chapels at Hastings and Windsor were in the same position as other appropriators, being also absentee rectors. So when Sir Walter de Manny[1] founded a collegiate chapel, he sought and obtained Papal permission to appropriate three benefices to it to the value of £100. Gascoigne does not excuse this. He goes on to relate that chronicles and histories tell that Pope Martin V used the superfluities of monasteries to endow the college of students founded at Pavia, and says that there is a sacred need to appropriate the superfluities of monasteries and great colleges and cathedrals to parish churches and their immediate cures, in which, for diverse reasons, men and souls perish. If anyone founds a college in increase of knowledge, virtue and teaching or of religious devotion, let him see that it is well endowed in necessaries, without the need of appropriations. Here Gascoigne lays his finger on the root of much of the evil, for too often laymen set out to found monasteries or colleges on insufficient means and eked these out with appropriated churches. Very seldom after the beginning of the thirteenth century was any such foundation made without the incorporation of churches, and there is a frequent plea that "the house was meagrely endowed from the beginning". Bishop Pecock[2], about 1449, considered it necessary to stress the need of ample endowments to all new convents and colleges, more, in fact, than was necessary to their original needs, if they were to be kept from beggary. He assumes that the property of such corporate bodies must deteriorate, or else that the needs of the corporations must grow beyond the capacity of the original endowments.

[1] *Cal. Pap. Let.* III, p. 396.
[2] *Repressor* (R.S.), II, pp. 345–7.

The evil of appropriations, says Gascoigne, was the cause of the destruction of the kingdom of Bohemia[1], for, though the University of Prague wrote to Martin V on this subject and on that of non-residence, no remedy was forthcoming, and the Hussite wars followed. While this theory of the cause of these wars is rather too simple to meet with complete scientific approval, these evils must undoubtedly have set many men criticising the whole rotten condition of Church government.

If monks prayed for men's souls, did not also the parsons who, beyond this, worked for the people and among them, and brought to them the things necessary for salvation "and to the parsons are the tithes and oblations due by reason and by law"[2]. The system is "the fourth River of Babylon, and of confusion, destroying the salvation of souls and many good works"[3], and from it follow many and great evils, "the destruction of the clergy and the want of students, and the lack of clerks busying themselves directly with the cure of souls: the silence and oblivion of God's word, through defect of preachers and instruction". Gascoigne would prefer the monks to do good to him than for him, to feed him when hungry, rather than feed another in his name or for love of him. The priest and parson do more good to the parishioners and in their presence, by word and example, than the monks do for them by their prayers[4].

> Many and innumerable are the souls which are damned eternally, and which would have been saved if they had had good rectors and the other good works aforesaid, which, through such miserable appropriation of churches, are omitted and lost, and thus the good works omitted through such appropriation among so many parsons and parishioners are probably more, in sum, than the good done or destined to be done by the score or two of Religious to whom these churches are appropriated[5].

The lay lords are deceived, thinking it better to have several sustained by the goods of a church than to have one proud rector living where he pleases[6]. They do not, however, consider that one does not solve difficulties by multiplying them. In fact, Gascoigne[7] had known a rector who possessed his church

[1] *Loci e Libro Veritatum*, ed J. E. T. Rogers, p. 5.
[2] *Ibid.* p. 21.
[3] *Ibid.* p. 70.
[4] *Ibid.* p. 113.
[5] Translation by Dr Coulton in *Hist. Teach. Misc.* IV, p. 5.
[6] *Loci e Libro Veritatum*, ed. J. E. T. Rogers, p. 148.
[7] *Ibid.* p. 112.

sole, who kept 20 young men at school and University, and made them priests. It must be feared that this was a most exceptional case, and that secular rectors very seldom showed any signs of this magnificent generosity. The monks themselves were required to send some of their number to the Universities, but this only formed an extra excuse for appropriation. Benedict XII in 1336 prescribed that all the larger monasteries should keep at least one of their monks at the University. As early as 1343 the Benedictine General Council[1] in England voted

a new tribute, to wit, one halfpenny in the pound, for sending messengers to the Roman Court, in order to appropriate some churches, if it may be done principally for the pension of the scholars, and secondarily, for other matters concerning Chapter business, to wit, for litigation against the prior of Canterbury and others who disdain to come to Chapter meetings.

On this pretext in 1349, St Albans appropriated Appelton, to keep five monks "at study", at a cost of £10 a year. The living was worth £46. 13*s*. 4*d*. which would just about cover the cost if the monks were actually allowed £10 each, a matter of grave doubt. In 1391 St Peter's Abbey, Gloucester[2], gained the appropriation of Chipping Norton (dioc. Lincoln), to help support three or four monks at Oxford or some other University, and to furnish each of them with 15 marks a year according to their statutes. The church was valued not exceeding 70 marks.

Another complaint made by Gascoigne is that recently, in the time of Martin V or of Pope Eugenius, an English bishop obtained a bull allowing him to have with him as chaplains either religious or rectors, or vicars. Hence it came to pass that vicars were absent as episcopal chaplains, idling in luxury and hunting with birds and dogs. It had been customary to grant permission for non-residence for a long time for bishop's chaplains, provided that suitable vicars were appointed and the cure of souls in no wise neglected. Such a permission was granted to the bishop of Exeter[3] about 1405. Gascoigne was scandalised that vicars themselves were thus granted permission for non-

[1] C. Reynerus' *Apostolatus Benedictinorum in Anglia*, 1626, app. p. 107 (transl. by G. G. Coulton in *Hist. Teach. Misc.* IV, p. 41).

[2] *Cal. Pap. Let.* V, p. 599.

[3] *Reg. Stafford*, p. 22.

residence[1]. In 1439 Thomas Cumpton, perpetual vicar of Chew Magna or Episcopi, in Somerset, a continual commensal chaplain of John, bishop of Bath and Wells, received Papal licence to let to farm or yearly pension the fruits of his vicarage and other benefices. This was for not only while he was in the bishop's service, but until seven years after his ceasing to be the bishop's chaplain, so that he could study at a University and not be bound to reside in any of his benefices. It is rarely, indeed, that one comes across such faculties to dispense for non-residence as that allowed to the bishop of Norwich in 1317, when he was permitted to dispense four perpetual vicars of his diocese to pursue their studies at a university for three years. The vicar was most essentially a resident, and it was more scandalous to have non-resident vicars following the bishop about than rectors. Papal licences for monasteries to have amovable vicars also came under Gascoigne's condemnation[2].

Sometimes the vicars of pluralists were made to swear before admission, by a legally binding oath, that they would pay to the rectors 20 marks or more. Bishop Philip Morgan of Ely would never admit anyone to a church before he had sworn that he had taken no such oath. He also made vicars swear that they had taken no oath not to plead against their monastic rectors for augmentation of their vicarages. "Therefore blessed be his soul, because he was the cause of vicarages being better endowed and augmented." This practice of exacting an oath from presentees appears to have been fairly common, and probably partly explains why there was no immediate rush for augmentation of vicarages after the Black Death. In 1278 William de Draycote, on obtaining the vicarage of Crich, promised *in verbo veritatis et sacerdocii* not to sue for augmentation[3]. A vicar of Selborne[4], having received an augmentation in 1272, was obliged to covenant never again to ask for augmentation. The rector of Eyton[5], in Shropshire, had been degraded from his rectory in 1327 and obliged to take an oath to pay two-thirds of his income to Polesworth Abbey. Finding that his income was not enough, he then obtained Papal annulment of the oath.

[1] *Loci e Libro Veritatum*, ed. J. E. T. Rogers, p. 173.
[2] *Ibid.* p. 132.
[3] MS. Cott. Titus CIX, fol. 47 *b*.
[4] *Selborne Charters*, I, p. 65.
[5] *Cal. Pap. Let.* II, p. 271.

The vicar of South Cerney, in Gloucestershire, in 1370 obtained Papal permission for a suit for augmentation to be heard by the bishop of Worcester, although he had taken an oath not to proceed against Gloucester Abbey for augmentation[1]. The vicar of Chalgrove, in Oxfordshire, said he was in danger from his rectors, the Cistercian abbot and convent of Thame, and that he was under an oath not to apply for augmentation. This oath was relaxed by the Pope in 1392 to enable the suit to proceed. In 1425 an inquiry was made into the alleged irregularities in Wigmore Abbey[2], and the abbot in his evidence said that he presented freely to all benefices but each one that was presented was bound in a certain sum of money not to proceed against the abbey for the augmentation of his benefice. Questioned further, he said that no one was admitted unless he was first bound in a sum of £20 or £40, and that this was of old custom. Walter Bacster, the *camerarius*, alleged definite simony, namely 8 marks from the vicar of Wigmore, 40*s*. from the vicar of Stanton, 4 marks from the vicar of Bishop's Castle, and 26*s*. 8*d*. from the vicar of Niensavage.

Gascoigne alleged that appropriations were sometimes matters of sheer bargaining, as when the Cistercians of Jervaulx gave £40 worth of their lands to an Earl and his heirs for the appropriation of the church of Haghkarth, worth £100 yearly, and when the monks of York gave a manor for the church at Ormshead[3]. Moreover, in the monasteries themselves "spiritual goods were often not increased, but rather superfluous or unnecessary ornaments or gluttonous dishes and vicious irregularities; and, if we destroyed the appropriations, the cause of these evils in many places would be destroyed....From such men shall the Lord take away the goods which they misuse". The monastic records themselves justify these remarks in substance, although the tone of them is rather intemperate. Dr Coulton has culled several such justifying remarks from the chronicles of St Albans showing how Abbot John I (1195–1214) was able to boast: "I have charitably given the church of St Stephen in this town for the kitchen of this community, which I have always

[1] *Cal. Pap. Let.* IV, pp. 85, 430.
[2] *Reg. Spofford*, p. 64.
[3] *Loci e Libro Veritatum*, ed. J. E. T. Rogers, p. 5.

embraced in the bowels of spiritual love, and shall embrace so long as I live, and in death".

Under his successor, William (1214–35): "Richard de Marisco, Bishop of Durham, gave us the church of Eglingham for the improvement of our beer".

The next abbot, John II (1235–60), assigned the church of Norton "for the amelioration of our beer, and for giving provision for the guests beyond what the abbot was wont to distribute"[1].

To these examples may be added one from the chronicle of Gloucester Abbey, to which William Rufus[2], thinking himself dying, had given the church of St Gundley of Newport. In 1231 Henry Foliot[3], the abbot, assigned 20 marks yearly of the church "for *caritates* of the convent of French wine". This was a very large sum for that purpose, and the sick of the convent could not have consumed so large a quantity. The *caritas* was a "charitable" allowance of liquor to a monk in consideration of the weakness of his stomach and was an institution strongly condemned by St Bernard.

About 1400 the abbot of Glastonbury[4] earmarked £30 a year partly from the "appropriation of a parish church for giving to each monk an allowance of private pocket money" which was even, in the strict sense, illegal.

Similarly on the Continent, at Rachen, in 1218, two churches were set aside for refectory expenses. At Limburg in 1279 a portion of parochial endowments went to increase the monks' allowances.

In 1319 the Premonstratensians of Mondaye[5] appropriated the vicarage of Juaye—the rectory having been in their hands for a century—and were allowed to apply its revenues for pittances[6] for the canons, lay brethren, servants and guests. The canon vicar was allowed to keep the *casualia* or occasional offerings, but the fruits for the pittances he was bound to give at due time to the cellarer, without keeping back anything or yielding any of them to anyone else. He was under obligation

1 In *Hist. Teach. Misc.* IV, p. 21.
2 *Hist. and Cart. Gloucs.* (R.S.), I, p. 102.
3 *Ibid.* p. 28.
4 *Hist. Teach. Misc.* IV, p. 23.
5 G. Madelaine, *L'Abbaye de Mondaye*, p. 138.
6 Pittance = extra allowance of food and drink.

to give an account to the abbot and convent at least once every year.

More laudable was the use of the small tithes of Sprimont[1] as early as 1127, of which the monks of Stavelot-Malmédy, it is true, received 4*d.* for fish and 3*d.* for wine on the feast of St Matthew, but on Maundy Thursday 100 poor people were to receive a penny each, besides wine and food.

As against this may be quoted the case of Charlbury, appropriated to Eynsham Abbey[2], where, in 1296, of the appropriated revenues, "near 40 per cent. went to the monks' creature comforts and little more than 10 per cent. to the actual poor". Even in the Sprimont case we must remember that it was only the small tithes that were given mainly to the poor.

As if it were not enough that the goods of the churches should be wasted on gluttony, continues Gascoigne, one appropriation leads on to another[3]. Mismanagement causes the parish revenues to fall from their ancient value, and soon the monks begin to labour to appropriate another church, pretending poverty, and so "deep calls deep". Indeed, as early as 1253, the order of Sempringham[4] had had 32 churches confirmed to it by Papal bull. Ely Priory[5] in 1276 had 18 churches confirmed to it *in proprios usus* by the archbishop of Canterbury. St Mary's Abbey, York[6], in 1396, had at least 14 churches in the diocese of York alone, and pensions in about 42 vicarages, churches and chapels in the diocese.

Then, going on to speak of the evil effects of monastic exemptions or privileges, he says: "It is known that many infants die without baptism because the parish churches have no fonts and diverse abbeys have licence and custom that all people of certain parishes shall be baptized in their monasteries, and yet they cannot in the night, or at other times, suitably gain access to the font there".

A most notorious instance of this is found at Sherborne[7], where the parishioners set up a font in the chapel of Allhallows

1 *Recueil des Chartes de...Stavelot-Malmédy*, I, p. 533.
2 *Eynsham Chart.* I, p. 340; *Hist. Teach. Misc.* IV, p. 22.
3 *Loci e Libro Veritatum*, ed. J. E. T. Rogers, p. 115.
4 *Cal. Pap. Let.* I, p. 284.
5 *Ely Dioc. Rem.* 1901, p. 123.
6 *Cal. Pap. Let.* V, p. 2.
7 Coulton, in *Hist. Teach. Misc.* IV, p. 94.

in defiance of monastic rights and a riot resulted in which the monastic mother-church was burned and defaced. Similarly annoying was the privilege of Pershore[1] in 1280, by which all the inhabitants from 35 parishes round must be buried either at Pershore or at Little Cumbrington. With regard to burial privileges, the vicar and parishioners of St Helen's at Abingdon[2] took matters into their own hands and made a new cemetery for themselves there, without permission of the abbey of Abingdon which had the right of burying all the parishioners in its cemetery and of taking the funeral oblations for itself. Consequently the disputants took the case to the Roman Curia, and the vicar was condemned in 1396 in costs to the amount of 60 gold florins of the camera, and the parishioners in 40. All the bodies, save two specially exempted for some reason or other, were to be exhumed from the new cemetery and reburied in the monastic cemetery, satisfaction being made to the abbey in respect of candles, mortuaries and other emoluments. The prior of Leominster[3], in 1276, had even to be forbidden to lock the doors of the church, which was both conventual and parochial, and prevent access for parochial uses, as had been done to the discouragement of reverence and devotion, and to the danger of those who came for sanctuary there. In 1397 the vicar and parishioners there were accused of aggressive acts towards the priory concerning matters of ceremony, such as new altars and the use of the amice[4]. In 1401 the parishioners of Winchcombe[5] were even forbidden to ring the church bells between curfew and prime "without evident necessity", so that the monastery should not be disturbed. These are only a few examples of the special privileges possessed by the monasteries at the expense of the parishes, mainly for financial reasons, for these restrictions on the parishioners, sometimes petty, sometimes exceedingly troublesome, resulted from a general tendency to regard everything, even the baptising of infants, primarily as a source of gain. These rights were of such value and were so often being attacked by harassed vicars and parishioners that there are cases where abbeys kept lawyers continually

[1] Dugdale-Caley, *Monasticon*, II, p. 420.
[2] *Cal. Pap. Let.* v, p. 5.
[3] *Reg. Thos. de Cantilupe*, p. 46.
[4] *Reg. Trefnant*, p. 140.
[5] *Cal. Pap. Let.* v, p. 439.

at Rome to defend them. Gascoigne[1] relates how, recently, a certain prior, having 16 churches appropriated to his house, kept a certain lawyer to defend it in the bishop's court, paying him a large annual pension and granting him the right of presentation to the churches. Consequently the parishioners and vicars could get no justice and were forced to have recourse to the law of the realm. This may be supported by the evidence of how the abbot of Gloucester, Walter Froucestre, soon after 1381, kept one William Bryt at Rome and so secured the appropriation of Holy Trinity, Gloucester, and other churches.

So, with "Heu! Heu!" and "Vae illis" and similarly impotent expressions of hopelessness, Gascoigne runs through the catalogue of evils that moralists had already been complaining of for two centuries and more. Had not Cardinal Humbert de Romans[2] in 1274 said that a vicar was a man "who would do a vicar's work at the lowest price"? Had not Archbishop Peckham[3] in 1285 complained to the mother house of Cluny: "We have passed the flower of youth and already are attaining to old age, and on careful retrospection we can hardly remember that, to the present day, we ever saw a man presented by the Prior and College of Lewes to the rule of souls in due sincerity".

In the same vein Bishop Guillaume Durand of Mende[4] in 1311 had complained to the Council of Vienne that in the churches of exempt religious there was a general lack of vestments and ministers and ornaments.

With similar complaints, as has been seen, the Commons under Richard II secured the passing of the Statute of Appropriations into law. In 1402 their successors[5] complained that this Statute had been broken, especially by the appropriation of the vicarages of the already appropriated churches. Now the cures were served by monks or canons regular or mercenary removable chaplains, incapable of giving the necessary alms. They therefore asked that every appropriated church should be bound to have its perpetual vicarage, notwithstanding indulgences or privilege of the kings of England or of persons of Holy

[1] *Loci e Libro Veritatum*, ed. J. E. T. Rogers, p. 147.
[2] Mansi, *Concilia*, XXIV, col. 131.
[3] *Reg. Peckham* (R.S.), III, pp. 902 *seq.*
[4] Coulton, in *Hist. Teach. Misc.* IV, p. 2.
[5] *Rot. Parl.* III, p. 499 *b*.

Church. The king replied that he wished the Statute of Appropriations to be firmly held and kept, and put in due execution, and that if any appropriations had been made by licence of King Richard or of the present king contrary to the Statute, they should be reformed by next Easter. If such reformation was not made the appropriations should be null and void, excepting only the church of Haddenham, in the diocese of Ely, which the king had allowed to be appropriated to the archdeacon of Ely. Henceforth there should be in every appropriated church a vicar, perpetual and canonically instituted, and suitably endowed by the discretion of the Ordinary and that no religious be henceforth made vicar. The general visitation of Premonstratensian houses in 1478 shows that, even if this Act had any temporary local effect (which may be doubted) it certainly did not have lasting effect. (See table on p. 173.)

The very next year after the Act was made, in fact, the Commons complained[1] that it was not kept, and the king only answered "let the statutes made on this point be kept and maintained". In 1432[2] Parliament rehearsed the same old grievances and asked that a penalty be attached to the Statute of Appropriations. Appropriators had allowed vicarages to lie void for many years whereby "old men and women had died unconfessed or without other Sacraments of Holy Church, and children have died unbaptised, and thereby many mischiefs and inconveniences have come to pass day by day, to the great dishonour of Holy Church". The Commons asked that if any vicarage were left vacant more than six months, the appropriation should be annulled. Henry VI, however, dared not affront the Church in this manner, and so endorsed the petition with the formal refusal "Le Roy s'advisera".

Archbishop Chichele[3] in 1439 remarked on the poverty of some vicarages and the difficulty that the vicars experienced in trying to procure augmentation. To relieve them, he ordered the Ordinaries to allow them to sue *in forma pauperis* and to see that they had endowments worth 12 marks, if the whole Church amounted to as much. This increased sum marks no real advance, only the depreciation of the coinage since the time of

[1] *Rot. Parl.* III, p. 542.
[2] *Ibid.* IV, p. 404.
[3] Wilkins, *Concilia*, III, p. 535.

the Council of Oxford. Nor does the Scottish rule[1] of 1549, that every curate or vicar pensioner residing and having cure of souls should have 20 marks Scots or its equivalent, the garden and fields adjoining the manse being included in the estimate.

In 1493 a Statute of the cathedral church of St David's[2] was made on the subject of appropriation, which declared that henceforth no appropriation should take effect without the assent of the chapter, six constituting a quorum. This was, in fact, going no further than the letter of definition sent by Innocent III to the bishop of Ely in 1204. The need for it reveals an exceedingly backward condition of the diocese. The preamble is very interesting as adding another to the numerous complaints of its kind:

> Seeing that by the debt of our pastoral office, and the zeal of our fatherly compassion we are bound to assist the necessities of our subjects, and seeing that for the nourishing of the children, without difficulty, there must be sufficient bread for the sustenance not only of their bodily but also of their spiritual food, according to the determinate ordinance of right in that behalf; and in order that such bread be not filched from our sons in future by mercenary persons as in the days that are passed it had been taken away everywhere in this our diocese; for this case we, weighing the so numerous appropriations and unions of benefices or churches of our diocese made in disregard of order of right by our predecessors before these times whereby the sustenance of the sowers of the Divine Word is taken away and want evidently increases every day among our subjects to the detriment not only of our cathedral church but also of our whole diocese of St David's, and fearing therefore very deeply such ruin of our subjects and poverty of the clergy in our aforesaid church of St David's, with the common assent and consent of our chapter of St David's aforesaid, decree, grant and ordain....

As the fatal day of the Reformation drew near the consciences of many began to prick them on this matter, and in 1529 several bishops exhibited bills in Convocation for the reformation of abuses in appropriated parish churches. In the following session the prolocutor[3] suggested that a constitution should be made about the appropriation of churches and about augmentations of vicars, and on March 16th, 1530, the archbishop discussed with the bishops dissolving some such appropriations and

[1] *Statutes of the Scottish Church*, p. 112.

[2] *Reg. St David's*, p. 661.

[3] Kennett, *Impropriations*, p. 117.

augmenting vicarages. These things, however, came to naught, and the bishops soon had matters of greater weight to occupy their minds.

At the same time the clergy in Convocation had complained about statutes limiting the practice of "farming" appropriated rectories, that is, of letting them out at a yearly rent. Their objection was that this practice had helped the poor vicars, who sometimes were the farmers of the rectories and made profits in this way to relieve their poverty. The practice arose from the difficulty of collecting and using tithes from distant parishes, and was early allowed to French monasteries for their English rectories. An instance is found at Fen Drayton[1] in the diocese of Ely in the time of Richard I when the abbot of Bon Repos farmed the church to the abbot of St Sergius in the diocese of Angers and its daughter house of Swavesey (dioc. Ely). Clearly the expense of collecting tithes at that distance must have taken most of the profits, and both the Cistercians of Bon Repos and the priory of Swavesey profited by this. In the sixth year of Edward I the abbey of Sawtre in Huntingdonshire farmed this church and three others from the abbot of Bon Repos. These two abbeys, incidentally, tried by collusion to avoid the difficulties experienced by the churches of aliens in England, but failed, the church being confiscated under the Act of 1414, and later granted to Christ's College, Cambridge. Similarly, in 1304 the church of Kirtlington[2] (dioc. Lincoln) was farmed by the Cistercians of Aulney (dioc. Bayeux) to Bicester Priory for a yearly rent of 40*s*. The church of Magor, in the diocese of Llandaff in 1239, had been granted to the abbey of Sta Maria de Gloria, Anagni, and was leased by that house to Tintern Abbey. John XXIII[3] confirmed a cession of the rectory made by the Anagni house to Tintern Abbey, whereby the laws about aliens and their possessions were evaded. In the time of Bishop Sutton of Lincoln a rector leased his church of Kirkby Mallory[4] to Leicester Abbey on condition that the farm should be given up if the bishop disapproved, but neither side saw fit to ascertain

[1] Mr H. Curtois, in *Christ's Coll. Mag.* no. 105, pp. 59, 62.
[2] Kennett, *Paroch. Antiquities*, I, p. 497; *Cal. Pap. Let.* I, p. 183.
[3] *Ibid.* IX, p. 266.
[4] Sister Elspeth of the Community of All Saints', in *Vic. County Hist.* (*Leics.*), I, p. 360, n. 43.

the bishop's opinion for four years after the agreement was made. Boniface IX would not withdraw permission to farm granted to Michelhouse, Cambridge[1], although Bishop Fordham of Ely particularly asked him to do so.

The Norman monastery of St Evroul[2] in 1257 farmed two-thirds of the tithes of the parish church of Boserinoult for two sextaries of corn, six of manure, and six of hay, yearly to the "rector" of the church. In 1266 the abbey farmed to Master Gerard of Marcheville, canon of Chartres, and rector of Montlissent, all the portions and tithes that it possessed in the vill and parish of Montlissent for £25 of the money of the place, as former farmers held them. In 1254 Peter de Lauda had accepted the farm of the rectory of the same church for £16 of Tours.

Papal licences to farm became common in the fourteenth century. In 1398 New College, Oxford[3], having hitherto been allowed to farm their churches for ten years at a time, obtained from the Pope, by intercession of the bishop of Winchester, permission to do so for as long a period as they pleased in spite of local legatine and provincial constitutions to the contrary[3]. King's Hall, Cambridge[4], in 1428, obtained licence to farm benefices even to laymen, provided that such renting did not extend to a fee or otherwise to alienation. Eynsham Abbey[5] in 1397 obtained an indult to farm to clerks or laymen, but not perpetually, any of their manors, pensions, stipends, portions, churches, chapels or other possessions, without requiring licence of the ordinaries. Similar permission and exemption was granted to Dunstable Priory[6] in 1426, setting, however, a limit of seven years to such leases[7].

Even vicars occasionally gained similar permission. In 1311 the vicar of Haltwistle[8], in the diocese of Durham, was allowed

[1] *Ely Dioc. Rem.* 1901, p. 123.

[2] Paris, MS. lat. 11056, fol. 82, col. 2, 148; col. 1, 146.

[3] *Cal. Pap. Let.* v, p. 87.

[4] *Ibid.* VIII, p. 21; VI, p. 393, for Selby Abbey 1412; IX, p. 351, for St Osyth's Abbey, London, in 1443.

[5] *Ibid.* v, p. 13.

[6] *Ibid.* VII, p. 436.

[7] For further examples see Coulton in *Hist. Teach. Misc.* IV, pp. 95, 96. For an interesting indenture in English concerning the farm of the church of Yeovil see Madox, *Formulare Anglic.* p. 149.

[8] *Reg. Pal. Dunelm.* I, p. 95.

by the bishop to farm his vicarage for one year to pay for his redemption from captivity by the Scots. The vicar of Middlezoy (Sowy)[1] in Bath and Wells in 1397 was John Preston and he was licensed by Papal letters to take and let, even to laymen, for ten years the fruits of his benefices, while he either resided in one of them, or studied letters at a University, or engaged in the service of his rectors, Glastonbury Abbey. At Aycliffe (co. Durham), in 1435, the vicar was in his sixty-sixth year and was almost continually ill[2]. The Pope allowed him to farm to any fit persons, even laymen, provided that a good and sufficient sub-vicarage was appointed.

As early as 1412 parishioners of the diocese of Norwich[3] protested to Pope John XXIII against permissions granted to appropriators to farm their churches to laymen without consent of the diocesan. These laymen, it was said, took the obventions of the altar, lorded it over the clerks and persons deputed to the sacred functions, dilapidated the rectories and committed very many excesses, whereby the devotion of parishioners had grown feeble, divine worship was diminished, and very many other evils had resulted. Consequently the bishop was ordered to cite such religious and laymen and take any measures that seemed suitable to him.

The *Valor Ecclesiasticus*, the great assessment of church property made by Henry VIII's order in 1535, reveals how exceedingly general the practice had become by then. Professor Savine[4] takes the following examples:

Markby Priory	5½	churches	of which	2	were farmed
Peterborough Abbey	6	,,	,,	5	,,
Shaftesbury Abbey	2	,,	,,	2	,,
Hartland Abbey	7	,,	,,	5[5]	,,
Cirencester Abbey	11	,,	,,	11	,,
Tewkesbury Abbey	16	,,	,,	15	,,

As Professor Savine[6] points out, this made the transition of monastic property to lay hands very easy, for farmers after the dissolution simply petitioned the Augmentation Court to renew

[1] *Cal. Pap. Let.* v, p. 124. There are several other licences of this kind on the same page and the two or three following.

[2] *Ibid.* VIII, p. 533.

[3] *Ibid.* VI, p. 310.

[4] A. Savine, *English Monast. at Dissolution*, p. 112.

[5] Two at the will of the monastery and three for years.

[6] Savine, *English Monast. at Dissolution*, p. 113.

their leases, or offered to buy the rectory, and the government was only too willing to accept such an easy solution of difficulties.

The *Valor* has been analysed by the Rev. E. L. Cutts[1] in the same careful way as the *Taxatio* of Pope Nicholas, and it affords a remarkable comparison between the number of vicarages in 1291 and 1535. A steady increase all round is noticed, and the number of appropriated churches had now reached more than one-third of the total, when it was stereotyped by the dissolution of the monasteries. Cutts' table is here reproduced without having been checked, a gigantic operation for which I have been unable to find time. The large proportion of vicarages in the northern dioceses and in Wales is only what might reasonably have been expected from the greater hardships of life there, and from the less severe discipline that accompanied these hardships. The figures are very much more reliable than those of the *Taxatio*, since the survey was much more thorough:

Dioceses	Rectories	Vicarages	Chapels	Chantries
Canterbury	225	108	13	23
Rochester	128	56	10	13
Bath and Wells	368	126	33	53
Chichester	279	124	13	39
London	731	201	31	310
Winchester	289	95	21	14
Salisbury	540	182	68	72
Oxford	167	64	8	10
Lincoln	1310	492	30	213
Peterborough	355	92	10	30
Exeter	524	185	43	36
Gloucester	246	106	35	30
Hereford	152	84	27	57
Coventry and Lichfield	466	207	29	106
Chester	197	78	5	127
Worcester	133	47	17	31
Norwich	1103	276	31	60
Ely	157	80	11	29
Llandaff	143	61	22	12
St David's	288	120	10	3
Bangor	110	27	45	4
St Asaph	157	83	4	0
York	581	305	19	424
Carlisle	75	38	0	19
Durham	114	70	1	18
	8838	3307	536	1733

By 1500 on the Continent complaints of abuses of the parochial system were more emphatic than ever, especially in

[1] E. L. Cutts, *Parish Priests*, p. 394.

Germany where the Reformation was brewing. Representatives of the German nation presented 100 complaints to the Emperor at the Diet of Nürnberg in 1522–3. One of these (No. 28) concerned pluralists who took pensions and proceeds of parish churches to convert to their own dishonourable and offensive uses, neglecting the cure. The complainants prayed that henceforth no one should be appointed to a benefice who was not suitable in doctrine, age and morals, who did not live an honourable life suitable to a priest, and was not prepared to administer one cure of souls, instead of several. Another complaint[1] (No. 86) ran as follows:

Moreover, many parish churches are subjected by appropriation[2] (as it is called) or by some other right, to monasteries, prelates and other rectors of churches with cure of souls: and although such [appropriators] are bound by Canon Law to provide themselves for these [churches] yet oftentimes [*plerumque*] when they let them out to be governed by others they keep to themselves the endowment and the tithes of the benefices, and also load and burden them with such enormous pensions of absences [*sic*] that these hired priests and their vicars, vice-parsons, chaplains, coadjutors, and other administrators of such hireling churches, cannot get therefrom a competent sustentation and a decent livelihood. Whereby it cometh to pass (seeing that such hireling and mercenary pastors must have whereby to live) they miserably plunder and ravage, by unlawful exactions, these sheep that are hired out to them, and all but consume all their substance. For inasmuch as the Sacraments of the Eucharist and Baptism are to be administered, or single or weekly or trental or annual Masses to be sung for the dead, auricular confession to be heard and corpses to be buried and other offices which are thought worth while to be observed for the dead, the priests never do this for nothing, but exact, extort, and suck out whatsoever their wretched flocks [*miserae plebeculae*] can afford, even with difficulty and at the utmost personal expense: and they daily increase and accumulate such exactions even to the utmost; moreover, they sometimes compel payment through the thunderbolt of excommunication, and attempt to compel many folk, whose poverty forbids it, to celebrate Masses for the dead, anniversaries, and other ceremonies of that sort.

The truth of these accusations is proved by the 1496 visitation of the diocese of Worms[3]. At the chapel of St Nicholas

[1] Browne, *Fasc. Rerum*, I, pp. 360, 372; transl. by Dr G. G. Coulton in *Hist. Teach. Misc.* IV, p. 6.

[2] *Incorporatio.*

[3] *Zeitschrift...Oberrheins*, XXVII, p. 254.

attached to Dienheim, there were endowments sufficient for two masses a week, but the monks hardly read one mass. In a number of cases where there was a chaplain for the purpose, the masses were neglected, although there were special endowments for them usually provided by the parishioners[1].

Cardinal Campeggio, at Ratisbon[2], issued constitutions reiterating all the rules, concerning the status of vicars and their suitable portions, "since it is better to have a few good and educated ministers than many uneducated ones, and since Bishops ought to surpass each other in being mindful of the poor, according to the customs of the Apostles and the primitive church". Whenever a historian finds such emphatic reiterations of old laws he may very safely assume that they were always being broken.

At the Council of Cardinals[3] held in 1536, it was declared that an abuse had crept in, of conferring benefices subject to a pension, and even of reserving the whole fruits of the benefice so conferred. No such pensions, it was stated, ought to be imposed unless for certain alms and for pious uses and for the poor.

For the income is annexed to the benefice, as the body to the soul: therefore by its nature it belongs to him who has the benefice, that he may be able to live honourably according to his order, and at the same time be able to bear the expenses for divine worship, and for the repair of the sacred buildings of the temple, and may turn what is left to pious uses: for this is the nature of his income. But as in the administration of the nature of things nothing is done by universal nature against the inclination of universal nature: so with the Bishop, who is the universal dispenser of the goods of the Church, if it shall seem that that portion of the fruits which ought to be spent in pious uses, or part of it, should be turned to any other pious use, or that more should be spent thus, that he can do without any doubt. So by worthy law he can impose a pension to help the needy, especially the clerk, that he may be able to lead an honourable life according to his order. Therefore to reserve all the fruits, and take away all that which should be paid for divine worship and the sustentation of him who holds the benefice, is a great abuse. Also that pensions should be given to rich clerks who can live suitably and honourably from the incomes that they have, certainly is a great abuse, and both should be abolished.

[1] See esp. pp. 244, 278, 312, 313–14, 366, 393, 412, 418.
[2] Browne, *Fasc. Rerum*, I, pp. 425 *seq.*
[3] *Ibid.* II, p. 232.

Clearly the Council was mainly considering absentee rectors sole, but the same arguments apply with equal force to the monastic rectors.

These complaints are the clouds attending the breaking of the storm of the Reformation, but that things in England at any rate were not immediately bettered by the Reformation appears forcibly from the tract of about 1542, called *The Complaynt of Roderyck Mors*[1], written by one Henry Brinklow, who had been a Grey Friar before the Dissolution. Brinklow cannot, of course, be regarded as an authoritative writer, nor as unbiassed: he was a reformer with a tendency to idealise some aspects of the past. Yet he confessed the old abuses, pleading in extenuation the worse condition that had followed.

"Your pretence", he says, "of putting down abbeys was to amend that was amysse in them. It was far amys, that a gret part of the lands of the abbeys (which were geuyn to bring up lernyd men, that myght be preachers afterward, to kepe hospitalyte and to gyue almesse to the poore) shuld be spent vpon a fewe supersticyos monkes, which gaue not .XL. pownd in almesse, whan thei shuld have geuen .ij. hundreth. It was amysse, that the monkes shuld have personages in their handys, and deale but the .XX. part thereof to the poore, and preached but ones in a yere to them that payed the tythes of the personages. It was amyse that thei scarsely among .XX. set not one sufficyent vicare to preach for the tythes that thei receyued. But see now how it that was amysse is amended, for all the goodly pretense. It is amended, even as the deuel mendyd his damys legg (as it is in the prouerbe) whan he shuld have set it right, he bracke it quyte in pecys! The monkes gave to lytle almesse, and set vnable parsons many tymes in their benyfyces. But now, where .XX. pownd was geuen yearly to the poore, in moo than an .C. places in Ingland is not one meales meat geuen. This is a fayre amendment. Where thei had always one or other vicar, that eyther preached or hyred some to preach; now is there no vicar at all, but the fermer is vicar and person, all to gether, and onely an old cast away monke or fryre, which can scarsely say his mattens, is hyred for .XX. or .XXX. shillings, meat and drinck; yea in some place, for meate and drinck alone without any wages.

"I knowe, and not I alone, but .XX.M. moo knowe, more than V.C. vycarages and personages, thus well and gospelly serued, after the newe gospel of Ingland."

[1] Brinklow, *Complaynt of Roderyck Mors* (E.E.T.S.), pp. 32 *seq.*

The farmer would say he had hired the parsonages of this or that lord, and the lord would say that it was the king who made him parson though a layman. Surely this was giving to the king and the Parliament the powers which the cardinal bishops gave to the Pope, who though he sent "infinyte thousandes to the deuyl, yet must no man speake agaynst him". The parsons that came in by Act of Parliament are no shepherds but thieves and murderers, for Christ has not sent them.

Brinklow says that the monks relieved many thousands of poor people, and would have done this even more "if thei had not had so many great mennes horses to fede and had not bene ouercharged with such idle gentylmen as were neuer out of the abbyes", and it is quite clear that the endowments of the monasteries set apart for charity went the same way as all the other endowments. Laymen were not likely to be a whit more careful of spiritual duties than the religious had been, and there was certainly a great depression of the parochial clergy. Not until the lawyers, from the later years of Queen Elizabeth onwards, took up the matter of augmentations, did the clergy lift up their heads again. Even then a Commonwealth re-organisation or a Queen Anne's Bounty was absolutely necessary to relieve the worst-endowed. The monks, by alienating tithes from their immediate uses, by farming them, even to laymen, accustomed even the least legal of lay minds to regarding them simply as personal property, without any spiritual significance. Above all, "farming" was responsible for that attitude of mind that made possible the transfer of tithe property to laymen.

APPENDIX A

EXAMPLES OF TWELFTH-CENTURY VICARAGES

THE monastery of St Mary, Newport[1] (co. Bucks.), at a date previous to 1154, received a charter from Bishop Robert de Chesney of Lincoln confirming to them several churches, including Newport, and containing also the provision that they should choose and present to the bishop vicars, to whom they would secure a vicarage therein. Bishop Gilbert Foliot of Hereford, in 1148, appropriated to the sacristy of Gloucester Abbey the church of Great Cowarne[2]. Until the rectory should fall vacant, the sacrist was to receive 15 marks yearly by right of the abbey's parsonage. Then the chaplain or vicar serving there was to have a sufficient and honourable sustentation to the value of 10 marks, all the rest going to the sacrist for the upkeep of the abbey lights and ornaments. Bishop Joscelin of Salisbury (1142–84) instituted the same abbey to the parsonage of Boyton[3] in the county of Wiltshire, the advowson of which parsonage had been granted to the abbey by Helyas Giffard and Walter, his son. They were to receive 40*s*., to encourage the hospitality of their house, from their presentee, who was a vicar but is not expressly called "vicar" in this deed. Presumably the vicar received all the rest of the fruits of the church. When (1217–28) Bishop Richard confirmed this deed he expressly called the incumbent a "vicar". A document of about 1176 shows the appointment of a vicar in a church of which the rectory was held by an absentee. Seffrid, the rector of Bloxham[4] (co. Oxford), granted to Robert of Porchester a "chantry" in the church, and detailed its emoluments, *scilicet altare cum omnibus oblationibus et diversis ad altare pertinentibus et decimam lini cum decimis minutis argenti cum medietate* [*digesarum*], that is to say, "the altarage with all and diverse oblations belonging to the altar and the tithe of flax with small tithes of silver and a half of the...". We know that one Seffrid[5] was archdeacon of Chichester (1176–8) and dean in 1180. Very soon afterwards Bloxham was promised by Henry II to Godstow Abbey after the death of Roger Clifford, its rector, and in the meantime the abbey was to receive 2*s*. pension. Another Godstow vicarage is mentioned at Lamyatt[6], in Somerset, about 1190. About 1180, in all probability, the prior of

[1] J. H. Round, *Cal. Docs. relating to France*, p. 444, no. 123.
[2] *Hist. and Cart. Gloucs.* (R.S.), I, p. 252; *Reg. Cantilupe*, p. 49.
[3] *Hist. and Cart. Gloucs.* (R.S.), I, pp. 208–209.
[4] *Godstow Chart.* (E.E.T.S.), I, p. 226.
[5] *Ibid.* I, p. 227.
[6] *Ibid.* II, pp. 582–3.

Bath granted the *perpetual* vicarage of Corston[1] to one Abel, with the consent of his own clerk Alured, who was to receive from Abel a rent of four besants, and the perpetual vicarage of Carempton with certain money payments to his clerk Walter. In 1181 or 1182 Hugh Pudsey[2], bishop of Durham, founded vicarages in his diocese, in the churches of Kelloe, Grindon, Sockburn, and Bishopton, which were then appropriated to the newly founded Hospital at Sherburn. The proctor of the Hospital was to present suitable and perpetual vicars who should receive all things belonging to their churches save three tithes only, namely, of corn, lambs and wool. The poor (that is, the lepers of the Hospital) were to receive these three tithes for their sustentation, and were not to be answerable to any man for any temporal service for them. The vicarage which the Rev. J. C. Cox[3] claimed to have discovered at Blakesley in Northamptonshire is the result of a mistake that is easily understood. The *Liber Antiquus* of Bishop Hugh de Welles, a book full of vicarage ordination details of very great value, refers to a vicarage ordained there by the late Bishop Robert and recorded in the rolls of his eighth year. The writing at this point is in a later hand, hence the late Bishop Robert was not Robert de Chesney, but Robert Grosseteste[4], as may be verified by reference to his registers printed by the Canterbury and York Society on p. 214, and in the rolls of his eighth year.

The church at Caddington[5], on the demesne of the canons of St Paul's, in 1181, had ten acres free from all secular service and received from the demesne of St Paul the third part of garbs, and served the chapel in the manor court three days a week if the farmer or his senechal wished it and was present. The church of Tillingham on the demesne of the canons had 40 free acres, and received the third part of the tithe of the demesne, both in small and great tithes, and all the tithes of the village. The canons received from Caddington from the clerks, Robert and Robert, 20*s*. and from Tillingham, through the farmers, 1 mark. The church of Chingford, however, we know was not appropriated, and it was not on the demesne. The parson received from the whole village the tithe of garbs only, and the villagers had never paid, nor did they then pay, any small tithes at all. The church of Sutton, in Middlesex, was founded on the canons' demesne, and had 16½ acres of arable land, and one of meadow. It received from the demesne of the canons the third part of all tithes, and from the demesne of the treasurer of Scotland the third part of all tithes, and from two villages all tithes save hay. It paid to the canons 10*s*.

1 *Bath Cart.* II, p. 4.
2 Allan, *Collections relating to Sherburn Hospital*, publ. 1771.
3 *Vic. County Hist.* (*Derbyshire*), II, p. 4; (*Northants.*), II, p. 18.
4 *Reg. Grosseteste*, p. 214.
5 *Domesday of St Paul's* (Camden Soc.), ed. W. H. Hale, 1858, pp. 146 *seq.*

yearly by the hand of the farmer. These details, and those of the other churches mentioned in the survey, are the result of purely local conditions and arrangements. They are totally unsystematic, and only serve to illustrate how utterly confused were the local arrangements about the tithes. They are the result of no theory, and no policy save that of immediate convenience and a deep reverence for customary rights in property.

Professor James Tait[1] refers to the appropriation of St Michael's on Wyre to the monks of Wyresdale between 1193 and 1196, when the archdeacon of Richmond insisted that there should be a definite (*certus*) vicar "with a portion sufficient for his food and clothing". Consequently the monks arranged with a certain chaplain that he should be their chaplain for life in his church of St Michael or find at his own cost another chaplain who should do fealty to the monks. "For this service they granted him land near the church and half a mark of silver yearly for his vicarage (*vicaria*) and for his faithful service." Yet Professor Tait also refers to certain cases where churches seem to have been treated in exactly the same way as those of the *prioratus curati* in France. He mentions Lancaster, Penwortham, Cockerham, Cartmel, Lytham and Ulverston as the Lancashire examples. The monk vicars, it appears, could at any time be removed by the appropriating monastery. The case of Lytham shows that, even where the prior of a cell was admitted to the cure by the ordinary, he could be removed at will by the convent.

On the foundation of Strood Hospital[2], in 1193, it was stated that the Master might present *conversi* (lay brothers) to the vicarages of Aylesford, Halling and St Nicholas of Strood, and to its daughter chapel of St Margaret. These *conversi* were to be free from all ecclesiastical dues save sinodals, which the master, with the bishop's consent, might force them to pay.

Merton Priory[3], in Surrey, held three churches, at least, in which there were constantly vicars before 1200. A perpetual vicar was presented to Sutton in Hampshire between 1186 and 1198 on condition that he paid 20*s*. yearly to the priory and paid the usual fees of the bishop and archdeacon and their officials, and provided all things necessary for church services. During the same period perpetual vicars were presented by the priory to the churches of Lulworth in Dorset, and St Mary's, Guildford, on similar conditions, save that they were to pay 40*s*. each year to the priory. The vicar of Lulworth was to hold the perpetual vicarage "as freely, peacefully and honourably as his predecessors had held it".

When Bishop Hugh of Coventry and Lichfield, between 1186 and

[1] *Vic. County Hist.* (*Lancs.*), II, p. 14.
[2] *Reg. Hethe*, p. 1.
[3] Heales, *Records of Merton Priory*, p. 39.

1199, appropriated the church of Duckmanton[1] in Derbyshire to Welbeck Abbey, it was stipulated that the abbey was to provide an honest chaplain to be presented to the bishop and serve the church. The abbey was to keep the anniversary of the bishop's death.

In 1200 a deed of Bishop Godfrey of Winchester certified the admission of one Simon de Petrager to the perpetual vicarage of Hurstbourne on the presentation of the bishop of Salisbury, on condition that Simon paid a pension of 5 marks yearly to the prebendary of Burbage[2]. Somewhere about the same time (? 1198) Eynsham Abbey[3] was allowed to appropriate the church of Cassington, saving a vicarage of 5 marks in it. Massey, in the diocese of Lincoln, was said to have been ordained by St Hugh, as is stated in Hugh de Welles' records, and several other vicarages are mentioned as having been ordained long since (*exdudum ordinate* or *ordinate ab antiquo*) in Hugh's Rolls and in his *Liber Antiquus*. Swinford Vicarage, however, was ordained by Hugh de Welles, not by St Hugh, as one writer following a misreading of the Rolls has stated.

Lalore's collection of cartularies for the diocese of Troyes show that proper detailed vicarage ordinations were quite common in that diocese in the twelfth century. There is no such evidence available for other parts of France, but wherever evidence does occur, it is of a similar kind and seems to me to show that Troyes was not unique, although it may have been one of the best dioceses in this respect.

In 1143, or a little before, there were appointed several vicarages in the diocese by the bishop. In the churches of the abbey of Montiéramey, Bishop Haton, who had appropriated them to the abbey, made very precise rules concerning the service and the payment of the vicars. Iterius, the rector of Cléry[4], was to receive during his lifetime half of the proceeds of the church, but after his death there should be appointed a priest who should receive the cure of souls from the bishop and answer to the abbey for temporalities. Two-thirds of the whole proceeds of the church were then to belong to them, while the priest, who is not expressly called a vicar, was to receive the other third. The oblations of All Saints' Day, Christmas, and Easter Day, however, were to belong to the abbey, save 12*d.* (*nummos*) on each feast day which belonged to the vicar. If any cultivated or uncultivated land should have been bequeathed to the church, it was to belong specially to the monks, but the priest was to have for himself the fees of weddings, purses (*pere*), churchings and confessions. He was to pay all the customary dues of the church. The church of Faux-Fresnay, which the bishop also appropriated to the abbey, was to belong for the rest of his life to the rector, but, for

[1] Cox, *Notes on the Churches of Derbyshire*, I, p. 379.
[2] *Reg. St Osmund* (R.S.), I, p. 240.
[3] *Eynsham Chart.* I, p. 47.
[4] E. L. Cutts, *Parish Priests*, p. 101.

their investiture of the church, the monks were to receive 5*s*. a year and 12*d*. in each of the feasts of All Saints, Christmas, Easter, Whitsun and the dedication of the church. After the death or translation of the rector, similar arrangements were to prevail as in the case of the other church[1]. The same bishop gave to the abbey of St Loup the churches of Auzon and Longsols[2], which could either be served by secular priests or by canons, who were to be presented to the bishop for institution. These vicars were to answer to the bishop for procurations and sinodals, but otherwise were to be free from all kind of exaction. These dues amounted to 8*d*. twice a year, save in the third year when it was 2*s*., in the name of these dues. In another document by which Haton conceded to St Loup the church and tithe of Lusigny[3], he made similar arrangements as in the case of the churches, Auzon and Longsols. The "chaplain" was to answer for procurations and sinodals, to the extent of 8*d*. three times a year, save in the third year when he was to pay 5*s*.

In 1175 Bishop Mathieu[4] set out the details of the division of the church of St Nicolas of Nogent-sur-Seine between the abbey of Montier-la-Celle, the rectors, and the incumbent. (Apart from the document of 991 the word *vicarius* is not found in these examples, its place being supplied by *presbiter*, *sacerdos* or *capellanus* or even *persona*.) The oblations received by the priest in his masses and in tithes were to be divided, one-third to the monks and two-thirds to the priest. The monks were to receive two-thirds of all candles, but the priest all confessional and marriage fees. The sinodals and *circade* (cathedral dues) were to be paid from the small tithes, and whatever was left over was to be divided equally between rectors and priest. These regulations were to hold equally of the chapel of St Patroclus of the mother church of St Nicholas.

About 1185 Bishop Manasses[5] found the task of dividing the portions too involved for him, and so gave up trying to deal with one or two minor points about the churches of Puellemontier and Brienne-la-Vieille, belonging to the monks of Montiérender. The monks claimed all candles in all masses at Puellemontier, but the priest negatived this claim; also they claimed all kinds of oblations of anniversaries and absolutions "which had been translated from Sunday to Monday". In the church of Brienne-la-Vieille they claimed two parts of the Sunday offerings, but the priest said they should only receive a half, while he himself ought to receive a half of the legacies of the church. Also there were difficulties about offerings at churchings and marriages and baptisms. All these things the bishop left to the discretion of his successors, a timid proceeding which

[1] Lalore, *Cartulaires du diocèse de Troyes*, VII, p. 60.
[2] *Ibid.* I, p. 23.
[3] *Ibid.* I, p. 25.
[4] *Ibid.* VI, p. 274.
[5] *Ibid.* IV, p. 215.

probably left the victory in the hands of the monastery which, after all, had the *force majeure*. Obviously these disputes were about details that could not be cleared up on the general ordination of the vicarages of the abbey a little before in the same year. It had been decreed about the church of Puellemontier—

in the church of Puellemontier, you shall have the presentation of the priest. The whole benefice in general masses is yours, save Christmas, when the priest shall have 12*d*. at Easter 12*d*. at Whitsun 4*d*. at All Saints' 12*d*. On the feast of St Nicholas at Droyes, the whole benefice is for the expenses of the clerks. On the feast of All Souls the clerks have a heaping measure of wheat between Droyes and Puellemontier [*i.e.*, I imagine, between all the clerks whether they were attached to the chapel of Droyes or the mother church of Puellemontier]. Be it known concerning marriages that on the morrow of the marriage the oblation of husband and wife, and suit (*secta*) is yours. In small tithes the priest shall have 3 little pigs, 3 geese, 40 measures (*massas*) of hemp, the rest is yours. In great tithe the priest shall have one measure (*modium*) of corn and one of hay. On the day of Purification all the oblation is yours. On Sundays the priest has a penny and a candle of holy bread. Baptismal and confessional offerings and offertory wine are the priest's. On the feast of All Saints, you owe 2*s*. for the custom of the church. You owe vinage on the day after Christmas and at Easter, and incense in the annual feasts. Purses (*pere*), the oblations of pilgrims and reconciliations of brawlers (*pugilum*) and women are the priest's, but the suit (*secta*) is yours[1].

The striking thing about this most interesting ordination is its complicated nature, and the idea of it seems to have been to supply the priest with some of each of the profits in kind for his own personal use, rather than to assign certain things to him which he could sell in order to supply himself with a monetary income. The hay is included in the great tithe, this being one of those rare instances that lend some colour of justification to the tendency of post-medieval lawyers to include them. Similarly elaborate ordinations are set out in full for the churches of Rosnay, Braux-le-Comte, Braux-le-Saint-Père, Aulnay, Joncreuil, and other places owned by the abbey. In the ordination of Aulnay not only is hay included in the great tithe, but also rye and manure. There the "customs" were to be paid in common by the rectors and the parish priest, as also at Ville-sur-Terre, Rances, and at Braux-le-Comte. If the priest of Brienne-le-Château made holy water in the castle he was to receive a penny for it. The priests of all these churches on being appointed were to take an oath of fidelity to the monastery that they would preserve the portion of the monks. Besides the quarrels at Puellemontier and Brienne-la-Vieille, there also arose one immediately after this at St Leger

[1] Lalore, *Cartulaires du diocèse de Troyes*, IV, pp. 206 *seq*.

sous-Brienne, upon certain tithes which the priest claimed, but this was settled in 1186 by the gift to the priest of an endowment of 24 sextaries of corn, half of frument and half of hay, whereupon he surrendered all the other claims.

A similar document of the year 1185 exists, by which Bishop Manasses defined the portions of rectors and vicars in the churches belonging to the abbey of Montier-la-Celle[1].

In Normandy the priest of the castle church of Briouze of which the rectory was owned by the monks of St Florent, in 1097, had his portion set out as a third of the revenues of the church, save candles, of which however, one-quarter should belong to him at Christmas, Easter and All Saints[2]. He was to pay one-third of the sinodal and visitation dues, and was to serve assiduously the monks at the priory of Briouze. The clerk of Berneville (1157–9) was assigned the benefice of the altar and one-third of the tithes[3].

In the diocese of Bayeux, in 1186, a vicarage was ordained in the prebendal church of St Georges of Lison, which belonged to the canon of Cartigny[4]. The priest was to receive a third of the garb tithes with the altarage and was to take an oath of obedience to the canon, and also one to the bishop and archdeacon that he would pay all episcopal dues.

Passing further north into the country now known as Belgium we find that there, too, vicarages were coming into existence as fully endowed perpetual benefices. The abbot of St Trond[5], as early as 1119, set apart as the portion of the priest of Donck one-third of all great and small tithes, the whole dowry, *i.e.* glebe, three *bonniers* (*bonnaria*) of land at Rotthem, and as many of meadow at Donck, and the whole poll-tax (*capitecensum familiarum*) of his parishioners, alive or dead, and the proceeds of the first mass whenever anyone from outside the parish was buried there. In 1127 the terms of the vicarage were arranged between the abbot of Stavelot-Malmédy, and the priest of Sprimont[6], it being stated that formerly the priest had a third of all the tithe and of the seven and a half manses which comprised the dowry of the church, one manse free from all kind of service. He had to pay 20*s*. yearly to the abbey, but, in the previous year, 1126, because the priest could not pay the pension and because he wanted a prebend from the monks for his foster-father (*nutricius*) Wido, the terms had been re-arranged. Now the new presentee was to receive the portion as before. The cellarer of the abbey, who

[1] Lalore, *Cartulaires du diocèse de Troyes*, VI, p. 276.
[2] P. Marchegay, *Chartes de St Florent*, p. 45.
[3] *Ibid.* p. 9.
[4] *Antiquus cartularius ecclesiae Baiocensis*, ed. V. Bourienne, I, p. 289.
[5] *Cart. St Trond*, I, p. 39.
[6] *Recueil des Chartes de...Stavelot-Malmédy* (Belg. Hist. Comm.), I, p. 295.

received the portion of the abbey, was to pay to the archdeacon, in leap-year, 10*s*. for the procurations (*obsonium*) but the priest was to pay 30*d*. in the year preceding the bissextile year for the sinodals (*circatio*). In 1148 at Alburg a sub-vicarage of Herpt was set up in a most unusual manner, which reflects no credit on a monastery that allowed such things to come to pass and then, holding tight to their own tithes, stood by benevolently consenting while other benefactors paid the bill.

The abbot of St Trond[1] recites how:

the poor folk of the village of Herpt besieged our predecessors and us with frequent and lamentable cries, complaining with truth that they lacked the service of God, and all kinds of Christian consolation ...children died sometimes unbaptized, the sick were unvisited, and the dying departed without the communion of our Lord's Body and Blood. Since, therefore, we were grievously afflicted for some years —*per aliquot annos*—by these miseries we held counsel with our reeve Humbert and the seniors of the church[2], by the advice and assent of the parson of Alburg and we have permitted this church of Herpt to have a priest of its own, with the income which we have noted here below. A noble lady, Hildegund by name in the presence and with the assent of Humbert, our reeve, hath carefully conferred upon us and St Trond, for the good of her soul and of all her kinsfolk, three acres of land for the stipend of the aforesaid priest; the inhabitants of the village have given five acres and a half, with a free croft [for his house] and have added free participation in their rights of pasture, of woodland, of water, and waterways. The parson of Alburg, whose vicar this priest will be and through whom he will enter into his office, in consideration of the burden which will thus be removed from him, will grant him from his own income the altar-offerings, and the gifts from live or dead parishioners [of Herpt]....These gifts of the faithful made to St Trond in the days of our prelacy for the stipend of the vicar, who is put in by our own free will on account of the aforesaid necessities, we do [hereby] transfer [to him] except the tithes which as before, we keep in our own hand, to be received by our reeve and disposed for the prebend of our brethren.

Dr Coulton adds his opinion:

The tithes, it need hardly be said, were by far the greater part of the parish revenues. It would be difficult to express more clearly than in this document the spiritual neglect which was possible for years under monastic regime, and the extent to which, when reform entailed expense, such expenses were met by outsiders under encouragement from the monks.

[1] *Cart. St Trond*, I, p. 76 (transl. Coulton, in *Hist. Teach. Misc.* IV, p. 92).

[2] Either of the abbey or of Alburg, the mother church to which Herpt was a hamlet.

A later example is found at Bevingen[1] to which church the abbot of St Trond in 1208 collated a priest saving to himself in all things the right of removing and substituting. In this case the church had not been sufficiently served in the past, and Arnold and Salutarius with all their neighbourhood had asked for a priest at their own expenses. The abbot granted them permission to present yearly priests to him. It was clearly a parochial chapel, not a regular parish church, and the case is very like that of Herpt.

In 1160 the archdeacon of Liège ordained that the *persona* ("parson", but really vicar) of Aelst[2] should receive one-third of the proceeds of both the small and great tithes. In 1184 Pope Lucius III confirmed the goods of the priory of Cons[3] and the arrangements made by Archbishop Alberic of Trèves concerning the portion of the "chaplain" of the parish church there. This consisted of one-third of all the parochial revenues, the tithe and the dowry of the altar, the whole tithe of cultivation of the lord of the vill, and the funeral offerings of each of the parishioners in alms or *tricenarium*[4] or oblations. In a burial mass, when the body was present, he was to receive half the profits whether the body was that of a parishioner or from outside the parish. Half of the offerings at masses at Christmas, Palm Sunday, Easter, Whitsun, Ascension and the dedication of the church were also to be his.

[1] *Cart. St Trond*, I, p. 161.

[2] *Ibid.* I, p. 94.

[3] *Chartes de St Hubert-en-Ardenne*, I, p. 139.

[4] The *tricenarium* was the mass said on the thirtieth day after death—here it may mean special payments for masses or other services during this period of 30 days.

APPENDIX B

DETAILED EVIDENCE OF THIRTEENTH-CENTURY VICARAGE ORDINATIONS

THE detailed assessments of vicarages, in the diocese of Lincoln, are interesting as showing the comparative value of the various emoluments, but it is impossible to say what was typical of an average vicarage, because the conditions of local agriculture can never be reduced to a type. For instance, flax tithes in one village might be extremely valuable, and yet in the next might be quite negligible. In 1212, at Upton[1], in Buckinghamshire, the vicarage was appraised as follows:

Offerings at Christmas, Easter, and other Feast days	30*s*.
Confessions in Lent and Holy Week	—
Flax tithes	10*s*.
Tithes of wool, lambs, pigs, geese	10*s*.
Tithe of cows, calves and geese with milk	10*s*.
All casual emoluments with a courtyard but not corn	5 marks

Besides these things the vicar owned half a virgate of land and a messuage.

At Bygrave[2], in Huntingdonshire, the vicarage consisted of the following:

Oblations of All Saints' Day	1*s*. 0*d*.
Carruage of All Saints' Day	9*d*.
Oblations of Christmas Day (7*s*.), Bread (8*d*.) ...	7*s*. 8*d*.
Oblations of day of Purification of B.V.M. ...	3*s*. 0*d*.
Confessions and Whitsunday	2*s*. 0*d*.
Eggs	1*s*. 0*d*.
Cheese	8*s*. 0*d*.
Oblations of St Margaret's Day	16*s*. 0*d*.
Oblations of Easter Day	6*s*. 8*d*.
Bread	8*d*.
Lambs, wool and flax	20*s*. 0*d*.
Small tithes and all other obventions	10*s*. 0*d*.
2 qrs of wheat and 3 of hay from the parson's barn	6*s*. 8*d*.
Summa totius	6 marks 3*s*. 5*d*.

While there is nothing particularly unusual about either of these assessments, they cannot be taken as more than they claim to be, ordinary examples. They are not typical, for there is no such thing as a typical vicarage for the simple reason that there was no typical village agriculture. Yet the proportion between small tithes and

[1] Heales, *Records of Merton Priory*, p. 67.
[2] *Reg. H. de Welles*, III, p. 40.

oblations is interesting and corrects the tendency to exaggerate the value of small tithes at the expense of the oblations. Eggs, for example, as perishable commodities, could not have been very valuable, even if plentiful. Fruit is very perishable, and consequently would not be of much value to the vicar. The penny marriage offerings and offerings at churchings, baptisms, funerals, and masses of all kinds might prove much more valuable simply because they would "keep". Such matter-of-fact considerations must have meant a great deal to the vicar, who, after all, was essentially a member of an agricultural community.

The ordinations of the vicarages in the diocese of York are very similar to those of the diocese of Lincoln. Colston Basset Vicarage, ordained in 1228, consisted in the altarage, a toft and a croft, a particular rood and 14 bovates (? *sic*) of land, the tithe of hay and two mills, and the rather exceptional endowment of the tithe of corn[1]. Radford[2], ordained in 1223, consisted in the whole altarage with four bovates belonging to that altarage with their tithes, the tithe of two mills and a toft. This endowment conforms exactly to the simple type that has led to the growth of an idea that the rector necessarily got the great tithes, and the vicar the small tithes. That is a rough and ready rule, whose efficacy is not seldom impeached by such ordinations as that of Colston Basset. The vicar of Leeds[3] at first received one-third of the garbs, and one-third of the altarage, according to an ordination deed of 1240, which then altered his endowment to the whole altarage with the tithes of mills, save those of the Earl of Lincoln, and save the church land. He was to pay back ten pounds of sterling in half-yearly instalments at Whitsun and at the feast of St Martin in the winter. This arrangement was a diminution of the vicarage made at the request of the rectors, Holy Trinity Priory at York. So it is plain that the archbishop had no less sympathy with the claims of the monasteries, if he thought they were well-founded, than with those of the vicars. The vicar of Conisborough[4] urged against the prior and convent of Lewes that his vicarage should be taxed, and the archbishop lent a ready ear to his prayer. He was granted the small tithes with two tofts, which were assigned for a manse. Exceptional arrangements were made at Pocklington and Pickering[5], the former of which had six chapels and the latter four. These chapels were united two by two as separate vicarages, and were only required to pay a small sum each to the mother vicarages in the name of their subjection. These mother-vicarages were to have a chaplain serving in each, besides the vicar. It was, indeed, an exceptional

[1] *Reg. Gray*, p. 22.
[2] *Ibid.* p. 8 n.
[3] *Ibid.* p. 89.
[4] *Ibid.* p. 113.
[5] *Ibid.* pp. 212–3.

diocese in the size of its parishes and, while Archbishop Gray may have been slightly more generous than Hugh de Welles to the vicars, it is most probable that it was the sheer size of the parishes and their burdens that made vicarages of 15 marks, like that of Dalton[1], or 20 marks, like that of St Mary's, Lancaster[2], quite common. There are many cases mentioned in Gray's register where the vicar held the whole church from a non-resident rector. The vicar of Ruddeby[3] had to pay 15 marks, the vicar of Gargrave[4] 10, the vicar of Burton Agnes[5] 15, and the vicar of Cottam[6] 40*s*. Yet again, as in Lincoln diocese, where the triple relation existed, a fully ordained vicarage was quite common. The vicar of Wath[7] received all the altarage and paid 10 marks pension to the parson, and all dues to the bishop and archdeacon. No fresh exactions, it was stated, were to be taken from the parishioners without the consent of the rector. Similarly, ordinations in kind were made at Skipsea and at South Kirkby, and for a mediety at Rillington[8, 9].

A brief survey of the appropriations and vicarages in the other dioceses will be sufficient to prove how widely spread were the same features that have been noticed in Lincoln and York, and that, while the authorities might vary in strictness and efficiency, the main theme of the story is everywhere the same. In the diocese of Worcester[10] the most important appropriator was Gloucester Abbey, which in 1191 had obtained a bull from Pope Celestine III enabling them to appropriate a number of churches of which they had the advowsons, when vacancies should occur, notwithstanding the prohibitions of the recent Council of Lateran (III) or of the bishop of the diocese. In 1198 Bishop John conceded to the abbey a pension of 4 marks from the vicarage of Kempsford. About 1217 a pension of 5 marks from the vicarage of All Saints', Cerney, was confirmed to the abbey. In these cases the vicars probably held the whole church minus the pension. Yet a properly ordained vicarage is to be found at Mickleton in Gloucestershire, as early as 1180–94, owning the altarage, the small tithes, a considerable amount of land and a manse. Tewkesbury Abbey[11] in 1221 obtained a Papal bull allowing them to appropriate seven churches, already granted by Pope Lucius on condition of their appointing fit vicars. They could also hold as appropriated certain other churches previously granted to them by the bishops of Llandaff and Exeter, but which some of the former abbots had given to secular clerks to the great hurt of the monastery. Sudbury and Bromsgrove[12], granted to the sacristy of Worcester Priory, had

[1] *Reg. Gray*, p. 160. [2] *Ibid.* p. 203. [3] *Ibid.* p. 31.
[4] *Ibid.* p. 7. [5] *Ibid.* p. 67. [6] *Ibid.* p. 71.
[7] *Ibid.* p. 8. [8] *Ibid.* p. 29. [9] *Ibid.* p. 35.
[10] *Reg. Giffard* (Worcs. Hist. Soc.), p. 59. [11] *Cal. Pap. Let.* I, p. 81.
[12] *Ann. Mon.* (R.S.), IV, p. 427.

vicarages ordained in them about 1236. The bishop, William of Blois, seems to have ordained vicarages systematically in the churches of his cathedral priory[1], the details being usually of the simple type according to which the vicar received the altarage and small tithes with slight differences occurring in each. Bishop Walter de Cantilupe[2] in 1240 issued Constitutions ordering the religious to present to their appropriated churches if there were no vicars there, and to augment all insufficient vicarages within two months, after which the official and the archdeacon should act in the matter, forcing assent where it was not readily forthcoming. In 1242 he attempted to put vicars in the churches of St James of Bristol and Tewkesbury[3], contrary to the Papal privileges of Tewkesbury Abbey, but apparently failed in this. This time the bishop was less successful than his predecessor, who in 1231 decided against the claim of the abbey to serve the church of Fairford[4] by a monk. Frederick, who claimed to be rector, entered the church with an armed force and threw out the monks, and his claim was recognised by the bishop. Not for another century did the abbey regain the church *in proprios usus*. The register of Bishop Giffard[5] at the end of the century reveals quite a large number of appropriations in process, and a note under the year 1300 mentions nine churches in which vicarages were to be ordained. It is also added that vicars non-resident without license for a year are by law deprived. This note at the end of the century reveals the flaws that were still left in the system, and checks any undue optimism. This incompleteness may be attributed to monastic obstruction, but there was no question of any misunderstanding as to the powers of the bishop. As early as 1222 the abbot of Gloucester[6] had said in a pleading that he had not *given* certain churches, and if he had given them this would not stand because it was for the bishop of the place to assign churches *in proprios usus*, but he said that he had presented his clerk to a disputed church. This statement reveals that the abbot recognised the bishop's authority over his churches, and that the bishop's authority alone could institute anyone, whether he be abbot or clerk, to benefices.

In the neighbouring diocese of Hereford there had been some sort of vicarages since 1100, when Bishop Gerard appropriated Preston and Churcham[7] to Gloucester Abbey on condition that a reasonable sustentation should be reserved to honest chaplains, who should minister in the churches. This by no means necessarily implies that the benefices were perpetual, for the word "chaplain" always

[1] *Reg. Worcs. Priory*, pp. 35 *a*, 86 *a*, *b*, 88 *b*.
[2] Wilkins, *Concilia*, I, p. 674.
[3] *Ann. Mon.* (R.S.), I, p. 126.
[4] *Ibid.* I, p. 82.
[5] *Reg. Giffard* (Worcs. Hist. Soc.), pp. 5, 17
[6] *Hist. and Cart. Gloucs.* (R.S.), I, p. 211.
[7] *Ibid.* I, p. 251.

suggests that the incumbent could be removed by the person who presented him. At a later date the word could be taken as certain evidence that he was not perpetual, but in the early days, when nomenclature was uncertain and shifting, one cannot be quite sure. Most probably the chaplains were amovable secular priests, not monks, and the stipulation only meant that they were not to be "sweated". About 1148 the incumbent of Great Cowarne[1] was called a chaplain or vicar, and was to receive emoluments to the value of 10 marks. About the same time St Lawrence's, Teignton[1], was appropriated to Gloucester Abbey, whose abbot was to present vicars to these two churches, but if they did not serve as they should, he could remove them with the knowledge of the bishop. In the early years of the thirteenth century a vicarage of 100*s*. was reserved on the appropriation of the church of Foy[2] to the same abbey. Dewchurch[3] was ordained in all the altarage and mortuaries with certain garb and lay tithes, a house rent-free and pasture for a horse. For this the vicar had to pay the *senagium* (sinodals) and the archdeacon's visitation dues, and to find a deacon to do the work of a modern curate. This was the work of Bishop Hugh Foliot, whose successor, Peter de Aquablanca, ordained vicarages worth 14 marks each at Dymock and Newent[4], and reserved *porciones congrue* at Ledbury and Bosbury when he appropriated them to his own "table" by Papal authority, and at Stottesdon when he appropriated it to Shrewsbury Abbey in 1243. The rights of the chapter of Hereford[5] gained Papal confirmation in 1245, when they were confirmed in three churches with the right of presenting vicars, and in 1246 when the bishop was licensed to revoke all appropriations of pensions, tithes or churches that had been made without the consent of the chapter. The Hospitallers and Templars, however, were favoured by exemption even from this.

Bishop Geoffrey Muschamp of Coventry and Lichfield (1199–1208) made an arrangement by which the vicar of St Helen's, Etwall, which then consisted of the whole church minus a pension to Welbeck Abbey, should be revised on the death of the vicar, who then held the benefice, so that the abbey should have two-thirds of the church and the vicar one-third. At Rochdale[6] a vicarage of 5 marks and 4 bovates of arable land was ordained about 1217. The vicar of Youlgrave[7], whose portion, endowed in 1224, consisted of the oblations and altar dues, and certain corn and hay tithes, found himself obliged to bear all the customary burdens and support at his own

[1] *Hist. and Cart. Gloucs.* (R.S.), I, p. 252; III, p. 5.

[2] *Ibid.* I, pp. 300, 301.

[3] *Ibid.* II, p. 224.

[4] Mus. Brit. Add. MS. 18461, fols. 13–14.

[5] *Cal. Pap. Let.* I, pp. 222, 229.

[6] *Vicars of Rochdale* (Chetham Soc.), I, p. 6.

[7] Cox, *Notes on the Churches of Derbyshire*, II, p. 316; Harl. MSS. 4799, fol. 44.

cost two chaplains and one deacon. The chapter of Coventry, like the cathedral chapters already mentioned, was anxious not to be trampled down in the scramble for parochial revenues, and acquired[1] from the Pope in 1221 a letter inhibiting anyone from transferring to other uses churches granted to them, or from exacting more than was due from them. This sounds as if they required protection from their own bishop, for no one else save the archbishop would be in a position to commit these offences. The bishop himself acquired the church of St Michael's, Coventry[2], for his own uses in 1241. In these cases where the bishop received permission from the Pope to appropriate churches to himself, for he could not do so by his own authority, the usual clause was inserted "saving a suitable portion for the vicar", but the Pope never indicated what the suitable portion should be. There is no evidence to hand of any dissatisfaction with the ordinations made by bishops in their own appropriated churches, and we may assume that his own dignity and the jealous vigilance of monasteries that smarted under his ordinations of their vicarages sufficed to prevent signal abuse of this power by the bishop.

For the diocese of Salisbury the documents of St Osmund's Priory, the cathedral chapter, reveal quite a thorough and business-like application of the 1215 Lateran decrees, at least from about 1220 onwards. Before 1191, indeed, there had been a vicar with an endowed portion at Stoke Abbot, but from the few early instances like this the number of endowed vicarages rapidly increased after 1220 by fresh ordinations. Wivelsford[3], Blewbury[4], Box[3], Faringdon[3] in 1227, and Harberton in 1236[5], are a few examples of the work of the bishop. In 1240, however, when he ordained the vicarages of Beaulieu Abbey at Inglesham and its chapel of Coxwell[6], he adopted the unusual but not unique policy of reserving the collation of the vicarages to himself[7]. This would have been a very sound policy, were it not for the sometimes lengthy vacancies of the see during which the king had the right of advowson, used by him in the interests, not of ecclesiastical discipline, but of lay power. Consequently, the collations of spiritually minded bishops might be cancelled against the political collations of the king and his chancellors, and of bishops, whose own elections were brought about by the use of political authority. Hence the general adoption of this policy would not have had the beneficial effects one would have expected at first glance.

The cathedral priory itself showed a quite praiseworthy although

[1] *Cal. Pap. Let.* I, p. 84. [2] *Ibid.* I, p. 198.
[3] *Sarum Chart. and Doc.* (R.S.), pp. 185–7.
[4] Rev. J. C. Cox, *Vic. County Hist.* (*Berks.*), II, p. 8.
[5] *Sarum Chart. and Doc.* (R.S.), p. 239. [6] *Ibid.* pp. 255 *seq.*
[7] Archbishop Boniface of Canterbury in 1264 on appropriating the church of Romenal to Pontigny Abbey made this same stipulation. Paris, MS. lat. 9887, fol. 33, col. 2.

perhaps spasmodic, interest in the welfare of its parishes, as a visitation of St Andrew's, Sonning[1], in 1220 reveals. They found there a perpetual vicar named Vitalis, who produced a charter of Dean Jordan, *c.* 1185, by which he had been granted the "chantry" of the church and Ruscombe Chapel for 40*s.* yearly pension to be paid by him to the chapter. The "chantry" consisted of the altarage, mortuaries, and the tithes of flax, wool, and cheese. It was found that four chaplains employed by the vicar were grossly ignorant, while a fifth was so old and infirm that he could not minister properly. The four ignorant ones were summarily dismissed and the fifth prohibited from ministering, while the vicar was severely rebuked, presumably for trying to increase his own income by employing cheap and incompetent labour.

For the diocese of Winchester, the Rev. J. C. Cox[2] says that he believes the ordination of the vicarage of Andover in 1246 to be the earliest ordering of a vicarage now extant. This may be true as far as details are concerned, but the end of the century reveals this diocese as not essentially different from any other in the matter of appropriations and vicarages. The vicarage of Kingston-on-Thames indeed was defined, if not fully ordained, in 1211[3] and again between 1231 and 1238[4].

The vicarages in four churches of Montacute Priory[5], in the diocese of Exeter, were ordained on the appropriation of those churches in 1236. Two years later a vicarage was ordained in the church of Uplyme[6], newly appropriated to Glastonbury Abbey. Beaulieu Abbey[7] acquired license to appropriate the Cornish church of St Keverne in 1235, for the needs of their hospitality, but the rector wrote to the legate, Otto, denouncing the appropriators as debauching in their monastery. He declared also that they were in a desert place, where there was no need for hospitality, and they admitted scarcely a single guest, that they had £1000 a year in rents, that they could support many more monks, and that they had turned St Keverne's Church into a grange. Garbled as this tale may have been by vituperation in a truly medieval vein, and by a desire on the part of the rector for a good fat pension, which was adjudged to him to the tune of 20 marks, our knowledge of Beaulieu Abbey indicates that a rich monastery hereby became richer, and a rich parish poorer. Such was the effect of many of these appropriations, which caused the monasteries to be rich, and reduced the parishes to a level of mediocrity verging on poverty. While it is possible to contend that a celibate

[1] Rev. J. C. Cox, in *Vic. County Hist.* (*Berks.*), II, p. 5.
[2] In *Vic. County Hist.* (*Hants.*), II, p. 23.
[3] Heales, *Records of Merton Priory*, p. 67.
[4] *Ibid.* p. 95.
[5] *Cart. Montacute Pr.* p. 196.
[6] Dugdale-Caley, *Monasticon*, I, p. 28 *b*.
[7] Rev. J. C. Cox, in *Vic. County Hist.* (*Hants.*), II, pp. 141 *seq.*

servant of God had no right to claim riches or even much comfort, this argument surely applies more to the monks who had renounced the world than to the parish priests who did not deny that they were of the world.

St Albans Abbey, that had previously succumbed to the attack of Hugh de Welles, in 1228 was obliged to set up vicarages in its churches in the diocese of Norwich[1] by Bishop Thomas. The vicarages, however, appear to have been poor ones amounting either to one-sixth of the old estimate of the churches or to one-eighth of the new estimates to be made by the chapter.

The augmented vicarage of Ilminster (dioc. Bath and Wells), in 1268 belonging to Muchelney Abbey, had even more detailed assessments than those I have reproduced from the diocese of Lincoln. These are as follows[2]:

	£	s.	d.
Christmas oblations		13	0
Purification and Dedication oblations ...		12	0
Holy Friday and Easter Oblations ...	1	0	0
Oblations of Assumption		15	0
Confessions and Altar Bread		5	0
Purifications of women		3	0
Marriage money		2	0
Occasional masses and trentals		13	4
Oblations of Burials and Mortuaries ...		10	0
Wool tithes		16	0
Cheese tithes		10	0
Cow tithes		4	0
Calves and foals in tithes		2	0
Apples	1	5	0
Mills		13	4
Lambs		14	0
Little pigs		3	6
Honey		1	6
Geese		1	6
Heypeni (Haypenny)		13	0
Flax	3	0	0
Pigeons			8
Hemp			8
Land		8	0
Hay of Richard Maloysel		1	4
1 qr wheat		4	0
1 qr rye		3	0
1 qr barley		2	0
1 qr beans		2	0
2 qr oats		3	4
Livery of the court of the abbot against Christmas			5
	£13	2	11 (*sic*)

[1] *Gesta Abbatum Mon. Si. Albani* (R.S.), 1, pp. 278, 279.
[2] *Muchelney Cart.* p. 54.

There is a very interesting composition between the first vicar of Chesterton, near Cambridge[1], Stephen Rampton, and the abbey of Vercelli, the patrons, of about 1273. The vicar was to have ground for his house, all altarages, various small tithes, oblations of the four chief feasts, and also oblations of churchings, weddings and requiem masses. The vicar was to be free from attending the court of the abbey, but had to come to the dinner then held, with his clerk. He was to receive the mortuary for the father or principal person of the house, namely, the best animal, but not a pig, because that was contrary to the use of the church, unless the vicar wanted it. If he preferred, he might have something of equal value. For the wife or second person in the house, the second best animal had to be given. The vicar also received the four candles, placed about the corpse on the funeral day. All persons celebrating in the church were to do first reverence to the abbey's proctor, and second reverence to the vicar, who had the governance of the church "because of the English tongue". The parish clerk was to be prepared day and night for administration of the mass when required. The vicar need not do any servile work for the lord of the manor, although he might help his parishioners in their agriculture, "for in these matters he is as free as we". Every parishioner who had a fire in his house had to pay 1*d*. to the vicar, before receiving Easter mass, of which "smoke pennies" ¼*d*. went to the Papal collector, ¼*d*. to St Peter's Altar at Ely Cathedral, ¼*d*. for the Paschal candle in the parish church, and ¼*d*. for the round candle over the beam in the chancel before the Sacrament of the Altar. By special request of the parishioners, it was also determined that the first vicar should receive garb tithes of any curtilages and gardens that should be turned to the plough.

[1] *Ely Dioc. Rem.* 1913, p. 64.

APPENDIX C

THE MORTUARY

THIS lengthy document analysed above is a most valuable statement of the social status of the vicar, who was in a more favourable position than the vicars of the monks of Depyng[1] Priory in Lincolnshire, if the animals taken from their stock by the priory after their death, *nomine Principalis*, were really heriots from them as feudal bondmen[2]. This, however, seems to me unlikely, for the words *principale legatum* were used frequently in the sense of mortuary. Probably these vicars were tithe-payers to the priory, and so were liable for the "legacy" for forgotten tithes. The vicar of Chesterton seemed to have occupied a perfectly self-respecting position on his vicarage, which was taxed at £6 in 1291, showing that it was not considered an exceptionally large one. Far from being a bondman, the abbey declared him in the matter of feudal services as free as itself. The mortuaries received by him were so divided and distinguished as to suggest a possible corrupted meaning of the words *primum legatum* (first legacy) and *secundum legatum* (second legacy). Possibly the first or principal legacy sometimes meant the legacy or mortuary of the principal person in the house, and the second legacy that of the second person of the house. This might explain the case of Bicester where, as Mr Snape says, there were two mortuaries[3]. Sometimes, again, a distinction is made as in the case of the church of Oakley[4], belonging to St Frideswide's Priory, between the live heriot that was received by the priory, and the dead by the vicar. The vicars of churches of Oseney Abbey[5] in the diocese of Lincoln received the *secundum legatum*, that is, the mortuary, up to the value of 6*d*. and half of any surplus beyond that. This was a very frequent division in Hugh de Welles' ordinations. In the 1403 ordination of the vicarage of Chesterton in Lincoln diocese it is stated:

Item vicarius post ejus decessum dabit heriettam rectori et conventui domus de Asherugge[6].

Item, that after his death the Vicar shall give a heriot to the rector and convent of the house of Ashridge.

1 Coulton, in *Hist. Teach. Misc.* IV, p. 68.
2 Dugdale-Caley, *Monasticon*, IV, p. 168 *b*.
3 Or is it a heriot and a mortuary?
4 Kennett, *Paroch. Antiquities*, II, Glossary. a.v. Herietum and Legatum.
5 *Lib. Ant.* p. 1.
6 Kennett, *Paroch. Antiquities*, 1818, ed. II, p. 203.

Whether this was a feudal heriot or an ecclesiastical mortuary is not definitely decided, I think, by the use of the word "heriot", for it is conceivable that, by the beginning of the fifteenth century, the ideas of heriot and mortuary were so confused that the words could be used indiscriminately. They were, doubtless, customary payments for which the original reason was forgotten. Even to-day, at Bicker, in Lincolnshire, as I am told by a native who has paid it for his father, the vicar receives a sum called "mortis money" on the death of some of his parishioners, and this seems fairly obviously a commutation of the ancient mortuaries. The whole subject of heriots and mortuaries is very confused, and I would sum up by saying that, while *herietum*, *principale legatum*, and *primum legatum* all properly mean the lay feudal due, and the *mortuarium* and *secundum legatum*, mean the payment *pro decimis oblitis*, in practice the phrases become so indiscriminate that it is quite frequently impossible to say which is meant.

In considering these matters it must, above all, be borne in mind that local customs remained stronger than either national or Catholic law until the end of the Middle Ages. If the vicar of Chesterton, near Cambridge, was as free from feudal services as his monastic rectors, it does not follow that all vicars were as free as that. If the vicar of St James', Depyng, was subject to certain servile dues, it does not follow that all vicars were.

I do not for one minute believe that the social status of the vicar, as such, was any different from that of the resident rector. Differences, which were very large, between that of one incumbent and another, were due to family and to the size of the benefice. Either vicar or rector might be a scion of a noble family, or like Chaucer's Poor Parson, the brother of the village ploughman. In fact, the Host[1] did not even know whether the Parson was vicar or rector, for

> Sir Preest, quod he, artow a vicary?
> Or art a Person? sey sooth, by thy fey.

The commonest Latin expression for the mortuary is as at Sempringham (dioc. Lincoln): *Habebit etiam secundum legatum suum* (*Reg. H. de Welles*, III, p. 77); Humberstone (dioc. Lincoln): *Et in secundo legato* (*Reg. Grosseteste*, p. 49).

Examples of the use of the word *mortuarium*, also very common, are at Wotton (dioc. Winton), 1300: *Item volumus quod idem vicarius habeat mortuaria quecunque provenientia* (*Reg. Pontissara*, I, p. 92); Tadcaster (dioc. York), 1290: *cum mortuariis sponsalibus purificacionibus, etc.* (*Reg. Romeyn*, I, p. 106); and at Pinchbeck (dioc. Lincoln), 1275: (*Reg. Gravesend*, p. 62).

[1] *Chaucer's Works*, Oxford ed. 1915, p. 674 *a*.

Less common is the phrase *primum legatum* with the meaning mortuary, but many examples can be found as in the *Statuta Sinodalia Johannis Episcopi Wyntoniensis* (*Reg. Pontissara*, I, p. 233).

De primo autem legato quod alio nomine Mortuarium appellatur, ut tollatur contencio et solucionis ipsius uniformis sit modus in nostra diocesi apud omnes, sic duximus faciendum quod si vir masculus testatus vel intestatus seu vidua in fata decedat pro decimis suis indiscrete vel ignoranter detentis seu minus plene solutis secundum melius averium quod in particione bonorum in porcione defuncti computari volumus matrici ecclesie seu capelle secundum loci consuetudinem assignetur, nisi forte moriens ita pauper fuerit quod soluto averio hujusmodi apud heredem vel liberos nichil sit equivalens remansurum. Quod si forte contigerit volumus quod cum de paupertate hujusmodi canonice doctum fuerit nil de bonis mortui exigatur nisi quod ecclesie specialiter duxerit relinquendum. Si autem aliquid nomine secundi melioris averii et quid ecclesie relinqui debeat cum mulier conjugata, Civis, Burgensis, Mercator aut quivis alii terras non tenentes decedunt, consuetudini locorum duximus relinquendum.

Concerning the first legacy, which is by another name called Mortuary, that contention should be stopped and that there should be a uniform solution of it with all in our diocese, we so rule that if a grown man, testate or intestate, or his widow shall pass away, we will that the second best beast which is valued in the parting of the goods belonging to the defunct, be assigned to the mother church or chapel according to the custom of the place, for his tithes that have been indiscretely or ignorantly withheld, or less than fully paid, unless perchance he die so poor that when the beast has been paid in this manner, there be nothing of equal value left to his heir or children. But if by chance this happen, we will that when this sort of poverty be canonically proved, nothing of the goods of the dead man be demanded save what he has specially left to the church. If, however, there is anything under the description of second best beast and anything ought to be left when a married woman, Citizen, Burgher, Merchant, or any other dies, not holding lands, then we determine that it should be left to the custom of the place.

This last sentence may explain Mr Snape's difficulty of the two mortuaries, and bears out the evidence quoted for the church of Chesterton, near Cambridge. Apparently local custom varies, so that in one place the wife might be liable for a mortuary, as well as the husband, but in another she might not.

In the ordination of the church of Betchworth in the diocese of Winchester in 1286, the mortuary is referred to as follows: *exceptis principali et legato in vivis animalibus existentibus* (*Reg. Pontissara*, I, p. 27).

Most exceptional is the use of the phrase *principale testamentum* which occurs in Hugh de Welles' *Rolls* (Cant. and York Soc.), I, p. 251, although *principale legatum* is very common.

BIBLIOGRAPHY

I

MANUSCRIPT SOURCES

Bibliothèque Nationale

MS. lat. 11059. Chartulary of Silly Abbey, dioc. Sées, 13th century MS. with 14th century additions.

MS. lat. 5413. Chartulary of the Abbey of St Magloire, Paris, 14th century with additions until 1440.

MS. lat. 5649. Chartulary of Abbey of Thenailles, dioc. Laon, 13th century.

MS. lat. 15057. Chartulary of Prebends of the Abbey of St Victor, 13th century.

MSS. lat. 11008, 11009, 11010, 11011, 9994. Chartularies of Abbey of Grandselve, dioc. Toulouse, 12th and 13th centuries.

MS. lat. 9901. Chartulary of Abbey of Vauluisant, dioc. Sens, 13th century.

MS. lat. 5528. Chartulary of the Cathedral Church of Meaux, 1260.

MS. lat. 18355. Chartulary of the Cathedral Church of Meaux, 14th century.

MS. lat. 13913. Chartulary of Bishopric of Angoulême, 13th century.

MS. lat. 17725. Chartulary of the Abbey of Régny, dioc. Auxerre, *c.* 1500.

MS. lat. 5526. Chartulary of the Bishop of Paris, 13th century.

MS. lat. 9887. Chartulary of Pontigny Abbey, dioc. Auxerre.

MS. lat. 11056. Chartulary of St Evroul's Abbey.

Coll. Dom. Grenier. Vol. 97. Concerning the Bishopric of Amiens.

MS. n.a. lat. 428. Formulary of ecclesiastical acts dedicated to Archbishop Pecham.

MS. n.a. lat. 1828. Le Livre Rouge de l'Évêché de Bayeux.

MS. n.a. lat. 1502. Treatise by Cluniac doctor, Peter Alberti.

MS. Coll. Moreau. Vol. 905. Copy of the Register of Bishop of Lausanne.

British Museum

MS. Cott. Titus. CIX. Chartulary of Darley Abbey.

MS. Harl. 862. Formula Book.

Add. MS. 18461. Cartularium Monasterii de Newent, co. Glouc.

Public Record Office

Early Chancery Proceedings. Bundle 13 no. 37; bundle 15, no. 169; bundle 47, no. 76. (Selected from P.R.O. Lists and Indexes.)

II

PRINTED ORIGINAL SOURCES

A. Episcopal Registers

Athens, École française

Bibliothèque. Série II, t. 5. Les Registres de Nicolas IV. Ed. E. Langlois. Athens, 1877.

Bannatyne Club, Edinburgh

Registrum Episcopatus Moraviensis. Ed. C. Innes. 4°. Edinburgh, 1837.

Registrum Episcopatus Glasguensis. 2 vols. Ed. C. Innes. 4°. Edinburgh, 1843.

Registrum Episcopatus Brechinensis. 2 vols. Ed. C. Innes. 4°. Aberdeen, 1856.

Canterbury and York Society

Rotuli Hugonis de Welles Episcopi Lincolniensis. MCCIX–MCCXXXV. Vol. I. (No. 1.) Ed. W. P. W. Phillimore, M.A., B.C.L. London, 1909. Vol. II. (No. 3.) Ed. several editors. London, 1907. Vol. III. (No. 4.) Ed. Rev. F. N. Davis, B.A. London, 1908.

Rotuli Roberti Grosseteste Episcopi Lincolniensis. MCCXXXV–MCCLIII. (No. 10.) Ed. Rev. F. N. Davis, B.A., B.Litt. London, 1913.

Rotuli Ricardi Gravesend Diocesis Lincolniensis. (No. 31.) Ed. Rev. F. N. Davis, with additions by C. W. Foster, M.A., F.S.A. and A. Hamilton-Thompson, M.A., D.Litt., F.S.A. Oxford University Press, 1925.

Registrum Thome de Cantilupo, Episcopi Herefordensis. MCCLXXV–MCCLXXXII. (No. 2.) Ed. Rev. R. G. Griffiths, M.A. London, 1907.

Registrum Ade de Orleton, Ep. Heref. MCCCXVII–MCCCXXVII. (No. 5.) Ed. Rev. A. T. Bannister, M.A. London, 1908.

Registrum Ricardi de Swinfield, Ep. Heref. MCCLXXXIII–MCCCXVII. (No. 6.) Ed. W. W. Capes, M.A. London, 1909.

Registrum Johannis de Trillek, Ep. Heref. MCCCXLIV–MCCCLXI. (No. 8.) Ed. J. H. Parry, M.A. London, 1912.

Registrum Thome de Charlton, Ep. Heref. MCCCXXVII–MCCCXLIV. (No. 9.) Ed. W. W. Capes, M.A. London, 1913.

Registrum Ludowici de Charltone, Ep. Heref. MCCCLXI–MCCCLXX. (No. 14.) Ed. J. H. Parry, M.A. London, 1914.

Registrum Willelmi de Courtenay, Ep. Heref. MCCCLXX–MCCCLXXV. (No. 15.) Ed. W. W. Capes, M.A. London, 1914.

Registrum Johannis Gilbert, Ep. Heref. MCCCLXXV–MCCCLXXX. (No. 18.) Ed. J. H. Parry, M.A. London, 1915.

Registrum Johannis Trefnant, Ep. Heref. MCCCLXXXIX–MCCCCIV. (No. 20.) Ed. W. W. Capes, M.A. London, 1916.

Registrum Roberti Mascall, Ep. Heref. MCCCCIV–MCCCCXVI. (No. 21.) Ed. J. H. Parry, M.A. London, 1917.

Registrum Edmundi Lacy, Ep. Heref. MCCCCXVII–MCCCCXX. (No. 22.) Ed. J. H. Parry, M.A. London, 1918.

Registrum Thome Spofford, Ep. Heref. MCCCCXXII–MCCCCXLVIII. (No. 23.) Ed. A. T. Bannister, M.A. London, 1919.

Registrum Ricardi Beauchamp, Ep. Heref. MCCCCXLIX–MCCCCL. (No. 25.) Ed. A. T. Bannister, M.A. London, 1919.

Registrum Thome Myllyng, Ep. Heref. MCCCCLXXIV–MCCCCXCII. (No. 26.) Ed. A. T. Bannister, M.A. London, 1920.

Registrum Ricardi Mayew, Ep. Heref. MDIV–MDXVI. (No. 27.) Ed. A. T. Bannister, M.A. London, 1921.

Registrum Caroli Bothe, Ep. Heref. MDXVI–MDXXXV. (No. 28.) (Also Edward Foxe, Edmundi Boner, in Appendix). Ed. A. T. Bannister, M.A. London, 1921.

Registrum Radulphi Baldock, Gilberti Segrave Ricardi Newport et Stephani Gravesend, Episcoporum Londoniensium. MCCCIV–MCCCXXXVIII. (No. 7.) Ed. R. C. Fowler, B.A. London, 1911.

The Register of John de Halton, Bishop of Carlisle, 1292–1324. 2 vols. (Nos. 12, 13.) Ed. W. N. Thompson, Esq. London, 1913.

Registrum Johannis de Pontissara, Episcopi Wyntoniensis. MCCLXXXII–MCCCIV. (Nos. 19, 30.) 2 vols. Ed. C. Deedes, M.A. London, 1915, 1924.

Visitations of Religious Houses in the diocese of Lincoln. 2 vols. (Nos. 17, 24.) Ed. A. Hamilton Thompson, M.A., F.S.A. London, 1915.

Registrum Simonis de Sudbiria, dioc. London. A.D. 1362–1375. Vol. I. (No. 34.) Ed. R. C. Fowler. London, 1927.

Also the following incomplete publications:

Registrum Johannis Pecham, Archiep. Cantuar.

Registrum R. Winchelsey, Archiep. Cantuar. Ed. Miss Rose Graham, M.A., F.S.A., F.R.Hist.S.

Diocesis Roffensis Registrum Hamonis Hethe. Ed. C. Johnson, M.A., F.S.A., F.R.Hist.S.

Registrum Simonis de Gandavo, Ep. Sarisbur. Ed. C. T. Flower, M.A., F.S.A.

Cymmrodorion,

Honorable Society of the; Episcopal Registers of the Diocese of St David's. 2 vols. 1397–1518. (Record Series, No. 6.) London, 1917.

Ely

Diocesan Remembrancer. 1885 onwards. Extracts from Ely Episcopal Registers.

A. W. Gibbons. Calendar of Ely Episcopal Records. 8°. 1891.

Exeter

Series of Episcopal Registers. Alphabetically summarised by the Rev. F. C. Hingeston Randolph, M.A. 1257–1455. London and Exeter, 1889 onwards.

Hampshire Record Society

Register of William of Wykeham. 2 vols. Ed. T. F. Kirby, M.A., F.S.A. London and Winchester, 1896.

Registers of John de Sandale and Rigaud de Asserio, Bishops of Winchester (A.D. 1316–23), with an appendix of contemporaneous and other illustrative documents. Ed. F. J. Baigent. London and Winchester, 1897.

Historical MSS. Commission Reports

re Carlisle Registers Report IX, App. pp. 178–97.

Presutti, P.

Regesta Honorii III. 2 vols. Rome, 1888.

Rolls Series

Registrum Epistolarum Fratris Johannis Peckham Archiepiscopi Cantuariensis. Ed. Chas. Trice Martin, B.A., F.S.A. 3 vols. London, 1882–6.

Roberti Grosseteste Episcopi Quondam Lincolniensis Epistolae. Ed. H. Richards Luard, M.A. London, 1861.

Historical Papers and Letters from the Northern Registers. Ed. James Raine, M.A. London, 1873.

Registrum Palatinum Dunelmense. Ed. Sir Thomas Duffus Hardy, D.C.L. London, 1873–8.

Calendars of Entries in Papal Registers relating to Great Britain and Ireland. Letters. Vols. 1, 2. Ed. W. H. Bliss. Vol. 3. Ed. W. H. Bliss and C. Johnson, M.A. Vols. 4, 5. Ed. W. H. Bliss and J. A. Twemlow, B.A. Vols. 6–11. Ed. J. A. Twemlow, B.A. 1893–1921.

Petitions. Vol. 1. 1897.

Rome, Institut Historique Belge de

Analecta Vaticano-Belgica. Vols. II and III. 2 vols. in 3 pts. Lettres de Jean XXII. Pub. Arnold Fayen. Rome, 1908–12.

Rouen

Registrum Visitationum Archiepiscopi Rothomagensis (Odonis Rigaldi), 1248–69. 4°. Pub. Th. Bonnin. Rouen, 1852.

Somerset Record Society

The Registers of Walter Giffard, Bishop of Bath and Wells, 1265–6, and of Henry Bowett, Bishop of Bath and Wells, 1401–7. Ed. Thomas Scott-Holmes, M.A. 4°. London, 1899.

Calendar of the Register of Bishop John de Drokensford, Bishop of Bath and Wells, 1309–29. Ed. Rt. Rev. Bishop Hobhouse. London, 1887.

The Register of Ralph of Shrewsbury, Bishop of Bath and Wells, 1329–63. Ed. Thomas Scott-Holmes. 2 vols. 4°. London, 1896.
The Register of Nicholas Bubwith, Bishop of Bath and Wells, 1407–24. 2 vols. 4°. London, 1914.

Spalding Club, Aberdeen
Registrum Episcopatus Aberdonensis. Ed. Cosmo Innes. 2 vols. 4°. Edinburgh, 1845.

Surtees Society Publications, Durham
Register of Walter Gray, 1225–55, Archbishop of York. (No. 56.) 1872.
Register of Walter Giffard, 1266–79, Archbishop of York. (No. 109.) 1904.
Register of William Wickwane, 1279–85, Archbishop of York. (No. 114.) 1907.
Part of Register of Richard d'Aungerville, of Bury, Bishop of Durham. (No. 119.) 1910.
Register of John le Romeyn (1286–98) and Henry of Newark (1298–9), Archbishops of York. 2 vols. (Nos. 123, 128.) 1913, 1916.

Sussex Record Society, Lewes
Register of Robert Rede, Bishop of Chichester, 1397–1415. 2 vols. 8°. Lewes, 1908–10.
Register of Richard Praty, Bishop of Chichester, 1438–45. 8°. Lewes.

Worcester Historical Society
Register of Godfrey Giffard, Bishop of Worcester, 1268–1301. 4°. Ed. J. W. W. Bund. Oxford, 1900, 1901, 1902.
Register of William Ginsborough, Bishop of Worcester, 1303–7. 4°. Ed. J. W. W. Bund. Oxford, 1907.
Register Sede Vacante, 1301–1435. 4°. Ed. J. W. W. Bund. Oxford, 1897.

B. MISCELLANEOUS, BEING MAINLY CHARTULARIES AND CHARTER BOOKS

(Where there are several publications of an academy I have indexed these under the name of the Academy and not under the names of the editors.)

Barris, C. Lacave La Plagne
Cartulaire de l'Église Ste-Marie d'Auch. Archives historiques de la Gascogne. 2me Série, fasc. III. Auch and Paris, 1899.

Belgique, Académie Royale de (Belgian Royal Commission)
Recueil des Chartes de l'Abbaye de Stavelot-Malmédy. Pub. Jos. Halkin et C. G. Roland. Brussels, 1909.
Cartulaire de l'Abbaye du Val Benoît. Pub. J. Cuvelier. Brussels, 1906.

Cartulaire de l'Abbaye de St Trond. 2 vols. Pub. Charles Piot. Brussels, 1870, 1874.
Cartulaire de l'Abbaye d'Orval. Ed. le P. Hippolyte Goffinet. Brussels, 1879.
Les Chartes de l'Abbaye de St Hubert-en-Ardenne. Ed. G. Kurth. 2 vols. Brussels, 1903.
Chartes de l'Abbaye de St Martin-de-Tournai, O.S.B. 2 vols. Ed. Armand d'Herbomez. Brussels, 1898, 1901.
Chartes du Chapitre de St Wandru-de-Mons. 3 vols. Ed. Léopold Devillers. Brussels, 1899, 1903, 1908.

Bled, O.
Diocèse de Thérouanne, Regestes 500–1553. 4 parts. (Société des Antiquaires de la Morinie.) Saint Omer, 1902.

Borderie, Arthur de la
Recueil d'Actes inédits des ducs et princes de Bretagne. Rennes, 1888.

Bourrienne, Abbé V.
Antiquus Cartularius Ecclesiae Baiocensis (Liber Niger). Société de l'histoire de Normandie: Rouen. Rouen and Paris, 1902, 1903.

Brown, E.
Fasciculus Rerum Expetendarum (O. Gratius). 2 vols. fol. London, 1690.

Cambridge Antiquarian Society
Publication XLVIII, Octavo Series. Vetus Liber Archidiaconi Eliensis. Ed. D. J. Stewart. 1844.

Camden Society
LXIX. Domesday of St Paul's. Ed. W. H. Hale. 1858.
XCI. Registrum...Prioratus B. M. Wigorniensis. 1865.
N.S. XIX. Christ Church Letters. 1877.
N.S. XLIII. Visitations of the Diocese of Norwich (A.D. 1492–1532). Ed. A. Jessopp. 1844.
N.S. LV. Visitations of the churches belonging to St Paul's Cathedral in 1297 and 1458. Ed. W. S. Simpson. 1895.
3rd Series. VI, X, XII. Collectanea Anglo-premonstratensia. Ed. F. A. Gasquet. 1904, 1906, 1906.

Charmasse, A. de
Cartulaire de l'Évêché d'Autun. 4°. Autun, Déjussieu. (Publication de la Société Éduenne.) 1880.

Chetham Society
N.S. Vols. 38, 39, 40, 43, 56, 57, 64. Cockersand Chartulary.
N.S. Vol. 79. Chartulary of Chester Abbey, Pt I.

Coussemaker, I. de
Cartulaire de Bourbourg. 3 vols. 8°. Lille, 1882–91.

Devillers, Léopold

Description des cartulaires et des chartriers du Hainaut. 8 vols. Mons, 1865–78.

Duchet, Th. et Giry, A.

Cartulaires de l'Église de Thérouanne. 4°. (Société des Antiquaires de la Morinie.) Saint Omer, 1881.

Duckett, Sir G. F.

Charters of Cluny. 2 vols. London, 1888.

Visitations of English Cluniac Foundations. London, 1890.

Early English Text Society

The English Register of Godstow Nunnery, nr Oxford, written about 1450. 2 vols. (Original Series 129, 130.) Ed. Andrew Clark, M.A., LL.D. London, 1906, 1911.

Sixty-three Lincoln Diocese Documents 1450–4. (Original Series 149.) Ed. Andrew Clark, M.A., LL.D. London, 1914.

Henry Brinklow's Complaynt of Roderyck Mors (*c.* 1542). (Extra Series 22.) Ed. J. Meadows Cowper, F.R.Hist.S. London, 1874. Reprinted, 1904.

English Historical Review

Visitation of the Archdeaconry of Totnes (1342). Jan. 1911, vol. XXII, pp. 108 *seq.* Ed. G. G. Coulton.

Gibbons, A. W.

Liber Antiquus Hugonis Welles. Lincoln, 1888.

Guérard, B.

Cartulaire de Notre-Dame de Paris. 4 vols. in-4°. (Collection des documents inédits.) Paris, Impr. nat. 1850.

Haigneré, Abbé D.

Chartes de St Bertin. 4 vols. Saint Omer, 1886–99.

Hampshire Record Society

Charters and Documents relating to Selborne and its Priory. Ed. W. Dunn Macray, M.A., F.S.A. London and Winchester.

Hautcœur, E.

Cartulaire de St Pierre-de-Lille. Lille and Paris, 1894.

Historical MSS. Comm. Rep. X, pt v, pp. 234–42

Taxation of diocese of Ossory, *c.* 1320. London, 1885.

Hollebeke, L. van

Cartulaire de l'Abbaye de Saint Pierre de Loo. 4°. (Société d'Émulation de Bruges, Recueil de Chroniques, etc., Sér. 1.) Brussels, 1870.

Hudson, W.

Collation of Norwich Taxation with Taxation of Pope Nicholas, Norwich. (Norfolk and Norwich Archaeological Society in Norfolk Archaeology, XVII, pp. 46–157.) Norwich, 1908.

Jourdain, Rev. Francis

Charters connected with the Church of Ashbourne in Derbyshire. (Derbyshire Archaeol. and Nat. Hist. Soc. Journal, XIII, pp. 52–107.) London, 1891.

Lalore, Ch.

Collection des principaux Cartulaires du diocèse de Troyes. 7 vols. 8°. Paris. Troyes, 1875–90.

Ancienne Discipline du diocèse de Troyes jusqu'en 1788. 3 vols. (Nos. 2–4.) 8°. Troyes, 1882–3.

Lyndwode, W.

Provinciale aut Constitutiones Angliae. Oxford, 1679.

Madox, Thomas

Formulare Anglicanum. London, 1702.

Marchegay, P.

Cartulaires de Bas-Poitou (La Vendée). Les Roches Baritaud, 1877.

Chartes Normandes de l'Abbaye de Saint-Florent près Saumur. Les Roches Baritaud, Vendée, 1879.

Merlet, Lucien

Cartulaire de l'abbaye de la Sainte-Trinité de Tiron. (Société archéologique d'Eure-et-Loire.) Chartres, 1883.

Oxford Historical Society

Chartulary of St Frideswide's. 2 vols. (Nos. 28, 31.) Ed. Rev. Spencer R. Wigram, M.A. Oxford, 1894, 1896.

Eynsham Chartulary. 2 vols. (Nos. 49, 51.) Oxford, 1906–7, 1908.

Putte, F. van der

Chronique et Cartulaire de l'abbaye de Groeninghe à Courtrai. 4°. (Société d'Émulation de Bruges, Recueil de Chroniques, etc., Sér. I.) Brussels, 1872.

Rogers, E. Thorold

Loci e Libro Veritatum (Gascoigne). London, 1881.

Reynerus, C.

Apostolatus Benedictinorum in Anglia. Douai, 1626.

Rolls Series

Chronicles and Memorials:

S. Petri Gloucestriae, Historia et Cartularium Monasterii. 3 vols. (No. 33.) Ed. W. H. Hart. 1863, 1865, 1867.

Annales Monastici. 5 vols. (No. 36.) Ed. Rev. H. R. Luard, M.A. 1864–9.

Registrum Malmesburiense. 2 vols. (No. 72.) Ed. Rev. J. S. Brewer, M.A. and C. T. Martin, B.A. 1879–80.
Register of St Osmund. 2 vols. (No. 78.) Ed. Rev. W. H. Rich-Jones, M.A. 1883–4.
Cartularium Monasterii de Rameseia. 3 vols. (No. 79.) Ed. W. H. Hart and Rev. P. A. Lyons. 1884, 1886, 1894.
Chartularies of St Mary's Abbey, Dublin. 2 vols. (No. 80.) Ed. J. T. Gilbert. 1884, 1886.
Letter Books of Christ Church, Canterbury. 3 vols. (No. 85.) Ed. Rev. J. B. Sheppard, LL.D. 1887, 1888, 1889.
Register of St Thomas the Martyr, Dublin. (No. 94.) Ed. J. T. Gilbert. 1889.
Taxatio Ecclesiastica Angliae et Walliae Auctoritate P. Nicholai IV, *c.* A.D. 1291. (ed.) 1802.

Royce, D.
Landboc sive Registrum Monasterii...de Winchelcumba. 2 vols. Exeter, 1892, 1893.

Scottish History Society, Edinburgh
Chartulary of Lindores Abbey 1195–1479. (No. 42.) Ed. Rt. Rev. J. Dowden. Edinburgh, 1903.
Statutes of the Scottish Church. (No. 54.) Ed. D. Patrick. Edinburgh, 1907.
Chartulary of Inchaffray Abbey. (No. 56.) Ed. W. A. Lindsay, J. Dowden, J. M. Thosom. Edinburgh, 1908.

Société de la Suisse Romande
Mémoires et documents, 2e Série, tome XI. Visitation of the churches of the diocese of Lausanne 1416–17. Lausanne, 1921.

Somerset Record Society
Two Chartularies of Bath Priory. Ed. Wm Hunt, M.A. London, 1893.
Two Chartularies of the Augustinian Priory of Bruton and the Cluniac Priory of Montacute. Ed. by members of the Council. London, 1894.
Two Chartularies of the Benedictine Abbeys of Muchelney and Athelney. Ed. Rev. E. H. Bates, M.A. London, 1899.
A Chartulary of Buckland Priory. Ed. Rev. F. W. Weaver, M.A., F.S.A. London, 1909.

Souancé, Vte. de
L'histoire et le cartulaire de l'abbaye de Notre-Dame-des-Clairets, dioc. Sées. Vannes, 1894.

Surtees Society
Cartularium Abbathie de Whiteby, O.S.B. 2 vols. (Nos. 69, 72.) Ed. Rev. J. C. Atkinson. Edinburgh, 1879.

Thorpe, John
Registrum Roffense. London, 1769.

Trémault, M. de
Cartulaire de Marmoutier. Paris and Vendôme, 1893.

Wilkins, D.
Concilia Magnae Britannicae et Hiberniae. 4 vols. London, 1737.

Zeitschrift für die Geschichte des Oberrheins
Vol. 27. Karlsruhe, 1875.

III

SECONDARY SOURCES

Baecker, L. de
Les Flamands de France. Gand, 1850.

Bonnard, Fourrier
Histoire de l'Abbaye de St Victor-de-Paris. 2 vols. in-8°. Paris, 1904.

Cauvet
Du droit du patronage ecclésiastique dans l'ancienne Normandie, relativement aux paroisses des campagnes. (Mémoires de la Société des Antiquaires de Normandie, t. xx.)

Charmasse, A. de
Les Origines des Paroisses Rurales dans le département de Saône-et-Loire. Autun, 1909.

Coulton, G. G.
Medieval Studies—Priests and People before the Reformation. London, 1907.
The Medieval Village. Cambridge, 1926.
Five Centuries of Religion. Vol. II. Cambridge, 1927.
Some Chapters in the History of Vicarages. (History Teachers' Miscellany. Vols. III, IV.) Cambridge, 1925, 1926.

Cox, Rev. J. C.
Notes on the Churches of Derbyshire. 4 vols. 8°. Chesterfield, London and Derby, 1875–9.

Curtois, H.
The Church of Fen Drayton, Cambridgeshire. (Christ's College Magazine. Vol. XXXIV, No. 105, pp. 52–71. Lent Term, 1925.)

Cutts, E. L.
Parish Priests and their People in the Middle Ages. 8°. London, 1914.

Delisle, Léopold
Le Clergé normand au XIIIe siècle in Bibliothèque de l'École des Chartes, t. VIII.

Dobiache-Rojdestvensky, O.
La Vie Paroissale en France au XIIIe Siècle. Paris, 1911.

Dénifle, P. Heinrich Suso

La Désolation des Églises, monastères, et hôpitaux en France, pendant la guerre de Cent Ans. 2 tomes in 3 vols. Paris, 1897, 1899.

Gasquet, F. A. (Antiquaries' Books.)

The Eve of the Reformation. London, 1900.

Parish Life in Mediaeval England. London, 1906.

Graham, Miss Rose

The Taxation of Pope Nicholas. (English Historical Review, XXIII, pp. 434 *seq.*) London, 1908.

Guillaume, J.

Recherches sur l'organisation de l'administration religieuse des paroisses en Normandie du XIe au XVIe siècle. (Positions des thèses des élèves de l'École des Chartes, année 1890.) Maçon, 1890.

Heales, A. C.

Records of Merton Priory, Surrey. London, 1898.

Imbart de la Tour, P.

Les Paroisses Rurales du IVe au XIe siècle. (See Stutz for review of same, Gött. Gelehr. Anz.) Paris, 1900.

Questions d'Histoire sociale et religieuse. Paris, 1907.

Jenkins, Rev. C.

The Register of Archbishop Odo Rigaldi of Rouen. (Church Quarterly Review, Vol. CI, No. 201, October, 1925.)

Jubainville, Marie Henri d'Arbois de

Histoires des Ducs et des Comtes de Champagne. 7 vols. 8°. Paris and Troyes, 1859–69.

Kennett, White

The Case of Impropriations and of the Augmentation of vicarages and other insufficient cures. 8°. London, 1704.

Parochial Antiquities. Enlarged edition, 2 vols. Oxford, 1818.

Langlois, Ch. V.

La Vie en France au Moyen Âge d'après quelques moralistes du temps. Paris, 1908.

Doléances du clergé de France au temps de Philippe le Bel. (Revue bleue, 9 Sept. and 14 Oct. 1905.)

Luchaire, A.

Manuel des institutions françaises—période des Capétiens directs. 8°. Paris, 1892.

Innocent III. Le concile de Latran et la réforme de l'église. Paris, 1908.

Madelaine, Godefroid
Essai Historique sur l'abbaye de Mondaye de l'ordre de Prémontré. 8°. Caen, 1874.

Maitland, F. W.
Roman Canon Law in the Church of England. London, 1898.

Makower, F.
Constitutional History of the Church of England. Translated from the German. 8°. London, 1895.

Maskell, Joseph
Berkynge chirche juxta Turrim. 8°. London, 1864.

Maskell, William
The Ancient Liturgy of the Church of England, pp. 191 *seq.* 8°. London, 1844.

Oxford Historical Society Publications
Wood. City of Oxford. Vol. II. (No. 17.)
Churches and Religious Houses. Oxford, 1890.
Three Oxfordshire Parishes—Kidlington, Yarnton and Begbroke. (No. 24.) Oxford, 1893.

Pegge, Samuel, The Elder
Life of Grosseteste. (Appendix on Vicarages.) 4°. London, 1793.

Phillimore, Sir R. J.
Ecclesiastical Law. 2 vols. New edition by Sir W. G. F. Phillimore and C. F. Jemmett. 8°. London, 1895.

Reichel, O. J.
Churches and Church Endowments in the 11th and 12th centuries. From Transactions of the Devonshire Association for the Advancement of Science, Literature and Art, etc. 8°. 1907.

Richardson, H. G.
The Parish Clergy of the 13th and 14th centuries. (Royal Historical Society Transactions, 3rd series. Vol. VI, pp. 89–128.) London, 1912.

Savine, A. R.
English Monasteries on the Eve of the Dissolution; in Vinogradoff, Sir P. G.'s Oxford Studies in Social and Legal History. Vol. I. Oxford, 1909.

Snape, R. H.
English Monastic Finances. (Cambridge Studies in Medieval Life and Thought.) Cambridge, 1926.

Stutz, Ulrich
Geschichte des Kirchlichen Benefizialwesens von seinen Anfängen bis auf die Zeit Alexanders III. Vol. I. Berlin, 1895.
Also in Göttingische Gelehrte Anzeige. Berlin, 1904, Nr. i.

Thomas, Paul

Le droit de Propriété des Laïques sur les Églises et le Patronage Laïque au Moyen Âge. (Bibl. de l'École des Hautes Études, Sciences Religieuses. Vol. XIX.) Paris, 1906.

Thomassin, L.

Ancienne et nouvelle discipline de l'Église. Paris, 1725.

Thompson, A. Hamilton

English Monasteries. (Cambridge Manuals Series.) Cambridge, 1913.

Whitaker, T. D.

History of Whalley. 4th edition, revised and enlarged by J. G. Nichols and P. A. Lyons. 2 vols. 4°. London, 1872–6.

Willis, Browne

Survey of the Cathedral Church of Llandaff. 8°. London, 1719.

Wilson, H. B.

St Laurence Pountney. London, 1831.

IV

REFERENCE ONLY

Calendars of Patent Rolls, 1216–1509. (Rolls Series.)

Calendars of Close Rolls, 1227–1396. (Rolls Series.)

Dugdale, W. Monasticon Anglicanum. Ed. J. Caley, etc. 6 vols. London, 1846.

Espen, Z. B. van. Jus Ecclesiasticum universum. Louvain, 1753.

Hefelé, C. J. Histoire des Conciles. Vols. IV, 1 to VII, 2. Paris, 1911–16. Translated from the second German edition by Dom. H. Leclercq.

Mansi, J. D. Sacrorum Conciliorum Collectio. Fol. Paris, 1759.

Migne, J. P. Patrologia Latina.

Neve, J. le. Fasti Ecclesiae Anglicanae. 8°. 3 vols. Oxford, 1854.

Sextus Decretalium Liber a Bonifacio Octavo in Concilio Lugdunensi editus.... Venice, 1572.

Stubbs, W. Registrum Sacrum Anglicanum. Oxford, 1897.

V

BIBLIOGRAPHY

Manuels de Bibliographie Historique. Vol. IV. Henri Stein. Bibliographie Générale des Cartulaires Français. Paris, 1907.

INDEX

ABBREVIATIONS:

Aug. = Augustinian   Ben. = Benedictine
Cist. = Cistercian   Clun. = Cluniac
Prem. = Premonstratensian